The Italian Financial System Remodelled

The Italian Financial System Remodelled

Pierluigi Ciocca

The original Italian edition of this book, *La nuova finanza in Italia:
Una difficile metamorfosi (1980–2000)* was published in 2000
by Bollati Boringhieri editore srl., Corso Vittorio Emanuele II,86 Torino

This English-language edition published 2005 by
PALGRAVE MACMILLAN
Houndmills, Basingstoke, Hampshire RG21 6XS and
175 Fifth Avenue, New York, N.Y. 10010
Companies and representatives throughout the world

PALGRAVE MACMILLAN is the global academic imprint of the Palgrave
Macmillan division of St. Martin's Press, LLC and of Palgrave Macmillan Ltd.
Macmillan® is a registered trademark in the United States, United Kingdom
and other countries. Palgrave is a registered trademark in the European
Union and other countries.

ISBN 1–4039–3479–7

This book is printed on paper suitable for recycling and made from fully
managed and sustained forest sources.

A catalogue record for this book is available from the British Library.

Library of Congress Cataloging-in-Publication Data
Ciocca, Pierluigi, 1941–
    The Italian financial system remodelled / Pierluigi Ciocca.
       p.   cm.
    Includes bibliographical references (p.) and index.
    ISBN 1–4039–3479–7 (cloth)
    1. Finance—Italy.   2. Financial institutions—Italy.   I. Title.

    HG186.I8C562 2004
    332′.0945—dc22   2004054297

10   9   8   7   6   5   4   3   2   1
14   13   12   11   10   09   08   07   06   05

Printed and bound in Great Britain by
Antony Rowe Ltd, Chippenham and Eastbourne

'Italy will be able to overcome this crisis . . . only if the fundamental rules governing its mixed economy are subjected to fresh, systematic scrutiny . . . if wisdom is exercised in both the economic and legal fields.'

—**Paolo Baffi**, The Governor's Concluding Remarks
to the Annual Meeting of the Bank of Italy,
Banca d'Italia, 31 May 1979

Contents

List of Tables

List of Figures

Preface

The events and prospects associated with the banking and financial sector in Italy can be summed up in just a few propositions.

Towards the end of the twentieth century the financial system built by Alberto Beneduce and Donato Menichella – for almost half a century the undisputed heritage of the Great Depression and its repercussions on Italy's economy – was replaced by a profoundly different one. Apart from the underdevelopment of pension funds – a serious shortcoming – the new system is similar in structure to those prevailing on the international scene (Chapter 1).

Legislation, taxation, supervision, the promotion of competition – economic and institutional policy – fostered that change. They now constitute a fitting framework for the financial sector, certainly one that does not differ from those of the other advanced market economies (Chapters 2–6).

Both the scope of operations and the performance of the financial industry have improved. Banks have progressed in volume of business, productivity and service prices. There has also been progress in the structure, breadth and efficiency of the markets. The principal weakness is per capita labour costs, which are too high. Banking groups of world size and standard struggle to make headway. There is room for improvement in the quality and availability of certain services. External, 'environmental' costs continue to weigh on Italian banks, putting them at a disadvantage in the international arena (Chapter 7).

The stagnation of the economy in the 1990s – one of the most disappointing decades for income growth since 1861 – cannot be blamed on the banking and financial sector, which was overcoming its inadequacies. Its causes lie elsewhere, in the 'real' economy, and are buried much deeper. Rather, the economic stagnation had adverse consequences for financial development (Chapter 8).

The banking and financial sector contributes, and could contribute more, to overcoming the contradiction that has characterized the Italian economy in recent years: although it is now better governed it is not growing as it could. The value of that contribution will depend on further economic and institutional policy measures. Even more, perhaps, it will depend on market operators: above all on bankers and financiers, but also on the ability of households and businesses to fully exploit – as they have failed to do so far – the potential of the instruments offered now and in the future by the financial system, in competition with international finance (Chapters 9–10).

These propositions, or theses, are developed on the separate and joint levels of law and economics in the pages that follow. They are illustrated by drawing on institutional elements, data and calculations based on sources found in the Bank of Italy's publications, culled painstakingly by many colleagues at the Bank, to whom the author, who has been a manager at the Bank since 1979, gives more than merely formal thanks.[1] The opinions contained in the book, however, are those of the author alone. They do not necessarily reflect the official position of the Bank.

This book follows on from two others written some years earlier.[2] At the start of the transformation that has now been completed, *Interesse e Profitto* (Interest and Profit) retraced its historical roots, emphasized its necessity, and examined the course it would probably take. Half way through the process, *Banca, Finanza, Mercato* (Banking, Finance, the Market) took stock of what had been achieved, denounced the delays, and called for improvements with a view to the introduction of the single European currency.

The English version of this book is the translation of the Italian text of 2000 exactly as it was published. Readers should note that 'today' – and the latest statistics and institutional arrangements – refer to 1999–2000. In the last four years the structure of the Italian financial system has not changed significantly. The radical transformation accomplished between 1980 and 2000 described here created a new and stable order; the adaptations being made – with regard to taxation, for example – and those that are foreseeable amount to a gradual evolution at the margin, with one exception: supervision. In 2004 a discussion began on Italy's supervisory authorities that has also involved the country's political forces and Parliament. The debate is far from over and it is difficult to predict when or how it will end.

PIERLUIGI CIOCCA

Santa Marinella

1
A Mutation

At the end of the 1970s Italy's financial system exhibited distinctive if not unique structural features. These reflected the country's economic history and the way the system had been shaped after the war; they were especially evident when viewed as deviations from the pattern of developments in the financial sector in other countries. In two decades of change, they have been attenuated and transcended. This evolution can also be read as progress in the direction taken by the financial systems of the richer countries, if not towards convergence. Considering the initial conditions, it constitutes a veritable mutation; under the impetus of internal and external forces a national financial system inherited from a very particular history gave way to a new system with markedly different institutional structures.

The premise of our analysis of the transformation of Italian finance in the closing decades of the last century is that the system was not quantitatively underdeveloped in 1980. On the contrary, the ratio of gross financial assets (liquid assets, loans and securities) to tangible national wealth (land, buildings, public works, machinery and stocks) – Raymond Goldsmith's financial interrelations ratio,[1] the best measure of the financial superstructure in relation to the real structure – can be estimated at 0.9 for 1980 (Table 1.1). This figure we can consider high, even if it was lower than the peaks recorded in the 1970s, which were anomalous in certain respects. It was comparable with the ratios in (West) Germany, France and Japan, countries that were and remain economically more advanced than Italy. Their average per capita income was more than 10 per cent higher than Italy's, their real wealth a third larger on average.

Since then, the volume of gross financial assets has risen in Italy from 1300 to 13300 trillion lire at current prices, or 3800 trillion at 1980 consumer prices. To this we should add the stock of trade credit

Table 1.1   Financial assets and real wealth (in billions of units of national currency)[a]

		Gross financial assets (FA)	Real wealth (RW)	Financial interrelations ratio (FA/RW)	Real wealth/ GDP	Per capita GDP
Italy	1980	1 342 318	1 546 861	0.87	4.05	73
	1998	11 414 730	8 519 888	1.34	4.16	67
France	1980	13 415	12 755	1.05	4.85	80
	1997	70 766	30 495	2.32	3.71	70
Germany	1980	5 426	6 693	0.81	4.55	90
	1998	824 892	17 899	1.39	4.87	71
United Kingdom	1980	1 489	1 104	1.35	4.76	65
	1996	8 334	2 914	2.86	3.92	65
United States	1980	13 816	13 007	1.06	4.67	100
	1996	58 267	27 932	2.09	3.66	100
Japan	1980	1 102 720	1 373 029	0.80	5.71	73
	1996	4 276 003	3 252 175	1.31	6.49	82

[a] Indices, United States = 100; 1995 constant prices, converted into dollars at 1995 purchasing power parities. For financial assets, the source is OECD, *Financial Accounts*; for France, the data for 1997 are from the Bank of France; for Germany, the data for 1998 are from Deutsche Bundesbank, *Financial Accounts for Germany 1990 to 1998*; for Japan, the data for 1996 are from EPA, *Annual Report on National Accounts*; the data on GDP are from OECD. Real wealth is defined as the sum of reproducible assets (dwellings and non-residential buildings, plant and machinery, stocks and durable goods) and non-reproducible assets (land). The data for Italy are derived from calculations by the Bank of Italy's Economic Research Department; for France from INSEE, *Comptes et indicateurs économiques. Rapport sur les comptes de la Nation*; for Germany from Statistische Bundesamt, *Statistische Jahrbuch für die Bundesrepublik*; for the United States from Board of Governors of the Federal Reserve System, *Balance Sheets*; for the United Kingdom from Central Statistical Office, *United Kingdom National Accounts*; for Japan from EPA, *Annual Report on National Accounts*. The other sources are national statistics for GDP at constant prices, OECD for purchasing power parities, and Eurostat and OECD for population.

outstanding between companies, which can be gauged only very roughly but far exceeds firms' bank debt (782 trillion lire). The financial interrelations ratio has also risen, reaching 1.3 in 1998. As in other countries, this is the consequence of higher prices of outstanding securities as well as of new issues of liabilities. In the 1990s the latter diminished in relation to income (Figure 1.1), more sharply in Italy than elsewhere. In the quantitative development of its financial system Italy, whose economy was slowing down, basically kept pace with Germany, labouring under the strains of unification, and Japan, gripped by crisis. Together,

Figure 1.1 Financial liabilities in Italy (changes as a percentage of GDP)

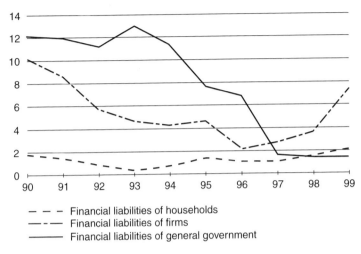

- — — Financial liabilities of households
- — · — Financial liabilities of firms
- ——— Financial liabilities of general government

Source: Banca d'Italia, 'Conti finanziari'.

the three countries recorded a widening gap *vis-à-vis* the United States (2.1), France (2.3) and especially the United Kingdom (2.9), unrivalled leader among the main 'industrial' countries. The UK's financial structures are increasingly oriented to satisfying international demand. The City of London presents itself as a sort of offshore centre. It is separated from the vicissitudes of the British economy, self-referential, important in its own right. It is protected by the political authorities, by the tax system and by the British press, which strives to promote it over other financial centres.

Matching the quantitative and qualitative progress of the financial sector is its growing contribution to employment, value added and the wealth of nations. In Italy the contribution of the sector to value added has climbed to 6 per cent, almost as high as in Germany though lower than the estimate for the United States (10 per cent) and for other countries typified by a deliberate, historical financial mission, such as the United Kingdom and Switzerland.

The new forms of the Italian financial system

On the basis of this premise, we shall consider the principal changes in the structure of the Italian financial system over a span of nearly 20 years dating back, as a matter of convention, to 1980. We have reduced the number of such changes to seven. The system's structure consists in its economic and legal forms, its ramification in different agents, markets and instruments, and its essential modes of organization. The structural changes will be described in this chapter separately from two other aspects. The first concerns the ability of economic agents – households, firms, government, non-residents – to utilize the services of the financial sector. The second, treated in the final chapters of the book, concerns the results achieved by banks, other intermediaries and the financial markets in terms of the quantity, quality and cost of services.

From intermediaries to markets

Until the 1970s Italy's financial system was 'bank-oriented' rather than 'market-oriented', even more than that of the other countries of continental Europe. Leaving aside its complex, debatable qualitative implications, this simple formula alluded to high or rising levels in the quantitative importance of the banks as measured by the financial intermediation ratio, that is the ratio of financial claims on credit institutions to total financial assets.

As had previously occurred in the years from 1880 to 1913, most notably in the Giolittian era after the turn of the century, between the end of the Second World War and the end of the 1960s, banks' new liabilities exceeded those of other issuers. Calculated on gross flows, the financial intermediation ratio fluctuated around 0.6, against an average of less than 0.5 in the other countries. Calculated on gross stocks, over the entire span from Italian unification until the 1970s the financial intermediation ratio displayed a rising trend. Its growth was faster than in other financial systems, which originated from the prevalently market-based capitalism of the mid-nineteenth century. In the 1970s anomalous phenomena of double intermediation drove the ratio in Italy up to peak levels. Partly under the compulsion of administrative constraints on their bond portfolios – constraints imposed in June 1973, eased at the end of 1978 and finally removed in 1986 – banks (operating at short term) increased their contribution to the funding of special credit institutions (operating beyond the short term): calculated on flows, from 35 per cent in the period between 1962 and 1972 to 75 per cent between 1973 and 1979; calculated on stocks, from one-third in 1971–2 to two-thirds in 1979. The liabilities of banks and other credit institutions tended to constitute the lion's share of the total stock of financial instruments in the economy (Figure 1.2).

Calculated on stocks, the financial intermediation ratio reached a peak of 0.5 in the mid-1970s. The spike induced by double intermediation

Figure 1.2   Financial intermediation and financial interrelations ratios in Italy [a]

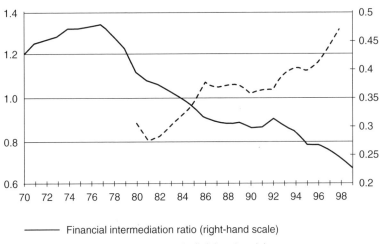

——— Financial intermediation ratio (right-hand scale)

- - - - Financial interrelations ratio (left-hand scale)

[a] The data on real wealth are the result of estimates by the Economic Research Department of the Bank of Italy. The data on stocks of financial assets and liabilities for 1989–94 are obtained from the financial accounts, produced according to the method used from 1989 onwards; for 1995–9 they are produced utilizing the ESA95 classification. For 1980–8 the data are the result of a reconstruction of the financial accounts on the basis of those produced earlier, aimed at rendering them compatible with those from 1989 onwards. For 1970–9 the data available earlier were normalized to permit comparison with subsequent data.

was rapidly reabsorbed. In 1980–1 the ratio had already fallen back to levels similar to those in France and Germany (0.4) but considerably higher than those in the United Kingdom and the United States (0.3 and 0.2 respectively). Over the subsequent years the ratio declined constantly, albeit less rapidly. In 1999 it stood at 0.2, lower than in Germany (0.4) and similar to the figures in France and the United Kingdom, though slightly higher than the ratio in the United States, which had fallen to 0.15.

In the last two decades 'primary securities', that is securities issued by prevalently non-financial spending units (households, firms and public bodies) and placed directly with ultimate lenders or their agents ('direct securities'), have grown much faster than 'indirect securities', that is securities supplied to ultimate borrowers by credit intermediaries following their acquisition of primary securities.[2] The expansion of the securities markets has been correspondingly large.

The growth of the markets has stemmed mainly from the expansion of the public debt, which soared from 58 per cent of GDP in 1980 to a peak of 124 per cent in 1994, and the private sector's capacity to absorb both the huge new public debt issues (amounting each year to approximately half of GDP) and the banking system's disposals of government paper. In December 1999 general government liabilities amounted to around 2450 trillion lire, or one-fifth of the national stock of financial instruments. The banking system, including the central bank, reduced the share of public debt it held from 60 per cent in 1980 to less than 20 per cent in the 1990s. Foreign investors, who had been virtually absent from this market, today hold around one-third of Italy's public debt. A decisive contribution came from MTS, the electronic secondary market in government securities, which Italy's leading intermediaries established in 1988 at the urgent recommendation, if not the command, of the Treasury and the Bank of Italy. Initially, trades on MTS were made by telephone, on the bid and ask price quotes displayed by primary dealers. Subsequently the market went over to an electronic platform, integrated with the trade settlement system. Its technology is among the most efficient by international standards.

The growth of the private capital market has been less pronounced, but not negligible. The stock market's capitalization, which amidst the economic difficulties of the 1970s had plummeted to just a few per cent of GDP, rose back in the 1990s, from 13 per cent at the start of the decade to 65 per cent towards the end. The capitalization:GDP ratio attained is comparable to that of the Frankfurt exchange (72 per cent) and the entire euro area (71 per cent). It is lower than the ratios of the Paris, New York and London exchanges (111, 180 and 200 per cent respectively). In the 1980s the growth of the Italian stock exchange was driven by the increase from 134 to 223 in the number of listed companies (most of the newly listed firms belonged to the private sector) and by the greater recourse of listed companies to new share issues. By contrast, in the 1990s it was mainly attributable to the rise in share prices and the privatization and listing of large public enterprises. The number of listed companies changed little over the decade and at the end of 1999 stood at 241, compared with 1043 in Germany, 968 in France and 718 in Spain. Their value added amounted to 8 per cent of GDP. In mid-1999 a new market was opened for the shares of small and medium-sized companies with high potential for technological innovation. Since the last quarter of 1993, when privatizations began in earnest, more than half of the growth of the stock exchange has come from privatized companies. The annual value of new share issues by listed companies fell from 8 per cent of the market's capitalization in the 1980s to 5 per cent in the 1990s. More than four-fifths of listed companies are controlled *de jure* or *de facto* by a single shareholder. Non-residents hold just over 8 per cent of the total value of shares.

The institutional and organizational transformation of the Italian stock exchange is recent but has been radical. The ownership structure of all the markets in corporate and government securities was privatized between 1996 and 1999; privatization came after almost a century during which the creation, operation and supervision of the markets had been set within a public-law framework. Market operating companies were created and given self-regulatory powers concerning the admission, exclusion and suspension of financial instruments and market partici-pants, trading rules, and the dissemination of information on trades. The procedures are specified in the rules of the operating companies approved by the authorities.

The money market is also broad and efficient today in its segments for government securities, interbank funds and repos. Italy's money market is an integral part of the euro market, indeed one of its most advanced components. It permits Italian banks, already accustomed to efficient treasury management, to compete on advantageous terms with European banks in borrowing and investing liquidity.

In the 1950s Treasury bills were issued at fixed rates and without limit; there was no secondary market. Change was first attempted in 1962 and came in the 1970s. The reform of 1975 strengthened Treasury bill issuance by suitably setting the floor price, permitting multiple price auctions and broadening the categories of intermediary admitted. The restored ability to fund the public borrowing requirement in the market, which received a boost from the introduction of variable-rate Treasury credit certificates in 1977, made possible the 1981 'divorce' between the Treasury Ministry under Beniamino Andreatta and the Bank of Italy under Carlo Azeglio Ciampi. The Bank's commitment to purchase the government securities not taken up at auction ceased; monetary policy's degrees of freedom increased. There followed the introduction of com-petitive price auctions for Treasury bills (in 1983 for three-month bills, 1984 for six-month bills and 1988 for the twelve-month maturity) and the suppression of the floor price (in 1988 for six-month bills and the following year for the other maturities). The reform of the Treasury current account with the Bank of Italy and the cessation of every form of financing of the Treasury by the Bank in 1993 constituted the final stages of this process, which was completed in spite of the state of the public finances, the size of the public debt, inflation and the fragility of the lira.

The interbank section of the money market was even more backward. Up to 1962 interbank deposits were prohibited, except for correspondent current accounts. This dovetailed with a policy of defending the role of local banks for their allocative efficiency and preventing the 'excesses' of competition. A multitude of current account advances by the Bank of Italy to banks (up to 1976 to their branches) was supposed to make up for the interbank market's underdevelopment, which it simultaneously perpetuated, however. In the 1970s the Bank of Italy began rationing the growth in banks' credit facilities, gradually killing off current account advances. The ratio to deposits of credit lines from the Bank of Italy fell from 2.8 per cent in 1970 to 0.9 per cent in 1980 and 0.5 per cent in 1985. Achieving efficiency gains, the banks gradually came to substitute market relationships for bilateral accounts as the basis for liquidity management.

Monetary policy was strengthened with repos (1979) and through changes in the classic instruments of refinancing, such as the application of a fee on current account advances (1985) and the introduction of penalizing rates on fixed-term advances (1991). The transition in monetary policy from direct administrative instruments, such as the ceiling on the increase in bank lending and the securities investment requirement for banks, to market-based instruments, such as open-market operations, was completed in 1988. The mobilization of compulsory reserves was introduced in 1990. The creation of the electronic interbank deposit market (MID) in the same year combined new rules and an advanced technology. The commitment to route interbank transactions between participants through MID and the binding nature of price quotes gave the market depth, transparency and efficiency. Innovations in the payment system helped to lessen the importance of correspondent current accounts.

There was positive synergy between monetary policy and the markets. The signalling effectiveness of monetary policy implemented in the markets increased as the markets progressed, while the markets grew more efficient because they now incorporated monetary policy interventions and information. In 1980 only 28 per cent of all potentially 'listable' financial instruments were actually listed on organized, continuously operating markets; today the proportion is 70 per cent.

Considered together, the fall in the financial intermediation ratio, the market's efficiency gains and its volume growth clearly signify that

Italy's financial system is no longer bank-oriented. However, the system remains bank-centred in a different sense. The decline in the relative importance of traditional bank instruments has not in fact coincided with a reduction in the role of the banks, which remains dominant. Outside the banking system, there is a lack of private investment in the financial industry. While deposits and loans were losing share, banks enhanced the value of their securities trading and custody operations. They accommodated customer demand for portfolio diversification. If, along with deposits raised directly from the public, account is also taken of the securities intermediation performed by banks directly and through subsidiary and related intermediaries, the share of financial savings managed by the banking system has not diminished. It stands well above 90 per cent, the level it had risen to in the 1980s starting from an already very high base (80 per cent) in the late 1970s.

The centrality of the banking system has important implications for supervisory activity. It is even reflected in the new, privatized configuration of the securities markets. Banks figure prominently among the shareholders of the markets. They are called upon to ensure the functionality and self-regulation of the Italian stock exchange and the electronic markets, to enhance the Milan marketplace in a strategic vision, to integrate it into the European financial network that is being formed.

More intermediaries, more organizational procedures, more instruments

The ascendancy of market-based activity over bank intermediation has been accompanied by an alteration and widening of the array of instruments, intermediaries and segments constituting the financial system.

The composition of financial assets has changed radically (Table 1.2). The decline in inflation and nominal interest rates beginning in the early 1980s, coupled with high real yields and rising rates of profit, contributed to this. The most liquid instruments – currency, deposits and Treasury bills – fell from 44 per cent of the total in 1980 to 33 per cent in 1990 and 19 per cent in 1999, while loans, especially those at short term disbursed by intermediaries issuing liquid liabilities, declined from 25 per cent in 1980 to 19 per cent in 1999. In correspondence, bonds (especially long government bonds), shares and other equity, insurance technical reserves and investment fund units rose to constitute the bulk of the total: almost 62 per cent at the end of 1999, compared with 31 per cent in 1980. Corporate bonds and commercial paper are still little used. Their issuance remains too costly and on too large a scale with respect to the normal needs of small and medium enterprises.

Table 1.2   Financial assets in Italy (stocks in thousands of billions of lire)

	1980	1990	1999
Gross financial assets	1342	5561	13263
as a ratio to GDP	3.5	4.2	6.2
Gross financial assets (1980 prices)	1342	2213	3768
Percentage composition by instrument			
currency, deposits, short-term securities	44.1	33.4	19.2
loans	24.9	23.9	19.4
bonds, shares, technical reserves, investment funds	31.0	42.7	61.4
Percentage composition by issuer			
banks (including the Bank of Italy)	39.7	29.3	22.6
non-banks	60.3	70.7	77.4
Italian investment funds	0.0	0.9	6.9
insurance companies, pension funds and staff severance pay provision	1.8	5.1	
public bodies	19.5	25.6	19.9
non-financial firms	25.8	25.3	22.1
non-residents	9.0	7.4	16.5
households	2.0	2.5	3.1
other Italian intermediaries	0.9	3.1	2.6
items n.e.c.	1.4	0.8	0.0
MEMORANDUM ITEMS			
Households' gross financial assets	392	2112	4695
Managed assets[a]	3	8	42
Listed Italian financial instruments[b]	28	41	70
Consumer price index (1980 = 100)	100	251	352
Nominal GDP (thousands of billions of lire)	385	1321	2128

[a] As a percentage of households' gross financial assets.
[b] Debt and equity securities traded on organized markets and units/shares of securities investment funds and SICAVs as a percentage of the total of such securities and units/shares.

The 90 per cent of Italian firms with fewer than 10 workers employ half the country's workers.

A greater variety of financial services other than credit intermediation is now available, as is a much wider array of contracts and technical forms embodying the classic instruments of loan, bond and share. The Consolidated Law on Banking (Legislative Decree 385 of 1 September 1993) and the Consolidated Law on Finance (Legislative Decree 58 of 24 February 1998) sanctioned these developments, providing for an extensive, contractually expandable taxonomy of financial services.

The banking component of the financial industry has been simplified through despecialization, while the non-bank component has expanded in its number and types of intermediaries. Mergers and acquisitions have reduced the number of banks. On the organizational level, at the point where the 'all-purpose' intermediary becomes unmanageable and specialization impracticable, recourse may be had to the intermediate solution of the 'multifunction' group. Simplification and despecialization have led most of the major banks to set up groups or federations, but others have chosen to take the universal bank route and yet others have opted for specialization.

The division of the credit sector into legally and institutionally distinct types has been overcome. In 1980 the banking component of the financial system consisted of 15 categories of banks operating at short term and special credit institutions operating at long term. At the end of 1990 there were still 1064 ordinary credit institutions and 94 special credit institutions. The ordinary credit institutions comprised 6 public-law banks, 3 banks of national interest, 106 other commercial banks, 108 cooperative banks, 75 savings banks, 7 first-category pledge banks, 2 second-category pledge banks, 715 rural and artisans' banks, 37 branches of foreign banks and 5 central credit institutions. The special credit institutions comprised 38 industrial credit institutions and sections, 19 sections for the financing of public works, 21 real-estate credit institutions and sections, 14 agricultural credit institutions and sections and 2 refinancing institutions. Today (end-1999) the system consists of 876 banks: 239 formed as public limited companies (*società per azioni*) plus central credit and refinancing institutions, 49 cooperative banks (*banche popolari*), 531 mutual banks (*banche di credito cooperativo*), and 57 branches of foreign banks (Table 1.3).

As 208 banks are members of groups, the number of independent banking units (groups or unaffiliated banks) is 747. Cooperative banks, mutual banks and the branches of foreign banks do not have the legal form of the public limited company.

There were 86 banking groups at the end of 1992. By the end of 1999 the number had fallen to 79, of which 64 had more than one component not engaged in purely instrumental activities such as data-processing or property management. The number of banks and foreign subsidiaries belonging to groups rose from 190 to 267 (including nearly every Italian bank of at least average size), that of group finance companies from 396 to 417. Above all, banking groups handle 88 per cent of lending, compared with 77 per cent in 1992. Banks individually or jointly control 29 Italian and 6 foreign insurance companies, whereas only 4 banks are controlled by insurance companies. Around half of the premium income of the life sector is collected through banking channels. The insurance, finance and, more in general, non-bank

Table 1.3 Financial intermediaries in Italy

	At 31 December 1998			At 31 December 1999		
	Intermediaries	Branches in operation		Intermediaries	Branches in operation	
		Italy	Abroad		Italy	Abroad
Banks	921	26 258	100	876	27 134	98
banks formed as public limited companies[a]	243	19 127	91	239	19 978	89
cooperative banks	56	4 275	9	49	4 205	9
mutual banks	563	2 772	–	531	2 862	–
branches of foreign banks	59	84	–	57	89	–
Investment firms	191	–	–	183	–	–
Asset management companies and SICAVs	72	–	–	86	–	–
Finance companies registered under Art. 106 of the Consolidated Law on Banking	1 427	–	–	1 339	–	–
registered under Art. 107 of the Consolidated Law on Banking	206	–	–	203	–	–

[a] Includes banks accepting medium and long-term funds and central credit and refinancing institutions.

component contributes around one-third of the consolidated profit of the largest banking groups, a lower proportion in the case of the smaller groups.

New institutions operate in the credit sector alongside the banks formerly classified as ordinary and special credit institutions, engaging in quasi-banking activities on an expanding scale. There are 1339 of these 'other credit intermediaries' offering leasing, factoring, consumer credit and venture capital services, with lending equal to around 10 per cent of that of the banks. The 18 Italian venture firms entered in the special register kept by the Bank of Italy under article 107 of the Consolidated Banking Law hold equity interests amounting to not more than 2 trillion lire. These investments absorb only one-fifth of their capital and reserves, which are underutilized because of a shortage of demand for their services on the part of firms. Among insurance companies, those operating in the life sector have grown and their premium income now exceeds that of the casualty sector. Among securities market intermediaries ('other financial institutions'), we have the birth or further growth of investment firms (numbering 183 today), asset management companies (85), and SICAVs (one Italian and 141 foreign). There are 1037 investment funds and 90 open or occupational pension funds.

The combined assets of 'other credit intermediaries' and 'other financial institutions' were equal to 5 per cent of the nation's gross financial assets in 1990. In 1999 the figure exceeded 13 per cent, thanks primarily to the 7-point increase in the share attributable to 'other financial institutions'. The latter had been less developed in Italy than in the other countries of continental Europe. In 1996 their assets were equal to 35 per cent of GDP in Italy, 42 per cent in Germany and 80 per cent in France. Over the next three years they rose to more than 80 per cent of GDP in Italy, closing or reducing the gap with the other European countries.

Pension funds, introduced recently, have a volume of assets that is still negligible. The coverage and generosity of Italy's pay-as-you-go, defined-benefit pension systems and the accordingly modest size of its funded schemes are mainly responsible for the lag on this front. The tax incentives offered have done little to accelerate the takeoff of pension funds.

From public to private

Private capital with the inclination and ability to control banks, intermediaries and other financial institutions and to manage them independently, profitably and prudently has historically been scant in Italy. The crises of the 1920s and 1930s confirmed this for the umpteenth time, and dramatically. The banks were in the hands of 'capitalists without capital', who controlled them not with their own money but with that of the depositors. They were commingled with industrial firms, which in fact held them captive. Even the Bank of Italy was involved in this 'monstrous Siamese twinship',[3] through losses in value of the loans it had granted. The collapse of such banks threatened to deprive the Italian economy both of a banking system of any sort and of an independent central bank. To preserve an essential mechanism of resource allocation and institutional defence, the State was forced to play banker, a role invented for it by Alberto Beneduce[4] and Donato Menichella.[5] Aside from the rhetoric of the times, in view of the manifest inferiority of private finance, this was more a product of necessity than of choice.

In 1980, and still in 1990, banks controlled by public bodies (the state, local government, foundations) had nearly 70 per cent of the total assets of the banking system, one of the highest shares in Europe. In 1999 the proportion referred to 61 banks out of a total of 876 and is 12 per cent, one of the lowest figures in Europe. It will fall further with the remaining disposals to be made by the foundations. If the privatization of public banks was executed within the span of a few years, its institutional preparation was long and complex. The reform developed in three phases: alignment of the rules for public banks with the provisions of the Civil Code governing banks in general, transformation of public banks into public limited companies, and removal of the restrictions on their ownership.

The sale of bank shareholdings by the state and the Institute for Industrial Reconstruction (IRI) produced almost 15 per cent of the proceeds of privatizations, a subject that Guido Carli (governor of the Bank of Italy from 1960 to 1975) was the first to mention openly in the late 1980s. Between 1993 and 1999, privatization receipts amounted to around 8 per cent of GDP. This proportion, with the sign changed, is comparable to that of the nationalizations of failed firms and banks carried out through IRI in the 1930s. However, the privatization of the banks adhered to the principle of separation between banking and commerce, the statutory restriction prohibiting an industrial firm from gaining control of a bank. What had been done under the pressure of the Great Depression was therefore overturned. This would have been impossible, inconceivable, if Italians' income, saving and wealth had not increased in real terms by factors of between 7 and 11 since the 1930s.

Calculating bank ownership in terms of percentages of total bank assets, in 1999 Italian banks were 27 per cent owned by other Italian banks, 4 per cent by foreign banks, 18 per cent by public or non-profit institutions, and 5 per cent by insurance companies and other financial institutions (the remainder refers to equity interests of less than 5 per cent, which are not reported to the Bank of Italy). Calculating control in similar terms, they were 65 per cent controlled by other Italian banks, 12 per cent by foundations and public entities, 5 per cent by insurance companies, industrial firms and other financial institutions, and 3 per cent by foreign banks.

The aspects of the ownership structure in the banking sector that often come under criticism – hard cores, cross-shareholdings, shareholders' agreements made after the privatization of publicly controlled banks – must be considered taking into account the scale of the privatization process, the very short time in which it was completed and the scarcity of institutional investors endowed with substantial 'financial' capital, such as pension funds.

International openness

The advances in the international integration of the economy and of the financial system are reflected in the volume of the transactions connected with capital movements recorded by the balance of payments (sum of the changes in gross assets and liabilities). In the 1990s these transactions increased tenfold for movements of Italian non-bank capital and sixteenfold for movements of foreign non-bank capital. Total transactions in the foreign exchange market tripled to almost $30 billion a day in 2000.

The Italian banking system has never been closed to international relationships since the Second World War. This was so even when residents' capital exports were discouraged or prohibited with sanctions, including penal sanctions, such as those established by Law 159/1976. That law cnvisagcd more severe penalties if bank officers were parties to the foreign exchange crime, imposed a fine where bank officers failed to perform the required checks on foreign transactions (for example, checks on the congruousness of the prices of merchandise exports or imports), and gave the judicial police access to banks for controls involving foreign exchange. Yet, the general intent of controls was to allow banks to deal with non-resident banks and individuals, providing these transactions did not deplete the country's foreign exchange reserves, or increased them. The objective was pursued essentially by controlling bank's overall external position in foreign currency and lire, regulating purchases of foreign currency for lire at the Italian Foreign Exchange Office (Ufficio italiano dei cambi, UIC), and applying 'spot-plus-forward' and 'spot -against-forward' ceilings on banks' foreign currency positions. The 1976 law upheld the criterion of restricting overall positions rather than individual relationships, although banks' scope for operations narrowed as a consequence of the prohibitions and obligations imposed on residents.

In the 1980s, and to an even greater extent in the 1990s with the removal of foreign exchange controls, Italian banks' international activity expanded across the board, reflecting their effective, competitive participation in financial globalization.

The assets held with non-residents by banks in Italy grew from $25 billion at the start of the 1980s to $88 billion in 1990 and $186 billion in 1998. Including the activity of Italian banks' branches abroad, between 1990 and 1998 residents' foreign currency deposits and non-residents' foreign currency and lira deposits grew from 8.2 to 10.2 per cent of total deposits, while lira and foreign currency loans to non-residents rose from 5.8 to 6.6 per cent of total lending.

Italian banks had 43 branches abroad in 1980; the number stood at around 100 in 1990 and remained more or less at that level through the decade. The number of foreign bank branches in Italy has increased continuously, from 25 in 1980 to 37 in 1990 to 57 in 1999. Italian banking groups' subsidiary banks and financial institutions abroad numbered 140 in 1992, 197 in 1999; foreign banks' subsidiaries in Italy numbered 7 in 1990, 12 in 1999. The foreign component of bank intermediation has grown significantly: between 1990 and 1999 the assets attributable to the branches or subsidiaries of non-Italian banks rose from 2.8 to 7.2 per cent of the total.

Outstanding loans and guarantee commitments by Italian banks and their foreign subsidiaries to non-OECD countries have reached $50 billion, or 44 per cent of their capital. The exposure is not negligible, although in relation to capital it is the smallest among the OECD countries with advanced financial systems.

The Italian banking system is established in offshore centres with 33 branches and 17 subsidiaries. At the end of 1999 deposits and other borrowed funds totalled $21 billion, of which only 1 per cent came from Italian non-banks. Lending to borrowers resident in offshore centres was equal to 6 per cent of total international lending by Italian banks, compared with 8, 11 and 20 per cent, respectively, for French, US and Japanese banks.

The payment system

Since the mid-1980s Italy's payment system has made a quantum leap in the efficiency and safety of cash settlement, in securities settlement, in technical infrastructure and in the payment services offered to customers. Manifold factors, several of them common to all the industrial countries, spurred this progress: technological and financial innovation, deregulation, European integration, competitive pressures, the growth in transaction volume and in exposure to systemic risk.

The settlement of interbank claims in monetary base has been furthered, giving certainty and finality to these transactions and assisting the growth of the electronic interbank deposit market. Between 1988 and 1998 (the last year before the euro) the volume settled in central bank money rose from 6 to around 41 times GDP, in line with the average ratio for the EU countries (43 times GDP). In parallel, the balances on correspondent current accounts fell from 34 per cent of total interbank liabilities at the end of the 1980s to 14 per cent in 1998.

The changeover from the clearing system to the BI-REL gross settlement system for large-value transactions strengthened the safety of payments, reducing risk significantly while the volume of transactions grew. With the launch of the European Monetary Union, in January 1999 Italy's gross settlement system become part of the backbone of TARGET, the European payment system. Monetary policy operations are carried out and financial market transactions settled through TARGET, which has fostered the integration of the money markets in Europe. The importance of TARGET is shown by its operating volumes: in its first year the system handled an average of more than 163,000 payments per day, worth a total of €925 billion; from the beginning of the year to December, cross-border payments settled per day rose by 29 per cent in number and 11 per cent in value. Italian intermediaries originated a large proportion of the total number of transactions made via TARGET, a smaller proportion of the total value (25 per cent as against 10 per cent).

The progress in payments was assisted by the creation of the interbank network, an electronic infrastructure providing efficient, safe and unified payment services. The merger between Società interbancaria per l'Automazione (SIA) and CED-Borsa offers the markets and payment systems a single technological platform. In April 2000 the Bank of Italy sold its equity interest in SIA.

The centralization of securities in dedicated depositories paved the way for securities to be transferred between intermediaries through book entries on their accounts with these depositories. The dematerialization of securities was completed with the measures issued for the introduction of the euro. The introduction of automatic trade checking procedures made it possible to automate securities trading and settlement. The Italian system has managed the growth in volume generated by expanding financial markets. Between 1988 and 1998 the value of transactions handled by securities settlement procedures grew by a factor of 48 at constant prices and rose to 26 times GDP, higher than the average in the European Union.

In the stock market the shift from securities settlement on predetermined dates to rolling settlement on a daily basis made it possible to reduce the time elapsing between a trade and its settlement from between 15 and 45 days to 3 days, in line with the other European Union countries. The safety of securities transactions has improved with the utilization of the BI-REL settlement system for the cash side; this helped to raise the share of gross settlements to 92 per cent of the flows settled in monetary base in 1999. Safety has also been enhanced through guarantee funds that insure the contracts concluded or the completion of settlement in the event of default by an intermediary. This has encouraged the entry of foreign intermediaries into Italy's markets and settlement systems.

In retail payments the gap between Italy and the other countries has narrowed in terms of the infrastructure and efficiency of services. In the 1990s the number of POS terminals per million inhabitants increased from 385 to 7,549 (to a total of 435,170), that of ATMs from 166 to 524 (to 30200 in all). The continuation of this trend will allow Italy to close the small remaining gap *vis-à-vis* the other main European countries in the endowment of such infrastructure. The introduction of specialized interbank procedures has shortened the time for executing payments with non-cash instruments. New channels have been developed as an alternative to the traditional branch network for contact with customers (remote banking) and innovative products have been promoted for business customers (interbank corporate banking).

Customer payments arranged with automated procedures have more than tripled since 1990. Payment execution time has been reduced: at the end of the 1980s credit transfers took an average of 6 days to complete; in 1999 the average was 4 days for credit transfers of less than 500 million lire, 1 day for 'urgent' and large-value transfers. The range of services offered has been widened with the creation of new instruments (electronic money) and the popularization of ones that had been scantily used (debit and credit cards). The pressure of competition has led intermediaries to invest in more innovative, higher-value-added services (home and corporate banking).

However, the prices of services are not always consistent with production costs. Only a limited number of intermediaries have product-based cost-accounting systems. There is still a bias in favour of opaque pricing systems based on value-dating. Some intermediaries still price payment services according to the amount. Gauged by payment execution time, the quality of services is probably sub par by international standards. It is affected by the presence of market niches.

As of March 2000, 312 Italian intermediaries offered internet banking. These included 237 banks, with an aggregate 87 per cent share of total bank assets. Internet banking customers numbered 480,000 (2 per cent of all account-holders), of which 90 per cent were households. Activity over the web centres involving securities trading, deposit-taking and lending are still limited and activity in the other segments is negligible.

Telephone banking is more widely used. At the end of 1999 there were 161 banks supplying this service to more than 1.6 million customers, or 4 per cent of the total number of bank accounts. The percentage is lower than the European average of 5 per cent; rates of penetration are high in some countries (10 per cent in France and the United Kingdom) but lower than in Italy in others (including several Nordic countries).

Despite the technical and organizational progress of the payment system, recourse by households and firms to the new services offered remains limited. Only 48 per cent of households have a 'Bancomat' debit card and 20 per cent a credit card. Though increasing in recent years, the frequency of cashless payments remains appreciably below the EU level (43 payments per capita in Italy, against 121 in the EU). The lower density of current accounts (0.5 accounts per inhabitant, against 1.4 in the other main European countries), the fragmented distribution network, and slower acceptance and utilization of payment cards explain part of the gap, which is also due to a lower propensity to use innovative payment instruments, notably on the part of firms. At the end of 1999 only 315,000 firms, just 9 per cent of the total, did business with their own bank using electronic systems. Households and firms stand to reap substantial efficiency gains by making more intensive and rational use of the services the financial industry offers.

Managed assets

Managed portfolios and institutional investors have grown remarkably since the beginning of the 1980s, when the share of Italian households' financial assets entrusted to others for management was negligible. They have contributed significantly to the strengthening of the money and securities markets.

As in other countries, the asset management industry has developed to serve the needs of savers as their stock of financial wealth has increased, the scope for diversification has broadened even for small portfolios and the volume of trading has expanded, in a setting of volatile, technically complex markets. The phenomenon is also rooted in a process that developed earlier elsewhere before getting underway in Italy. The hypothesis, attributed to Ricardo and Keynes, that the contribution of wage workers to national saving is modest or nil no longer holds, if it ever did. More than one-third of the flow of Italian saving is generated by payroll workers or pensioners and their households. They invest a large part of it – around one-half – in financial assets rather than in real estate. These households' net financial wealth constitutes around 70 per cent of the Italian household sector's total financial assets. Between 1987 and 1998 average net financial wealth rose from 37 to 75 million lire for payroll employee households and from 47 to 189 million lire for pensioner households, while it grew from 66 to 305 million for other households. The relative smallness of individual holdings, the cost of their direct administration and the great size of their aggregate value make it more advantageous for workers, having become rentiers, to entrust these funds to professional investors for management.

The birth of securities investment funds and the spread of individual portfolio management services in the early 1980s provided decisive impetus. Financial assets under management by intermediaries (securities investment fund units, individual investment portfolios, insurance policies and pension funds) rose to 10 per cent of households' total financial assets at the beginning of the 1990s and 42 per cent at the end of the decade (Table 1.4). However, this is still less than the average for the G-7 countries (55 per cent). Like others, this aspect of the remaining

Table 1.4   Percentage composition of the assets of institutional investors in selected countries[a]

	Italy	France	Germany	Spain	United Kingdom	United States
Institutional investors						
investment funds	44	43	44	61	12	27
insurance companies	17	57	51	36	49	20
pension funds	5	0	5	3	39	39
other	34	0	0	0	0	14
Total	100	100	100	100	100	100
Total/GDP	0.98	1.16	0.70	0.69	2.14	2.19
Total/households' financial assets	0.42	0.50	0.46	0.42	–	0.71

[a] The data refer to 1999 for Italy and 1998 for the other countries.
Sources: For Italy, Bank of Italy; for the other countries, OECD, *Institutional Investors. Statistical Year Book* (1999).

gap is largely ascribable to the social protection network provided by the public sector in Italy and the corresponding underdevelopment of pension funds.

A comparison of the main euro-area countries by ratio of the stock of managed assets to GDP shows Italy in an intermediate position with a ratio of 98 per cent at the end of 1999, against 70 per cent for Germany and Spain and 115 per cent for France. Continental Europe remains light-years behind the United Kingdom and the United States, where professionally managed assets exceed 200 per cent of GDP. In both the Anglo-Saxon countries the combined contribution of insurance companies and pension funds is preponderant (188 and 129 per cent of GDP, respectively); in Italy this aggregate is equal to 22 per cent of GDP. In France and Germany insurance companies but not pension funds have an important market share (more than 50 per cent of managed assets).

The banking industry has used local branches and numerous financial salesmen (more than 15,000 at the end of 1998) to market increasingly specialized asset management products. Banks directly provide management services for individual investment portfolios amounting to 431 trillion lire (21 per cent of total assets under management). Bank-controlled companies received nearly all of the flow of fresh funds to collective investment undertakings in 1999 and accounted for 95 per cent of the total assets of asset management companies, compared with 80 per cent at the end of 1996. Among the securities held for custody by banks, those owned directly by firms and households are diminishing while those deposited by investment firms and asset management companies are increasing and amount to 738 trillion lire, or 38 per cent of the total. The administration of assets has generated increasing fee income for banks: 13.5 trillion lire, or 14 per cent of total gross income, in 1998.

Derivatives

Derivatives are prominent among the financial instruments recently introduced or popularized in Italy. The value of these contracts and the obligations and entitlements they establish for the contracting parties depend on the value and characteristics of underlying assets or indices, hence the term 'derivatives'. The contracts establish the obligation (forwards and futures) or the right (options) to deliver or receive the underlying at a predetermined date. Alternatively, it is sometimes possible to settle the difference, calculated on the underlying, between the price agreed at the contract date and the price obtaining at the delivery date. Swaps are derivative contracts based on the settlement of the difference in value between two assets or indices at dates established in advance.

The contractual results can be made to depend on a potentially unlimited variety of events; for example, a ski-lift operator can issue bonds with coupons conditional upon snowfall. More efficiently than the techniques used in the past, derivatives facilitate the opening and closing of positions, both in order to hedge portfolios against risk and to bet on the direction securities and commodities prices will take. They allow risk to be split into separately tradable (financial and credit) components. They adjust portfolios to preferences in a way that cannot be achieved using primary securities alone. They make it possible to create new financial instruments 'synthetically' by calibrating the mix between derivatives and primary securities, and thus lend themselves to financial innovation.

The spread of futures trading on the stock exchanges has contributed decisively to the development of organized derivatives markets. A clearing house and standardized contracts constitute the basis of the arrangement. As the central counterparty to all transactions, the clearing house guarantees the execution of contracts; by setting the margin requirements for participants and managing their margin deposits and the marking-to-market of contracts, it neutralizes the credit risk inherent in the transactions. The structure of the futures market has been extended successfully to trading in options, which are written on securities similar to those underlying futures contracts. On the other hand, swaps and forward contracts are traded bilaterally in non-centralized electronic over-the-counter (OTC) markets in which dealers trade with any counterparty. The lower degree of standardization and the absence of margins and transparent marking-to-market make OTC markets more suitable for counterparties' particular needs and innovative contracts.

Italy's first organized derivatives market, the MIF futures market, created in 1991, is an electronic market for trading futures and options on government securities and futures on short-term interest rates. With the transformation of the markets into companies subject to private law, in 1998, MIF was acquired by Borsa Italiana S.p.A. Italy's first market in futures on equity securities, the IDEM derivatives market, was set up at the end of 1994 as an integral part of the stock exchange. The following year the introduction of the options market heavily reduced the volume of trading in traditional Italian option-style and stock-exchange repo contracts, which had been listed ever since the establishment of the stock exchange under public law in 1913.

The use of derivatives by Italian intermediaries, negligible until the end of the 1980s, grew very rapidly in the following years. Macroeconomic instability, flexible exchange rates after the crisis of the European Monetary System in 1993 and uncertainty about the convergence of interest rates in the European Monetary Union accelerated the learning process.

Forward contracts remain prevalent in foreign exchange trading with deferred delivery, as in other countries, but derivatives (swaps, futures and options) hold sway when it comes to contracts based on securities and interest rates. Only a part of forward and derivatives trading takes place on organized markets. The OTC component is predominant in foreign exchange forward trading, currency derivatives and interest rate swaps.

Derivatives activity in Italy is comparable with that in the other main countries. The volume of business in exchange-traded derivatives on Italian securities is one of the highest in Europe. Adjusting for the size of Italy's financial sector, it is in line with the volume recorded in the United States.

In 1998 average daily turnover in the organized markets of lira-denominated instruments exceeded 60 trillion lire ($35 billion), more than two-thirds of it involved money market and bond-based instruments. The latter component, nine-tenths of which referred to the London marketplace, contributed significantly to the formation of the euro-area derivatives market; in 1998 it accounted for 15 per cent of transactions in derivatives based on euro-area interest rates and bonds. The European market drew equal with the US market in size. With the introduction of the euro in 1999, the volume of transactions in money market and bond-based instruments fell to 5.3 trillion lire. In 1999 trading in equity index derivatives on the Italian stock exchange accounted for 14 per cent of total turnover in the European market, a share second only to that of Eurex (which combines Germany and Switzerland) and larger than that of the London and Paris exchanges.

Cassa di Compensazione e Garanzia S.p.A., the clearing house, was founded in March 1992 by the 22 primary dealers on MTS, who were interested in the nascent market in futures on government securities (at the end of October 1999 the Cassa had 149 members). It began risk management in August 1992 through the Settlement Guarantee Fund, charged with ensuring the closing of the clearing and the execution of stock exchange contracts. The following month MIF started operations and the Cassa began to perform clearing house functions by stepping in as central counterparty with appropriate risk limitation mechanisms and assuming contracts made by its own direct members. Its clearing house role was subsequently extended to the new types of contract traded on MIF and, from November 1994, to those traded on IDEM. In June 1999 the Cassa began clearing of the three-month Euribor contract traded on MATIF, the French futures market. The number of contracts handled by the Cassa rose from 0.8 million in 1992 to around 9 million in 1999. The Cassa protects the integrity of the markets by setting capital and organizational requirements for membership, setting initial margin requirements and marking positions to market on a daily basis, and requiring deposit of additional intraday margins in the event of market turbulence. The method of calculating initial margins have been refined over time and are in line with those used in the other European financial centres. Fees have been gradually reduced. There have been no defaults by direct members.

Unlike the data on the organized markets, available information on OTC trading is sketchy. The surveys do little else than measure the activity of the main participants. Italy accounts for a smaller share of OTC business than of exchange-based trading, although the percentage is not negligible.

Daily turnover in foreign exchange forward contracts and OTC derivatives in the Italian markets amounted to $33 billion in 1998, an increase of a little less than 50 per cent compared with 1995. The former rose from nearly $16 billion in 1995 to just over $22 billion in 1998, owing essentially to the growth of 127 per cent in foreign exchange swaps, whose share increased from 33 to 52 per cent. The proportion of total transactions attributable to non-resident counterparties remained broadly unchanged (around 75 per cent). By contrast, activity in derivatives based on exchange rates declined from $1 billion to $0.7 billion, owing to the reduced recourse to currency swaps and domestic currency swaps, while the volume of options increased.

Notional turnover in derivatives based on securities and interest rates rose from $2.5 billion to more than $6 billion per day between 1995 and 1998. In particular, activity in derivatives based on interest rates rose from $1.7 billion to $5.5 billion and from 62 to 88 per cent of the total. The sharpest increase was that in interest rate swaps, from $0.5 billion to $4 billion; daily activity in interest rate options rose from $0.2 billion to $0.4 billion.

As in the foreign exchange market, in 1998 the bulk of activity in OTC derivatives consisted of interbank contracts and transactions with non-residents (92 and 75 per cent, respectively); the majority of transactions were denominated in lire (88 per cent).

Finance and the sectors of the economy

The changes in the total gross assets and liabilities of the financial sector have interacted in various ways with the needs and resources of economic agents, with their propensity to issue and to hold financial instruments and to request financial services. These changes are reflected in the accounts of households, non-financial firms, general government and the 'rest of the world', the four major sectors, together with the financial sector, composing the economy. This purely accounting evidence shows that households and firms could have made and could still make much more intensive and efficient use of the possibilities permitted by the financial industry. In reality, the state has exploited those possibilities better and more extensively than households and firms, particularly in managing the enormous public debt and in carrying out large-scale privatizations.

Households

Although the propensity of Italian households to engage with the financial sector has increased, the scope for further growth remains considerable. The ratio of households' net financial assets to their disposable income rose from 1.6 in 1980 to 3.1 in 1999, in line with that of the other continental Europe countries but far lower compared with the Anglo-Saxon countries. In 1980 about three-fifths of Italian households' wealth consisted of tangible assets (mainly property) and two-fifths of financial assets. The latter's share grew uninterruptedly in the first half of the 1980s to reach one-half in 1986 and has subsequently fluctuated around that level.

In recent years the composition of households' financial portfolios has shifted almost everywhere in favour of less-liquid, higher-yielding and riskier instruments. In Italy the proportion of deposits plummeted between 1982 and 1999 from 50 to 20 per cent, with a corresponding increase in those of government securities and other bonds (from 15 to 17 per cent), shares (from 24 to 32 per cent) and 'other assets' (from 12 to 31 per cent). Pension funds constitute only 2 per cent of the household sector's portfolio. Direct holdings of fixed-income securities constitute a particularly large share by international standards: one-third, compared with an average of 7 per cent in the other European countries. Despite the improved structures of the payment system, households' cash balances still exceed 7 per cent of their disposable income, as in 1980, and cash continues to be widely used in transactions. A rising percentage of households hold risky assets, but it is still far lower than in other countries. In 1995 only 10 per cent of households in Italy held shares, investment fund units and individual portfolio management accounts, compared with 25 per cent in Germany, the United Kingdom and the United States; only 13 per cent held a diversified portfolio, compared with 22, 25 and 40 per cent respectively in the Netherlands, the United Kingdom and the United States. In 1998 the percentage of households declaring direct ownership of shares had risen but not surpassed 8 per cent.

However, it is on the liabilities side especially that Italian households' involvement with finance remains very limited. Over a span of 20 years households' financial liabilities grew from 1 to 17 per cent of disposable income, among the lowest levels for the main industrial countries. They do not reach 10 per cent of the value of the sector's financial assets, compared with 15 per cent in Germany and around 25 per cent in the United Kingdom, the United States and the Netherlands. The percentage of households in debt is twice as high in Germany, the United Kingdom and the Netherlands, and almost three times as high in the United States. While bank lending to firms in Italy is equal to around 40 per cent of GDP, as in the rest of the euro area, bank lending to households does not reach 20 per cent of GDP, compared with 44 per cent in the entire euro area. Three-quarters of bank loans to households are long-term, consisting primarily of mortgage loans for the purchase and maintenance of real estate, ownership of which is widespread among Italians. In fact, more than two-thirds of Italian households own their home.

These characteristics are consistent with the comparative levels of the financial interrelations ratio – similar to those of the main countries of continental Europe, lower than those of the Anglo-Saxon countries – and with the decline in the role of credit intermediaries owing to a decrease in the demand for deposits and a slow increase in the demand for loans on the part of Italian households.

There is still ample scope for recourse to finance by Italian households. In some respects this reflects surmountable supply-side limitations arising from banks' perception of consumer credit as especially risky. However, households underutilize services the demand for which the financial system is already able to satisfy. This is what happens in the field of payments. It happens in pension funds. It happens most notably in borrowing, especially to cover the expenses of enhancing 'human capital', which in Italy are not located at the top of the 'Engel curve', where consumption becomes investment. The ratio of household spending on education, books and foreign travel to GDP (3 per cent) has increased only slightly over the last 20 years. Comparing the structure of private consumption of the 15 EU countries, Italy is first in spending on clothing, second for furnishing, third for restaurants, but only ninth in spending on education and culture.

Firms

In the 1980s and 1990s Italian firms' fixed investment trended down-wards in relation to GDP while their profit margins rose (Figure 1.3). The average rate of capital formation fell from 24 per cent in the 1970s to 20.2 per cent in the 1980s and 19.2 per cent in the 1990s; it was 19.7 per cent in 1999. The decline was caused by the collapse of investment in construction, which was offset only partly by increased spending on plant and equipment. The annual flow of direct investment abroad exceeded 1 per cent of GDP in 1998–9. Gross profits in the economy as a whole rose on average from 29 per cent of GDP in the 1970s to 31 per cent in the 1980s and 32 per cent in the 1990s; in 1999 the ratio approached 35 per cent. There is a clear inverse correlation between profits and investment. Self-financing continued to be the main source fuelling investment in the 1990s in all the major economies. Internally generated resources cover a larger share of investment in the United Kingdom, the United States and France, approaching 100 per cent.

Figure 1.3   Rates of capital formation in Italy (percentages)

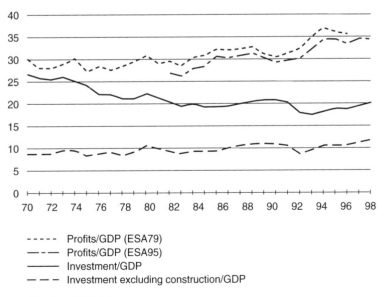

Source: Based on ISTAT data.

The ratio is lower in Germany and Japan. In Italy, after fluctuating around 50 per cent in the first half of the 1990s, it rose to more than 60 per cent in the second half of the decade, when peak values for profits coincided with lows for investment. This led to less recourse by firms to outside financing, thus restricting, as in the case of households, the growth of financial intermediation.

The last few years have seen diversification of the sources of corporate finance in continental Europe and the Anglo-Saxon countries, with a departure from earlier trends.[6] For Anglo-Saxon firms there has been an increase in the role of debt, especially at short term. For those of continental Europe the growth in self-financing has corresponded to a shift in the composition of the financial structure to the benefit of equity, less recourse to loans and a lengthening of the maturity of debt. Nonetheless, loans, particularly bank loans, still constitute the main source of external financing, especially in Germany.

Share issues by firms have been abundant in France, the United Kingdom and Italy; the volume has been smaller, but growing, in Germany. In Italy the bulk of equity issuance has taken place outside the stock exchange. Shares of listed companies make up less than one half the total value of shares and other equity of Italian firms. Bonds have been an important source of funds in the United Kingdom and the United States, far more than in the past. Despite the increase in Euromarket issuance in 1999, bonds are little used by non-financial firms in France and especially in Germany and Italy (where the amount outstanding was equal to only 2 per cent of corporate liabilities in 1999). As remarked earlier, few Italian firms use innovative payment systems, such as those permitted by electronic links with their banks. Their issues of commercial paper are virtually non-existent. Demand for advanced financial services supplied not only by Italian merchant banks and venture capitalists, but also by their more experienced foreign counterparts, remains limited. Between 1992 and 1998, tender offers for listed companies averaged fewer than 20 a year, with acceptances averaging 2.7 trillion lire a year; in 1999, under the new legislation on tender offers, the number of offers rose to 24 and acceptances soared to 107 trillion lire in connection with the bid for Telecom Italia.

Corresponding to the changes in flows are those in stocks (though these are also influenced by the rules for valuing shares), with a reduction in the share of debt in the liabilities of non-financial firms in Italy, France and Germany. The share of debt is relatively high in Germany, lower in France. In Italy it is low for the aggregate encompassing non-financial corporations and individual proprietorships but intermediate with reference to corporations alone. While the ratio of financial debt to the sum of financial debt and equity is 66 per cent for small firms, compared with 46 per cent for large firms, the leverage ratio of listed companies is around half that of unlisted companies. Listed companies are not only less numerous in Italy but also younger than those in other countries. Italian firms make abundant use of short-term bank loans and trade credit.

In the main economies there has been a continuing, moderately rising trend in the ratio of firms' financial assets to value added. The increase in Italy has been among the most regular, but the ratio is still less than one and the lowest among the major industrial countries. The composition of Italian firms' financial assets reflects the large drop in the share of deposits (from 42 per cent in 1980 to 15 per cent in 1999) and the corresponding increase in that of equity interests (from 26 to 58 per cent). After rising from 6 to 19 per cent in the 1980s the proportion of fixed-income securities fell back as interest rates declined, and stood at 8 per cent at the end of the 1990s.

The public sector

The public sector's liabilities began to mount in the 1970s. In the following decade the buildup became anomalous, proceeding at breakneck pace. The accumulation of debt was driven by growing budget deficits and high real interest rates. The budget deficit on current account – general government dissaving – reached peaks of 8 per cent of GDP. In view of the high level of interest rates and inflation and uncertainty about the future cost of the debt, it was considered advisable to suspend issues of medium- and long-term fixed-rate paper and to limit placements to short-term or indexed securities. The average residual life of the debt shortened dramatically, contracting to almost 12 months in 1982. It stayed below 30 months until the turn of the 1990s. Treasury Minister Guido Carli is to be credited for having rejected ideas and tentative proposals for solving the debt problem with instruments of 'extraordinary finance'.[7]

Strategic, market-oriented management of the Treasury's assets and liabilities was necessary. Orderly sales of government securities and limitation of the risks of financial instability were immediate priorities. A broad and efficient primary market and negotiability of the securities on the secondary market were the guidelines followed by the Treasury and the Bank of Italy in managing the public debt. The creation of a liquid and transparent electronic wholesale market in government securities, the success of the markets in derivatives, and the introduction of multiple-price auctions for Treasury bills and uniform-price auctions for other government securities were instrumental to this end. Direct access to the international markets with the placement of 'Republic of Italy issues' brought foreign intermediaries closer to Italian government securities. The Treasury's activity in the international market gradually became more sophisticated, with recourse in the 1990s to currency and interest rate swaps as means of hedging financial risks and to innovative technical forms such as issues of global bonds and commercial paper, still rarely utilized by Italian issuers. The new placement procedures and the wider array of instruments helped to curb the cost of the debt and reduced underpricing in placements on the primary market; that phenomenon began to diminish at the end of the 1980s and has virtually vanished today.

Public offerings of the Treasury's shareholdings have contributed greatly to stock market capitalization since the turn of the 1990s. More than 90 per cent of the privatization sales by the Treasury have been carried out by means of public offerings on the stock exchange. To apply privatization receipts to lowering the debt, the Treasury has bought back outstanding government securities through auctions with the primary dealers of the new issue market or directly on the secondary market.

The buildup of financial liabilities began to slow as the deficit on current account diminished, public investment declined and privatizations proceeded. The stabilization of the debt, the fall in interest rates and disinflation created propitious conditions for lengthening maturities. These opportunities were seized, and the average residual maturity of the debt rose from 18 months in 1995 to 70 months in 2000. Since 1993 the market has accepted 30-year Republic of Italy issues.

If Italy's ratio of public debt to GDP is almost twice that of other European countries, private financial liabilities are only a fraction of the corresponding amounts in the other countries: 71, 46 and 36 per cent, respectively, of those in Germany, the United Kingdom and France. Nations adopt different solutions to financing investment and social security systems. In contrast with other countries, in Italy private-sector debt has tended to contract in recent years, as have the total liabilities of the non-financial domestic sector.

These developments suggest the possibility of the crowding out of the private sector by the public sector. According to this hypothesis, the high level of interest rates, pushed up by the excess supply of government securities, helps to explain diminishing investment and debt issuance on the part of firms; meanwhile, the public pension system braked households' accumulation of financial assets in the form of private pension funds and held down their propensity to issue liabilities.

The second phenomenon no doubt occurred. Yet, the reduction in general government's liabilities in recent years has not been accompanied by an expansion in households' assets and liabilities; on the contrary, their financial balances diminished in relation to GDP during the 1990s.

From at least 1993 onwards, firms' high and rising profits and declining financial deficits, the availability of unutilized real resources (and not only of unemployed workers), the transfer of real resources to the rest of the world, the large gap between potential and actual output, and the reduction in interest rates starting in 1996 have characterized an economy under decreasing strain. A reduction in the liabilities of the state has not been matched by greater resource utilization on the part of firms, despite the absence of financial or real constraints. The high current and expected long-term level of the overall fiscal burden (taxes and social security contributions) necessary to service and reduce the debt has been the real obstacle to private investment. The public debt has held down investment by lowering the marginal efficiency of capital more than by raising interest rates.

The domestic sectors – general government, firms and households – recorded a simultaneous contraction in their financial balances in relation to GDP in the 1990s (Figure 1.4). Their contribution to the overall quantitative growth of financial intermediation decreased. The rest of the world, with a financial deficit from 1994 onwards, was the only sector whose contribution to the growth in Italian financial assets increased.

The rest of the world

The share of Italian financial instruments held by non-residents rose from 11.4 per cent in 1992 to 14.3 per cent in 1999. A similar increase occurred in Germany, whose openness is comparable to Italy's, and in the United States, which remain less open in this respect. In the Italian case, the growth in non-residents' exposure involved both fixed-income securities and equities.

Over the same period the proportion of foreign assets in residents' total financial assets increased by a larger extent, rising from 9 to 16.5 per cent. The growth was mainly in regard to loans (from 5.2 to 14.5 per cent), shares (from 10 to 26.2 per cent) and fixed-income securities (from 8.3 to 17.5 per cent). The international composition of portfolios did not change in the other countries, with the exception of France and

Figure 1.4   Sectoral financial balances in Italy (as a percentage of GDP)

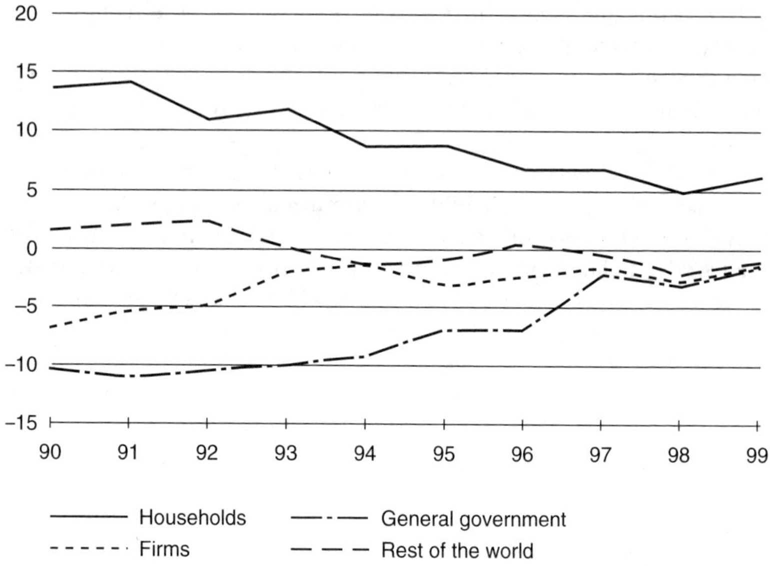

Source: Banca d'Italia, 'Conti finanziari'.

the United States, where the share of foreign assets rose slightly. Italy's international diversification is similar today to that of France and Germany.

The precondition for the growth in Italy's financial exposure to the rest of the world in the 1990s was the dismantling of the foreign exchange controls introduced in the 1970s. Nowadays Italy is among the OECD countries with the lowest institutional barriers to international trade and investment. The economy's greater openness to world trade is reflected in the ratio to GDP of exports and imports of goods and services at constant prices, which rose from 32 per cent in 1982 to 41 per cent in 1990 and 55 per cent in 1999.

The foreign exchange regime now in force is based on the principle of freedom. The previous reigning principle of prohibition with exceptions has been overturned. The state monopoly on gold and foreign exchange dated from 1917. In the 1960s it was made possible for residents to carry out a series of cross-border transactions through authorized banks. However, in the 1970s there was a reversal of this trend, with the intensification of restrictions and controls in 1973 and 1976. Law 159 of 30 April 1976, which possessed an autarkic stamp reminiscent of the 1930s, introduced severe sanctions for several violations, such as the illegal export of capital, holding foreign exchange abroad and failure to sell foreign exchange to the Italian Foreign Exchange Office. Liberalization resumed in 1984 and was confirmed in 1986, with the enabling law for the reform of foreign exchange legislation. The process was completed with the codified law on foreign exchange in 1988 and the abolition in May 1990 of the remaining constraints and restrictions, making Italians fully free to engage in financial transactions with the rest of the world. Since then the Italian economy has been fully immersed in the context that has been taking shape for the world economy – high capital mobility, competition between financial systems and centres, and the globalization of finance.

The turning-point for Italy's accounts with the rest of the world came in 1992. The trade balance and the external current account had been in deficit up to the end of the 1970s, leading to the accumulation of a net external debtor position equal to 11 per cent of GDP. Starting in 1993, in the wake of the depreciation of the lira, the disinflation of the economy and the stagnation of domestic demand, Italy ran a string of large surpluses on the trade balance and the external current account. These gradually reduced the country's net external debt, eventually giving Italy a net creditor position (equal to 4.5 per cent of GDP in 1999). They contributed to creating financial assets in a phase in which the surpluses and deficits of the other sectors were diminishing in relation to GDP.

A tendency to converge?

The foregoing presentation has sketched the Italian financial system's radical change over time, its mutation. Until a decade or two ago the comparative radiography of financial systems, conducted using institutional and statistical methods à la Goldsmith or Gurley and Shaw, would have found the Italian financial system overdeveloped in some segments and underdeveloped or totally lacking in other, innovative areas. Today, an analysis of this type reveals a morphological structure comparable with the major finance systems.

The change has followed the pattern prevailing in international finance, which in Europe is also reflected in the directives of the European Community. In some sectors and in several respects this conformity has led to the attainment of convergence. This is the case of the now dominant role played by the securities and financial markets and by intermediaries with a specific mission to operate in them and of private-sector ownership of the banks. In other fields convergence is clearly underway and is destined to be completed. This is the case of derivatives, of the use of the new payment systems, of international openness. In other respects Italy, though moving in the same direction, has progressed less rapidly than other countries and the gap has widened. This is the case of pension funds, whose underdevelopment, reflecting the approach used to fund expenditure for the elderly, is the principal anomaly persisting in the Italian financial system.

In the last twenty years the Italian economy has followed a different path from most of the other industrial countries in Europe and beyond. Inflation came down more slowly and less smoothly, from 20 per cent in the early 1980s to 1.7 per cent in 1999. Long-term interest rates fell from 22 per cent to less than 4 per cent in 1998, the lowest level in nominal terms since the 1930s. The general government budget showed a deficit, net of interest payments, equal to 5.4 per cent of GDP in 1981; in 1997 that deficit had given way to a surplus of nearly 7 per cent. For the fourth time since Italian unification – following the peaks of 1897, 1920 and 1943 – in 1994 the public debt rose above the threshold of 120 per cent of GDP, before turning downwards. The effective exchange rate of the lira weakened by 15 per cent in the summer of 1992 and by 10 per cent in the spring of 1995; it then strengthened by 10 per cent, up to the lira's re-entry to the EMS in November 1996, which was followed by the irrevocable locking of exchange rates in Europe, the advent of the euro in 1999 and the phasing out of the lira. The external accounts showed large deficits up to 1992, large surpluses thereafter. Between the 1970s and the 1990s the rate of capital formation fell by 15 per cent while the unemployment rate rose from 6 to 12 per cent, with widespread irregular use of immigrant labour as well as Italian workers. The rate of output growth diminished in the 1980s and fell by one-half in the 1990s.

This upheaval did not prevent the Italian financial system from being part of the international trends that globalization was powerfully reinforcing, but it did accelerate developments on some fronts and cause lags on others. The distinctive traits still to be found reflect not only the capabilities of the market's actors but also the latent propensity of Italian households and firms to exploit the potential of the financial system.

However, the crucial point is the change itself. It has occurred. The financial system that Beneduce and Menichella had to reinvent in 1933 on the ruins of the previous system[8] had remained unchanged, and basically unquestioned, up to the wage- and oil-shock-induced stagflation of the 1970s. Today that system and its institutional configuration of intermediaries, markets and financial instruments have ceased to exist.

A new system has been forged in a twenty-year transformation. Its basic configuration resembles the internationally prevailing model. Together with the features of the new system, with its morphology, which we have described in this chapter, we must evaluate the determinants and quality of the change, its implications for the Italian economy, and the both actual and potential utilization of the system by economic agents.

2
The Institutional and Analytical Framework

Among the causes of change we cited in the previous chapter were the impulses transmitted by the world financial system to Italy's increasingly open economy. We also referred to the Italian economy's own needs, expressed amidst acute tensions as it changed, in some ways falling into line with the trends in the other leading economies and in some ways diverging from them. Alongside these forces and in relation to the capacity of Italian bankers and financiers to adapt and bring in the new, we must examine how the financial system has been governed. During the period under scrutiny, governance was a very important factor, with the contributions of Parliament, the executive, the independent authorities and the Bank of Italy. The transformation of the financial system was realized by market forces, but it was also accepted, influenced and spurred by economic policy in all its manifestations: regulation, taxation, supervision and the promotion of competition.

Historical analysis and documentary research could determine whether this action was undertaken in the late 1970s and early 1980s as part of an overall plan, how precise and detailed such a plan was originally and how far it was adapted and extended over the years. Although at the start a precise and comprehensive 'official' design – a sort of national plan – was lacking, in the chapters that follow we shall see whether the course of events does not suggest, *ex post*, a coherent fabric, a logical sequence in the progressive configuration of the new financial system that the Italian economy adopted over two decades.

I am convinced, and can testify, that the Bank of Italy, in the unhappily brief governorship of Paolo Baffi (1975–9) and the first part of that of Carlo Azeglio Ciampi (1979–93), perceived the need for change. On the technical plane the Bank involved the successive treasury ministers and developed the principles that would later guide the transformation. This justifies this book's adoption of 1980 as a conventional starting date for the reform process, whose necessity and general thrust did not escape the Bank of Italy, at least. The central bank was convinced of the urgent need to strengthen the response of resource allocation and the financial structure to the economic crisis of the 1970s, the most severe and complex the country had experienced since the 1930s. The Bank's analysis of the crisis centred on the aggregate supply shock: oil and wages, the exogenous pressures that made for the stagnation of output and rising prices. The critique focused on the mechanisms propagating inflation: 100 per cent indexations and the loss of control over the public finances. In the 1980s the first of these would be defused, the idea of wages as an 'independent variable' overturned; but the second degenerated into the dissipation of public money. Baffi and Ciampi were among the few to grasp, early on, that in addition to this macro dimension, on which the Bank of Italy (long unheeded) never failed to insist, the crisis had a no less important micro dimension. The ultimate limit to the capacity to respond to shocks lay in the spheres that ought to have overcome the inconsistency between relative prices and the use of resources: the markets, imperfect; the state's presence, redundant; and the whole model of Italy as a mixed economy, inadequate.

The Bank of Italy's diagnosis stressed that the collapse in the terms of trade and the wage explosion had undermined the very foundations of Italy's mixed economy: that peculiar combination of state, market, public enterprises and financial institutions that had accompanied and embodied the material progress of a poor nation in the first two decades after the war. The constellation of prices and the ways in which resources were used were under fierce pressure. Only reformed mechanisms of allocation, not least the banking and financial system, would enable the economy to make better use of its productive capacity, to overcome the stagflation to which wage and oil price pressures had consigned it, and to resume stable growth. The financial system that had arisen out of the crisis of the 1930s and been consolidated in the 1950s – a system that over the decades had successfully intermediated large flows of savings and guaranteed some degree of competition between large industrial groups and small companies – was inadequate to the quintessential function of large-scale dynamic reallocation to which it was now called for the first time.

In the official documents of the Bank of Italy and internal analytical papers we can readily trace the identification of urgent problems and suggested lines for reform. We begin with Governor Baffi's 'Concluding

Remarks' to the Bank's annual meetings and the collected speeches and writings of Governor Ciampi.[1]

Baffi had never concurred with the mixed-economy paradigm. The philosophy of Ricardo, Walras, Keynes – fundamental economic theory, of which he was a scholar – could not accommodate any such model, which in Italy literally extended as far as a state-made pastry industry. Although those thinkers differed in their conception and their degree of acceptance of overall government action in the economy, Baffi saw them as sharing an analysis that hinged on market prices as the mechanism of resource allocation. Long before it was fashionable he had been a critic of the concept and the organization of the mixed economy. His 'Observations on IRI' in 1955 was a harsh, unflinching statement of the case against Italy's state holding company,[2] despite the fact that IRI had been created and directed by the governor of the day, Donato Menichella. As director general of the Bank of Italy he had ill tolerated these arrangements under what he called the 'dazzling' governorship of Guido Carli (1960–75), who tried to improve if not overcome the system, but working from within. When he succeeded Carli at the head of the central bank he attacked it openly. It was the backlash from the economic and political power structure that curtailed Paolo Baffi's term as governor, wounding him personally as well.

Unbinding a 'constricted credit system'; an equal footing for public and private banks; avoidance of the commingling of banking and commerce; the independence of the Bank of Italy in banking supervision as in monetary policy; competition in banking; reformed tax treatment of corporate finance; the discretionary powers of the banker, from designation onwards; efficient money and capital markets; the vices of subsidized credit: these were the financial issues that Baffi dealt with in his 'Concluding Remarks' from 1975 to 1979. The analytical framework implicit in his reports to the annual meetings of the Bank combined aggregate supply shock and disproportions in resource allocation. This is what he stated explicitly, in the untrammeled language of the scholar, in his introductory address, as president, to the scientific meeting of the Italian Association of Economists in 1981.[3]

Starting from this analysis of the causes of the crisis and its implications for financial structures – as well as for the public finances, industrial relations and market forms – the Bank developed a series of reflections, partly in collaboration with outside scholars. A significant contribution came from the Einaudi Institute under the leadership of former governor Carli in 1975 and 1976.[4] Another major event was the Institute's 1980 international conference on credit systems in the 1970s.[5]

In his own 'Concluding Remarks,' starting with the very first, Governor Ciampi reaffirmed and enriched this framework of analysis, drawing out its institutional and economic policy implications. This was the direction in which the Bank of Italy would proceed, in practical action as in policy proposal, during the 1980s and 1990s. Under Ciampi's tenacious and constructive leadership and, from 1993 onwards, under his successor Antonio Fazio, the Bank justified, promoted and realized the transformations in the financial system I have broadly described in Chapter 1.

In its spheres of competence the Bank acted directly: supervision, promotion of competition, the promulgation of regulations. Indirectly, through suggestions, technical collaboration, and public advocacy the Bank also influenced primary legislation, playing a major role in the drafting of the two consolidated laws on banking and finance and a lesser but still significant role in shaping tax measures in these fields.

Yet if our selection of the starting point is well founded, if guidelines for action were laid down decades ago, one wonders why was there no 'big bang' but instead a lengthy process of reform. Why was the metamorphosis so slow, difficult, laborious?

The change was not traumatic; it did not come, as in the 1930s, under the gun of a deep depression. So it was gradual, as may be proper to the financial sector. Financial instability can infect the entire economy, implicitly counselling Alessandro Manzoni's dictum, *'adelante con juicio'* (advance judiciously). Finance involves such special conceptual categories as agents' reputations, which are constructed over time, and information asymmetries, which are overcome with time. Markets and financial institutions are not created overnight, and as a rule they change only gradually.[6] With the benefit of hindsight, however, the impression is that not only the nature and depth of the *mutation*, which in itself implies a longer time-frame, but also a variety of factors combined to slow the change.

The arrangements inherited from the 1930s constituted a stand-alone system – legal scholars called it an *'ordinamento sezionale'*[7] – constructed, theorized and governed by overarching criteria. This made the system internally homogeneous in its watchwords and its established positions, and accordingly particularly inertial and resistant to change. For its merits or out of sheer coincidence, that system had accompanied the Italian economy from 1950 to 1973 in its extremely rapid growth and radical transformation, a period of extraordinary and perhaps unrepeatable success. It was Italy's true, belated industrial revolution and saw a country lacking in natural resources and decadent for centuries become newly rich. Above all that system corresponded to an idea adopted by the political system, government and opposition alike, in which at least in intention the economy would be publicly guided and planned. Until it was abandoned – cautiously and unwillingly – the concept of the mixed economy placed stubborn obstacles in the way of the technical demands for reform which the Bank of Italy put forward with the support of the Treasury, notably under Beniamino Andreatta as minister,[8] a brilliant economist and courageous politician, and Mario Sarcinelli, former deputy director general of the Bank of Italy, as director general. As always, there was the resistance of vested interests. But in the final analysis the obstacles were cultural: economic, legal, technical and organizational habits of mind. No few economists and legal scholars, once fervent theoretical backers and interpreters of the state enterprise system, of an economy to be commanded by policy-makers through the public banks and subsidized credit, became equally fervent advocates of some form of economic neoliberalism. But for many the conversion was difficult, not always convinced, rarely credible. 'The difficulty lies, not in the new ideas, but in escaping from the old ones, which ramify... into every corner of our minds.'[9]

Rules, taxation, supervision, competition: these are the four sides of the frame that delineates the environment in which intermediaries and financial markets act. External action – public intervention to foster the development and orderly operation of finance and so to contribute to economic growth and stability – can focus on this framework, on these elements. It is inadvisable for the governance of financial structures to go further. Overstepping this border would mean slipping into the direct hypermanagement of the financial industry, which would be extremely difficult to interpret, the source of inefficiency and institutional confusion, in contradiction with the principles of what can truly be called a market economy.

Yet an adequate environment, though important, is not the whole solution. It is a necessary but not sufficient condition for the efficiency, proper functioning and soundness of the financial system and for the fortunes of the enterprises that make it up. Ultimately, these fortunes depend on the behaviour and the capacities of those who supply and those who demand financial services.

Each of the next four chapters will take up one of the four constituent elements of this framework, recounting its practical impact on the Italian financial system over the past two decades and tracing its present configuration. As a premise to this examination, we now set forth a number of more general – if not theoretical – considerations concerning the *raison d'être* and role of the four pillars of financial policy, the specific contribution of each to this area of economic policy, and their potential synergies.

The legal order

Juridical norms – laws – are indispensable, or inevitable. They allow, encourage, require, or prohibit actions. They are never without effect.

All possible theses on the relationship between law and economy have been upheld and rebutted. The fire of controversy has never gone out of what is now a centuries-old debate on method: from Smith to Hegel, from Marx to Stammler, from Croce to Capograssi, from Hayek to Director, from Coase to the 'law and economics' school. Yet no one has ever maintained the irrelevance of laws or, more generally, of the legal dimension to the operation of a market economy, and all the more so to a modern economy to which a 'monetary theory of production', in Keynes's words, applies.

Those who believe that a *laissez-faire* market system cannot unleash optimizing forces naturally tend to see law and rules not only as an exogenous variable but as instrumental, a potent tool for economic policy. Even those who hold that the economy is 'structure' and law 'superstructure' do not rule out major feedback effects, and thus a significant impact of the latter upon the former. Those who hold that laws are necessary to the economy in order to minimize transaction costs, and that without them the market's tendency to the optimum, or at least to the 'better', would be impeded, call for legislation to devise the most suitable solutions. The solutions may well be technical and not political, but they cannot be neutral; they are important *per se*. Those who feel that the legal order governing the market tends to arise spontaneously still call upon legislation, the legal order, to recognize if not to create the most effective codes of conduct. The recognition must be quick and appropriate, to avoid delay and distortion.

Those who hypothesize the irrelevance of law to the economy, if indeed there are any such, are thus the exception, even among the most highly abstract economists. Rather, what prevails is the common-sense belief that good law can greatly assist the good operation and progress of the economy while bad law impedes them.

Norms and legal scholarship, together with developments in the economy and in society, constitute the 'legal experience', a notion that sees as

correlated and interactive within a solid relation, interwoven in a 'set' . . . the world of 'human behaviour' and with it the relationships, structures and institutions that human behaviour creates...and the world of norms of all types and origins...the world of activities... which as a group we see as comprising *scientia juris*.[10]

The interactions of these elements, among which the economic is crucial, are so close as to make separating them, in analysis and in policy, inadvisable.

Certainly such separation runs counter to centuries of European thought, the intellectual tradition from which all the positions we have just mentioned concerning the relationship between economy and law originated. In Europe at least

> until the eighteenth century...the economy lived in symbiosis with the law and with a *philosophia practica*, rhetorically and juridically oriented and engaged. So thinking was influenced by a community paradigm of resource use – not only rational but also ethical – that was the antithesis of the Utilitarians' *homo oeconomicus*. The concept of wealth did not postulate egoistic use: if *'iniuria' represented the limit to the legitimacy of enrichment*, the foundations of the economic order must be sought in a negative philosophy of justice beginning from the problems of exchange connected with the redressing of torts. This, perhaps, is the cultural setting in which to frame the economic work of Adam Smith, professor of rhetoric, *jurisprudence* and *moral philosophy*: 'The end of justice is to secure from injury.'[11]

These propositions become all the more pregnant if referred to money, credit and finance, a specific yet crucial and all-pervasive dimension of the modern market economy. 'Money' is the answer to the realization that we must decide and act in a state of uncertainty, to the need for an efficient allocation of risk in any enterprise, where both uncertainty and risk are typical in scale and in form of an advanced economy. If there is a response, if the economy becomes monetary, both the potential prosperity and the potential instability of the economy increase dramatically. Financial assets constitute claims upon a flow of future income. An appropriate legal order underpins confidence in financial assets. The true test of property rights is a crisis. Almost always, financial crises are not crises of returns due to a surge in risk but outright crises of confidence, which are frequently amplified if not actually provoked by the imperfections of the institutional framework. Hence the increasingly widely acknowledged importance of attending to legal orders with a view to the efficiency and stability of the financial system.

An appropriate and certain system of law is not only useful or necessary but also valuable for the proper working of the market machinery in a monetary economy. Law plays a particularly significant role in fostering changes in the monetary and financial system, or at least in accompanying and facilitating them.[12]

At any point in time the legal framework is given; it is one of the environmental conditions for the economy and finance. However, the economy and finance change, usually by gradual evolution but sometimes abruptly. Thus there is a permanent problem concerning the adequacy and adaptation of the rules. Legal policy has two ways of tackling the problem. One is to embody in the law itself the timing and forms of a periodic check – a sort of self-analysis – of the legal order's correspondence to economic realities. A country that has taken this approach is Canada, which has regularly scheduled reviews of the validity of primary banking legislation (statutes). The other method is to allow ample room for secondary legislation (regulation), under principles fixed by law but in practice more flexible than statutes. This is the established tradition of Italy. The pros and cons of the two solutions are evident: the former is parliament-centred but slower, the latter administration-centred but quicker.

The adaptation of the Italian legal order to economic and financial realities is also susceptible to influence from Italy's membership in the European Community (whether and how far this influence has been exerted will be considered in Chapter 3). Community legislation directly affects Italian law by virtue of the prevalence of European over domestic law, which is based on article 11 of the Italian Constitution: 'Italy shall consent to limitations of sovereignty...' The Community produces acts that are general and abstract in nature. In some cases (regulations) they arc of direct and immediate efficacy within member states, with no need for transposition into national law. In others (directives) they impose upon member states certain results that must be attained, but without detriment to national jurisdiction as regards the form and means to use. In still others (decisions) acts are addressed to single states or persons and are binding only upon these. Finally, some acts (recommendations, opinions) are not binding. The choice of legal instrument is not left to the Community institutions when it is the Treaties that make the choice. It may happen that directives contain provisions so finely detailed as to leave no scope for national legislation in the implementing rules. In these cases the European Court of Justice and the national courts ordinarily recognize the direct application of the directive to the domestic legal order in so far as relationships between the individual and the state are concerned but not (so far) as regards the relationships of private citizens with one another. These directives are treated, *de facto*, as regulations, even though they are issued in spheres where Community bodies lack regulatory powers. In Italy, Law 86 of 9 March 1989 governs the procedures for performing Community obligations. The yearly 'Community transposition law' approved by Parliament can empower the government to implement directives by means of regulations (in the matters already governed by law but not reserved exclusively to legislation). In some cases the 'Community transposition law' has provided for implementation of directives by ministerial regulation or simple administrative acts.

Taxation

The one sphere in which the legal order is unquestionably imperative is taxation. Economics has devoted special attention to the importance of the fiscal side of finance. A series of key questions have been raised, not always finding sure or convincing answers. Should capital be taxed, or only labour and current consumption? Should taxation be neutral or should it serve to promote finance? Should the nation's financial industry be freed from taxation, so as to keep savings and investment at home? Should the tax system be used to impede the free movement of capital or reduce its velocity? What sort of harmonization of the taxation of savings should prevail within a single monetary area like that of the euro?

The taxation of investment income (interest, dividends and capital gains) as part of direct taxation is justified by the principle of taxpaying capacity and the traditional philosophy of modern tax systems. In principle, the all-inclusive income tax that is the linchpin of such systems covers investment income. The alternative approach, namely taxing consumption and wealth, has not been systematically applied. The problem has been the difficulty of enacting radical reform, especially when the intention was to move a country's tax system far away from the established, internationally adopted norms.

At all events, actual fiscal systems are all hybrids, with significant deviation towards consumption taxes. A good number of countries, including Italy, tax income from capital at a flat rate, forgoing the principle of progressive taxation. Exemptions or lower rates for certain kinds of income – depending on type of issuer, instrument or amount – are more the rule than the exception, especially where capital gains are concerned. *De facto*, this very patchy taxation of capital gains leads the system away from the taxation of comprehensive income, which is the theoretical principle. Going by the Hicksian definition of income as potential consumption (what an individual could have spent during a given period without diminishing his initial wealth), one should also tax the capital gains accrued during the tax period (and allow a tax deduction for capital losses). The gaps and inconsistencies in this sphere spur the invention of new types of financial instrument designed to avoid or reduce taxes by making income take the form of capital gains. And they distort taxpayers' choices.

Apart from the straightforward effect of reducing one's disposable income, taxation may impose the further burden of modifying the taxpayers' economic decisions: the excess burden of taxation.[13] Over-taxation may cause a significant decline in welfare even if the taxpayer avoids the income loss by forgoing the consumption of the good or service subject to taxation. Excessive taxation and the related distortion are correlated with the elasticity of demand. They increase with the square of the increase in the tax rate: marginal excessive taxation is greater than the average. Neutrality is less likely to be violated by taxes that do not bite at the margin and by general rather than special taxes. Unless there are definite policy reasons to seek a given composition or resource allocation of resources, the tax system should interfere as little as possible with citizens' economic advantages and disadvantages; that is, it should observe the constraint of neutrality. 'In the choice of taxes . . . it is necessary to avoid those forms of economic distortion, unless they respond to a specific objective.'[14]

> The scope of Barone's theorem in the evaluation of tax measures depends strictly on the function one assigns to such measures. In some cases, in fact, the distortion is no longer a harmful by-product of taxation but the precisely intended effect of the fiscal instrument selected.[15]

In the case of finance, one must consider not only formal, explicit taxation but also implicit quasi-taxes. The stealthiest levy, that is the erosion of holdings of money due to inflation, can be accompanied by such implicit levies as reserve requirements on bank deposits, lending ceilings, portfolio constraints on banks, ceilings on interest rates and restrictions on international capital movements. These levies are frequently decided or managed by administrative or technical bodies, such as central banks. In this case they amount to a sort of 'taxation without representation', having fiscal implications if no fiscal intent, but other avowed purposes: monetary policy, foreign exchange policy or economic management. The obstacles that such measures place in the way of financial deepening, the distortions they create between different instruments and intermediaries may actually exceed those of formal taxation enacted by parliament.

At the same time, total observance of the principle of neutrality meets other obstacles as well, especially in the taxation of financial assets:

> A general, uniform tax on saving and on *all* forms of investment is a purely hypothetical case. Some form of investment of savings always avoids taxation (e.g., savings invested in another country). Nor is it possible, in practice, to tax the net income of all the various forms of investment uniformly, because the *risk* factor is different; it cannot be appreciated in advance, so taxation at a uniform rate would actually be very unequal.[16]

In so far as it is possible to evaluate risk differentials, it may be questioned whether the gross return incorporating the higher risk premium should be taxed at a higher or at a lower rate. The sensitivity of the demand for financial assets to rates of return depends on the degree of risk aversion. Assuming risk neutrality, in efficient capital markets the equilibrium expected return on financial assets must be uniform. In this case there must be no discrimination in tax rates, so as to keep the relative economic advantage of the various choices unaltered. Assuming risk aversion, taxing all financial assets at the same rate would be anything but neutral. The demand for risky financial assets becomes less sensitive to yield differentials (demand elasticity of less than one). The distorting effects of taxation are attenuated. If the relative degree of risk aversion increases with an increase in wealth, a relatively risky asset will tolerate a higher tax rate. By contrast, if relative risk aversion decreases as wealth increases (the elasticity of demand for risky assets is greater than one), then the less-risky assets should be more heavily taxed. Consistent with the assumption of an elasticity of demand for risky assets lower than one is the proposal to make risk-free investment income totally tax-exempt and, for risky assets, to tax only the portion of the return over and above the risk-free rate. The merit of this variant is that it avoids fiscal interference in the allocation of resources between saving and consumption.

These considerations on tax neutrality assume the existence of a financial market that is efficient in transferring risk, with minor liquidity constraints; that the tax system allows the deduction of losses (that it is willing to take risks along with the investor); and that the demand function for financial assets is known, so that tax rates can be appropriately graduated.

Empirical studies of demand functions and investors' attitudes towards risk have produced discordant results. Kenneth Arrow hypothesized that the relative risk aversion implicit in the demand for financial assets was constant or rising with the expected return (wealth).[17] For the United States, he maintained that the observed elasticity of demand for risky assets with respect to wealth was less than one, while up to that time the observed elasticity of the demand for money with respect to wealth had been greater than one. Ideally, therefore, risky financial assets should have been taxed at a higher rate. Some later estimates reached the opposite conclusion on the elasticity of the demand for risky assets. Yet the evidence bearing on the equity-premium puzzle – which indicated that the holders of shares demand an exorbitant premium – supports Arrow's thesis that investors are strongly risk-averse. The uncertainty of empirical knowledge in this field is confirmed by the econometric estimates for Italy, which unlike those of Arrow for the United States have found long-term elasticity of the demand for money with respect to wealth to be less than one. The sensitivity of the demand for long-term government securities and of that for bank credit denote long-term elasticity greater than one. So in the case of Italy, optimal fiscal policy would imply higher tax rates on the financial assets that are substitutes for money.

The gamut of forms of investment relevant to taxation has been extended by the emergence of derivative products. The possession of instruments by final investors has been flanked by indirect means of holding in connection with the rise of institutional investors (mutual funds, insurance companies, pension funds). The diversification of forms of investment and the proliferation of types of instrument have complicated the valuation of the fiscal impact on the propensity to save and on the structure of the financial system. The difficulty is aggravated by the wide variety of modes of taxation of financial assets. Taxes may be levied on the purchase of securities (transaction taxes), on their sale (capital gains taxes), on their possession (wealth taxes), or on the flow of income from them (taxes on interest and dividends). A thorough evaluation of the net incidence of taxation on finance would also cover any subsidies to the financial industry or its users: subsidized credit, government bail-outs of financial institutions, privileged access to central bank credit on special terms. The diversity of forms and the complexity of the interactions among components make it difficult in the extreme to trace a satisfactory concise summary of the effects of fiscal and quasi-fiscal rules on financial intermediation. The evaluation is further complicated in a dynamic framework, when there are significant changes in macroeconomic variables (inflation, interest rates) and in the forms of taxation.

In imperfect product and factor markets, far from the pure theory schemas of Pareto and Barone, the scale of investment projects and consumption differs from the optimal. Tax neutrality, then, may not coincide with uniform effective marginal tax rates. One must consider the externalities stemming from various types of goods, such as investment in human capital and research. In these cases deviations from tax neutrality may be socially accepted. The very impossibility, in practice, of tracing the process whereby taxes are incorporated in the evaluation of effective yields generates the 'fiscal illusion'.

In the past such factors as a widespread demonic concept of finance, the idea that speculators and rentiers – as such, or because they are 'idlers' or simply because they are 'rich' – should be taxed more heavily than other groups or persons, the lesser scope for tax evasion and avoidance in an industry hinging on correct accounting practices, and efforts to govern the entire economy through direct controls on financial flows have led to the enactment of explicit and implicit levies on the financial industry out of proportion to its weight in the economy. The incidence of fiscal and quasi-fiscal levies on finance were estimated at 7 per cent of GDP in some developing countries in the 1980s, far above the financial sector's share in the value added of the whole economy.[18] In Italy too, tax revenues deriving directly from financial intermediaries and the users of financial instruments, though now amounting to less than 3 per cent of GDP, long represented more than a tenth of total tax revenue, twice the financial sector's incidence on GDP.

These considerations and these difficulties might suggest the desirability of a consistent structure of tax-induced distortions, rather than tax neutrality, which may or may not coincide with equal tax rates on net yields. Yet the problem of tax neutrality, the need to avoid distortions, is of special importance in the field of financial instruments. Both the price elasticity of the demand for financial assets/liabilities and for the interest and dividend income they generate and the sensitivity of financial choices to agents' expectations are high (though not necessarily increasing with financial innovation).

The reasonable conclusion is that the taxation of financial intermediation, both explicit and implicit, can cause distortions in individual choices, excesses of tax pressure, and possibly very significant reductions in welfare. This is more likely the higher is the average tax rate on financial assets and the greater the dispersion of rates and tax bases, and the more high average taxation and dispersion are combined with a panoply of direct administrative controls on financial flows. In this spirit, Chapter 4 is based on the assumption that the abandonment of such conditions, which prevailed in Italy at the outset of the period under review, represented an approach to tax neutrality.

The question of neutrality and deviations from it intersects with that of the obstacles or impulses deriving from the tax system for the development of given technical forms of finance. Starting from conditions far removed from neutrality, the fiscal system may in fact evolve towards greater general neutrality while at the same time acting, during the traverse, as a factor accelerating or delaying specific transformations within the financial industry. In some periods and some economic and institutional contexts the promotion of financial change by means of tax rules and the tendency towards tax neutrality in finance are not mutually exclusive.

Other questions raised in this section share reference to the nexus between financial taxation and capital movements and to the future rather than to the past. In an open economy, capital flows may be heavily influenced by differences between domestic and foreign taxation. Yet relieving the domestic financial industry of taxation, or subsidizing it, may correspond not to neo-mercantilist intentions but simply to the aim of fostering its progress, so as to endow the national economy with a requisite for growth.

In a modern monetary economy, finance should be considered what Piero Sraffa called a 'basic commodity', one that plays a direct or indirect part in the production of all commodities, rather than a 'luxury good' or final consumption good, the productivity of which does not affect relative prices, the profit rate or capital formation. So the attention of economic policy to this industry, possibly even with favoured tax treatment, is understandable. And in any case, the tendency is international, presumably because of the increase in capital mobility owing to globalization and financial market integration. The threat of 'losing' national savings leads countries to shift the tax burden away from the most mobile factor, financial capital, and onto the least mobile, labour. The same conclusion, though based on a completely different argument, is suggested by the debatable thesis of no tax on capital. On this theory, capital should be totally tax-exempt for a number of reasons: the elasticity of demand for capital is high,[19] so taxing it would be tantamount to taxing future consumption more heavily than current consumption; investment income and free time are substitutes, so taxing capital would be tantamount to providing an incentive for leisure time and a disincentive to labour supply;[20] consumption taxes that rise over time should be avoided, because these imply a distortion by raising future consumption prices and placing an excessive burden on taxpayers.[21]

This is not just a problem of income distribution, of equity, complicated (or simplified) by the fact that workers have become rentiers, holders of financial assets (so that if labour as a productive factor is more heavily taxed, workers *qua* savers and investors will be less heavily taxed). On assumptions radically different from those of the zero-capital-tax proposal, private wealth should be curbed and taxed and labour relieved of taxation if unemployment is high and the aim is to reduce it, lowering the 'reservation wage' demanded by workers.[22]

In Europe, the adoption of the single monetary policy eliminates differences between jurisdictions in the monetary field. However, it heightens the remaining differences in such areas as commercial law, bankruptcy law and tax law. In tax law in particular, the harmonization envisaged by the Treaty on European Union (title VI, chapter II) is designed to remove barriers to trade between member states, with express reference to indirect taxation. Apart from these provisions, there is the principle of subsidiarity, under article 5 of the Treaty. In order to limit disparities introduced by national law, the Commission may initiate the consultation procedures provided for in articles 96 and 97. The Council may intervene under article 94 by unanimously adopted directives when differences between tax laws constitute barriers to the proper functioning of the single market. Other important clauses are those requiring member states to observe the code of conduct on the taxation of enterprises, or the 'Stability and Growth Pact', which prohibits fiscal policies from violating certain parameters.

However, these limitations shrink but do not eliminate individual states' room for action in determining levels of taxation. In the countries that have adopted the euro, the tax treatment of savings is a burning issue:

> Not taxing interest income accruing to non-residents...which is now a common practice in Europe, generates distortions that are incompatible with the single market, causes a generalized loss of revenue undermining the budget discipline imposed by Community accords and, paradoxically, makes EU member countries tax havens with respect to one another.[23]

Europe's fiscal problem is as simple to solve technically as it is difficult politically: that is, by coordinating the treatment of saving with a single withholding rate in settlement of non-residents' tax liabilities or through exchange of information between national agencies on tax returns. But the fiscal problem consists above all in making the basic choice: whether or not to tax capital and wealth in a situation of high public debt, high tax rates and high unemployment.

The idea of coordinating the rules on the taxation of investment income, in order to ensure a minimum of actual levy, would appear to be based on the thesis that the 'deterioration' in the composition of tax revenue, favouring capital and penalizing labour, will produce a sub-optimal configuration. A glaring contradiction would arise, for instance, if Europe, to spur employment, opted to tax capital while the United States – with its low public debt, low taxes and high employment – opted to exempt capital and wealth. A fiscal policy attentive to the external and internal equilibrium of the European economy should thus distinguish between the freedom of movement and the velocity of movement of domestic capital abroad. In general, a policy of taxing savings may not conflict with citizens' freedom to invest abroad. But to prevent a structural outflow of savings, in such a scenario it could prove necessary to use the fiscal lever to slow down short-term capital movements – without prejudice to the free movement of capital – in order to counter downward pressures on the currency and a decline in domestic invest-ment. We must not underestimate the practical difficulties of introducing an internationally concerted measure, such as the 'Tobin tax' on cross-border financial transactions,[24] but these do not affect the theoretical concept. In any event, globalization would be put under heavy strain.

Supervision

Virtually everywhere, financial services and banking services in particular are subject to rules and supervision. In most countries these controls are stricter than those on other goods and services. The economic and social repercussions of financial market failures are judged to be more serious than the distortions and inefficiencies that may derive from regulation. In the period we are examining, there has been growing international pressure to extend banking and financial supervision, to bring all countries up to historically high standards. The calls for upgrading have not been limited to the emerging economies with their weak supervisory structures or to the offshore centres with their collusive oversight.

These developments and the underlying policy choice are sustained in both theoretical and empirical economics. Again on this aspect of money, banking and finance, namely the *raison d'être* and the form of rules and supervision, theory lagged behind real institutional developments and the conceptual framework that central bankers and other practitioners had forged. Economic theory merely set these developments in the context of the accepted principles. But it has helped to disseminate a conventional wisdom that affects opinion and is thus important even aside from its actual validity, which we shall not attempt to discuss here.

According to these analyses, the financial markets are more imperfect than others or more subject to imperfections that can have severe repercussions. The 'failures' of the financial markets are traced to information defects, imperfect competition, externalities, and to transaction costs, which are seen as the cause of deviation from efficiency.

Transaction costs can impede the very creation of financial markets. By their nature, such markets require a larger minimum size than others. They are based on the reputation of the suppliers of services and on customers' getting used to their services; neither of these factors can be improvised. The financial markets deal in a basic commodity that pervades the entire economy. The amounts traded are without equal. The stock of gross financial assets is a multiple of gross output and even of total national wealth. Incompleteness and inefficiency in market systems stem from externalities, which work in favour of markets that are already broad and deep while impeding the expansion of thin, low-productivity markets. The result is a widening gap between the two groups. The entry of new producers is especially difficult in markets where information is decisive, which works to favour the incumbents. This undermines competition, and with it efficiency and distributive equity. Incomplete information is a form of market failure that cannot be overcome by the surrogate of perfect information, namely reputation. As a form of capital, reputation can safeguard the individual producer but not the industry as a whole. This is a form of capital that is easily expropriated unless there is regulation to safeguard the return on investment in reputation.

Incomplete information, *per se*, results in perverse selection in both the primary and secondary securities markets, a gap between social utility and private utility in gathering new information. The ultimate reason is that in finance prices have a special role: they must provide information on the quality of goods (assets) that are heterogeneous, offered to persons who may have widely differing degrees of awareness of their characteristics. More than in other markets, in capital markets organizational efficiency – low operating and transaction costs, spurred by competition – must be combined with efficient reflection of the available information by prices.[25,26] While competition and perfection tend to coincide in nearly all markets, in that the former leads to the latter, in financial markets the ability to make the best possible use of information may be present in oligopoly but lacking under competition. The dichotomy between social and private gain can impede the collection and dissemination of information.[27] Adverse selection can restrict the market to low-quality goods.[28] Both are mechanisms leading to inefficiency, rationing, imperfect competition.

Rules are deemed useful to correct the situation of potential imbalance of power and knowledge that favours those who manage enterprises (insiders) at the expense of the shareholders and creditors (outsiders) who finance them, and other stakeholders. In the absence of rules to counter this asymmetry, outsiders are exposed to possible expropriation by the diversion of profits or value to the benefit of a selected few. There is a clear, intimate connection between the aim of equity and that of efficiency, which is the purpose of laws and regulations – company law, rules for complete disclosure in offerings and periodic reports, against market manipulations, for investor protection. Investor protection fosters the flow of savings to the market, fuels its development and lowers the cost of capital, benefiting the entire economy.

These are the considerations from which we derive the analytical reasons justifying financial market oversight. They also imply the basic purposes, the intermediate objectives that are assigned to supervision:

- improving the utilization of information about securities, and about financial assets in general, or setting minimum quality standards for negotiable securities;
- countering the abuse of dominant positions, requiring transparency and punishing improper use of inside information;
- providing incentives for research, production, reciprocity in supply, and dissemination of new information;
- combating the manipulation of market prices, that is improper influence that causes prices to deviate from the levels at which ordinary speculation would otherwise have put them;
- preparing the defences against systemic instability, in the event that a financial crisis breaks out despite the preventive perfecting of markets.

The validity of the arguments underpinning market oversight as now conceived is not universally acknowledged by economic theorists. The *laissez-faire* school denies such validity, minimizing market failures and emphasizing supervisory and economic policy failures. Yet there is a perceptible international trend towards more extensive financial market oversight, not merely self-regulation, and towards greater uniformity of objectives, instruments and styles. One factor in the trend is the fact that episodes of financial instability around the world have multiplied in the last quarter-century, albeit not always with repercussions on the real economy. The prevalence of the conventional view favouring regulation and supervision has also contributed. In the age of global finance, any country that diverges from the dominant orientation may find itself isolated, in a sort of ghetto of high risk premia and economic costs.

The consensus in favour of supervision and oversight becomes even broader when the object is payment systems or banking. Payment systems depend on the activities of banks and non-banks, on the operation of shared infrastructure and on a multiplicity of norms. In the clearing and settlement of interbank transactions, if a participant is incapable of meeting its obligations it can trigger contagion, undermining overall financial stability and confidence in the currency. Such pathologies aside, payment system arrangements influence the velocity of circulation of money. They affect the maximum possible velocity and how promptly an increase in speed can offset a money supply shock. A payment system's efficiency is gauged by the volume of transactions it can handle using a given amount of money and by its flexibility. The task of oversight, therefore, is to ensure reliability, that is to guarantee that the system can absorb shocks and avoid interfering with monetary policy, and to ensure efficiency, making money circulate as rapidly as possible at low cost. Intrinsically bound up with the function of issuing money and supplying liquidity to the banking system, payment system oversight is one of the historical functions of the central bank, the 'bank of banks'.

Historically, banking supervision preceded market oversight. It is widely held that banks remain a special case not only among enterprises but even among financial enterprises, and thus require particularly close supervision. The essence of banking is the management of specific risks through direct bilateral lending relations. With the disbursement of credit and the use of depositors' resources, banks channel savings into investments with uncertain return. They take responsibility for the investment choices, staking their own capital and their reputation. They perform the delicate task of allocating capital resources, selecting the worthiest firms and investment projects on the basis of risk/return standards. By virtue of their role in allocating resources, they are high-powered enterprises, crucial to the growth and stability of the entire economy. Given informational asymmetry and agency costs, the banks cannot be entirely displaced in this role by financial markets or direct contact between savers (investors) and borrowers. Thanks to lasting relationships with firms, banks can sustain the information costs and, better than individual savers, monitor the companies that take funds. The funds they administer are equal to a multiple of the banks' own capital and reserves. For the most part, their liabilities are repayable in the short term and at face value, against which they hold longer-term assets whose value is subject to variations that may be quite substantial (securities) and others whose real value is hard for outsiders to estimate (loans). This high debt leverage and the difficulties of valuing assets make the fiduciary relationship with the bank's creditors crucial. The latter may be insufficiently protected by the bank's capital. In case of insolvency, the losses tend to be borne not only by the bank's shareholders but also by depositors and taxpayers. And given interbank relations, problems at one bank can have repercussions on others, engendering systemic risk with an impact on payments in the rest of the economy.

The very foundations of money, which is now fiduciary and virtually coincides with bank deposits, would be undermined if people were to doubt the sufficiency of banks' assets to meet their liabilities. Credit intermediation has an importance that transcends the interests of banks' shareholders and even of savers. From the standpoint of society more severe regulation than that directed to other market agents is considered necessary.

As for the form of such regulation, institutional practice has not applied the radical solution. This would consist in distinguishing in balance sheets between the banks' monetary function – to be discharged by the full, compulsory coverage of deposits by monetary base – and the selection and assumption of credit risk, which would be entrusted to the market and whatever risk coverage it devised.[29] Deposit insurance, moreover, far from being a substitute for supervision, is its complement. Only through regulation and prudential supervision can it be guaranteed that (less than total) deposit insurance will not be vitiated by less than responsible conduct by banks and by depositors themselves in assessing risk.

In fact, the alternative solution has been chosen and is increasingly prevalent the world over. This alternative centres on prudential regulation. It also centres on an authority mandated to make sure that banks' capital does not fall below a minimum considered consistent with their risks, given the monetary nature of their liabilities. Shifting the emphasis from maturity transformation to risk intermediation, prudential regulation relies less than in the past on liquid reserves against deposits (compulsory reserves). Supervision leans increasingly towards risk limitation (credit ratios), capital requirements against risky assets, and reliance on the individual bank's capacity to combine return and risk (internal organization for risk assessment and management).

The supervisory authorities take on the role of insider *vis-à-vis* the banks in protecting depositors and in the general interests of system stability and efficiency. Informational asymmetries make it advisable to delegate the checking to an institution endowed with specific expertise and enjoying economies of scale. In part, this is the mirror image of the role played by banks *vis-à-vis* firms. Banks' internal governance is supplemented by an external screening, over and above that to which non-bank enterprises are subject.

Banking supervision, even more than supervision of financial markets and their participants, must not limit itself to strengthening information, requiring transparency, imposing correct conduct. Only to a very limited extent can self-regulation be a surrogate for banking supervision. Risk containment, efficiency, outside checks on banks' operation, and pressure exerted upon them by an authoritative institution and not just by the market are the features that make banking supervision inherently technical. Inevitably, it must be associated with a degree of discretion in technical assessments, in a field dominated by uncertainty and not always commensurable probabilities. The magnitude and the configuration of financial risks are extremely variable. They force adjustments even in the safeguards against instability. Without prejudice to the distinction between external screening (the job of the supervisor) and the entrepreneurial management of the bank (the job of the bank's governing bodies), banking supervision checks and promotes sound and prudent management in a key sector of the economy. The presumption is that the supervisor can have thorough, continuous information on the state of the accounts, the business strategy, the risks, and the ownership, control and organizational structures of individual banks. The evaluation centres on the quality of management. In many countries, including Italy, supervisors assign a rating to each bank and certain technical aspects of its activity, based on study of prudential reports and on-site inspections. This supervisory action is intended to spur banks' managements to efficiency and prudence.

Oversight of conduct within the financial markets, by contrast, is directed chiefly to enforcing the rules of the game: transparency and correct conduct, which are necessary conditions if the market is to make proper evaluations. The end purpose is to put investors in a position to evaluate markets and issuers on their own. Yet – albeit less so than the banks – financial market participants and structures are also subject to rules and controls that go beyond matters of legitimacy, proper conduct, and transparency to touch on competition, efficiency and stability. Rules and controls of this kind also apply to capital markets and their participants with a view to consolidating the intrinsic systemic stability of the financial industry as a whole, hence that of the entire economy.

Both history and theory warn of the danger that the banking and financial sector may cause instability in a market economy or may reflect such instability, suffering from and amplifying it. The possibility of financial crises and of crises that are at once real and financial adds a dimension of economic policy discretion to the supervision of banks and financial markets in the interests of stability. Supervision for stability transcends ordinary oversight designed to elicit and verify conduct in conformity with the rules and standards of normal, proper working of markets. It touches on three special matters: the distinction between illiquidity and insolvency, the assessment of the likelihood of a crisis being spread by 'contagion', and the selection and timing of methods of intervention that are effective but that also minimize moral hazard, the risk of irresponsible behaviour. Illiquidity must not be allowed to degenerate into insolvency. Insolvent institutions must leave the market. Both keeping a bank that is in irreversible crisis afloat in the market and expelling one that has good prospects for recovery are a waste of wealth, of professional, financial and technological resources. The solution depends on the objective state of the enterprise but also on the opportunities offered by the environment. A deep crisis may turn out to be reversible if someone is willing to sustain the cost of adjustment. Even what appear to be definitive crises can be overcome without going out of business, through suitable restructuring. On the other hand, a crisis that is objectively soluble may prove to be irreversible if there is no interest in financing a restructuring. Neither the insolvency of a part of the system – nor, a fortiori, a lack of liquidity – must be allowed to spread throughout the system, with repercussions on the entire economy. Support must not come late but neither must it be overhasty, overgenerous or taken for granted, in such a way as to prompt opportunistic, irresponsible behaviour. These dictates and objectives imply that the authorities must make evaluations and discretional decisions in the context given: that is to say, supervision as economic policy.

The special nature of banking explains the drive, over the years, to international convergence in banking supervision on very high prudential standards, notably as regards capital adequacy. The 1975 Basel Concordat led the authorities of the G-10 countries to coordinate their action to make sure their own banks' business did not escape their supervision, even when projected abroad. In 1978 came the recommendation to supervise banks' international business on a consolidated basis. The revised Concordat in 1983 explicitly introduced the concept of supervisory adequacy, implicitly calling on members to raise their standards towards the most stringent. The 1988 Accord on minimum capital requirements for banks was intended not only for prudential purposes but also to level the playing field for internationally active banks. Then came the crucial turning-point, the shift from coordination to harmonization of the rules on a world scale. The 1990 Addendum strengthened the portion of the Accord bearing on cooperation among supervisory authorities, including inspections.

Oversight on financial markets was developing along similar lines at the International Organization of Securities Commissions (IOSCO), formed in 1983, and on insurance markets at the International Association of Insurance Supervisors (IAIS), formed in 1994. In the 1990s, as financial globalization required, the Basel Committee extended cooperation among banking supervisors to non-G-10 countries. Above all, there was increasingly close cooperation with the international institutions engaged in the oversight of non-bank finance. The fruit of the collaboration among authorities of the G-10 and many other countries was the promulgation in 1997 of the 25 'Core Principles of Effective Banking Supervision'. This was followed, in September 1999, by the 'Core Principles Methodology' that the International Monetary Fund would use to check each country's compliance with the supervisory principles. A radical reinforcement of the Capital Accord for banks is at an advanced stage of development. In 1999 the G-7 countries created the Financial Stability Forum to coordinate initiatives for financial stability worldwide and in all its forms and manifestations: banks, financial and insurance intermediaries, markets. Participation in the Forum extends to national and supranational institutions engaged in supervisory activities. The Forum's first commitment was to close reporting, regulatory and supervisory gaps on hedge funds, which are heavily financed by banks, and on offshore centres, where the banks are abundantly present.

The tendency of financial and banking supervisory systems to converge in terms of purposes, intermediate objectives and instruments does not appear to extend to the identity of the institutions responsible for supervision. Here, the situation is quite varied, even among the leading countries. In France and the United States supervisory responsibility is divided among a large number of institutions. In the United Kingdom these responsibilities were brought together in a single new institution, the Financial Services Authority, constituted in 1997. In Japan responsibility has been assigned to two institutions, with the prime jurisdiction going to the newly created Financial Supervisory Authority (1998). Somewhere between these extremes, but basically closer to diversification than to centralization, we find Italy.

Within the European System of Central Banks (ESCB), instituted in 1999, the European Central Bank (ECB) is responsible for liquidity management and oversight of the payment system. The other supervisory tasks remain under the responsibility of national institutions (which coincides with the national central banks to the extent that each of these is responsible within its own country). The European Union leaves crisis management to the troubled institution's national authorities, in keeping with the accepted principle of home country control, with Community directives and with decentralized supervision. The type of intervention depends on the particular situation to be faced, with four distinct cases: crisis prevention, liquidity crisis, solvency crisis and systemic crisis.

Prevention requires national supervisory authorities to put an adequate regulatory framework in place and to conduct monitoring to pick up anomalies in time. The European interbank market is much more highly developed than many of the national markets that preceded it. Financing of a bank that is merely illiquid is consequently easier, without bringing public resources into play. The ESCB also has an Emergency Lending Assistance agreement to provide credit of last resort to an illiquid bank. The national central banks have the primary responsibility for such financing, sustaining its cost and risks. It is up to the ECB to take account of the impact of the operation on the overall liquidity of the Eurosystem. In the case of an insolvency without systemic implications (often very small institutions are involved) it is up to the home country authorities to prepare the orderly exit of the troubled bank from the market (the takeover of its assets and liabilities by other institutions and then its liquidation). European Union legislation provides a framework for national situations. The rules on deposit guarantees, for example, offer uniform protection for all a bank's depositors under the rules of the home country, regardless of the location of the branch at which the account is held. A planned directive on the reorganization and winding-up of credit institutions takes the same approach, assigning those procedures to the home country authorities. In the case of an insolvency with systemic and even international impact, the nature and magnitude of the crisis need to be assessed in order to decide whether to intervene with public resources. Such a decision would stem from close coordination between the technical authorities and those responsible for the public finances. It would be counterproductive to predetermine the procedure for dealing with insolvency, because each such crisis has its own characteristics. Precise indications in this regard would aggravate moral hazard. The troubled bank's home country supervisory authorities will inform the other authorities affected in order to keep the repercussions to the minimum. Information will be followed by coordinated intervention, decided upon taking the contingent variables into account.

Yet even in this changeable institutional setting, some common features can be identified. The first concerns the central bank. To varying degrees and in various forms, this institution is always involved not only in the payment system but also in banking supervision. A crucial function is its role as lender of last resort, which is entrusted to its independence and technical expertise. There is now a nearly universal consensus that the best antidote to banking instability, transcending Bagehot's rules, is 'constructive ambiguity'. To be effective it requires ample liquidity, timely and detailed information, technical competence and powers of sanction. These are the characteristics of the central banks that also enjoy supervisory powers and whose action is sustained by strong legislation. To base the assignment of supervision to the central bank rather than to a special public agency merely on its 'distance' from the executive power would be reductive; even more valuable is the synergy stemming from the combination of supervision, control of the monetary base and the technical expertise acquired through continuous presence in the markets.[30] In the spectrum of institutional arrangements, the Bank of Italy has always been the most heavily engaged on this front, the Bank of England now the least involved. Nevertheless, the linkage between monetary management and attention to the financial structures of the economy is universally viewed as essential and not to be severed, not least for purposes of the stability of the financial system.

Here as in other fields there is a general tendency on the part of parliaments to rely on independent authorities rather than on executive agencies and to shift policy guidelines and political control to a higher level:

[I]n many cases the ideal size for the unit of control and organization lies somewhere between the individual and the modern State...

[P]rogress lies in the growth and the recognition of semi-autonomous bodies within the State...bodies which in the ordinary course of affairs are mainly autonomous within their prescribed limitations, but are subject in the last resort to the sovereignty of the democracy expressed through Parliament.[31]

On a less refined level of argument, decentralization may prove practical, opportune, where decision implies thorough technical expertise and knowledge of the probabilities, a long-term engagement, transaction costs, zero-sum games. If voters find it hard to evaluate arguments and choices that are imbued with technicalities, then elected officials and government will also be subjected to less-stringent political control. Imperfect information, which is typical of the political marketplace, thus embodies a conflict between democratic rules and economic rationality that can be overcome by an agency separate from the politically elected executive.[32]

In Britain and Japan, as we have seen, the solution adopted was to bring most supervisory responsibilities under a single, gigantic state institution. The financial system of the City increasingly coincides with the national interest of the United Kingdom, political as well as economic. At the same time it serves not just the British economy but the whole world. The Japanese financial system had fallen into unprecedented disarray, even though Japan was the world's largest net creditor country. Apart from special cases, total supervisory centralization may well be inappropriate. A mega-authority would wield such enormous power that the political system could hardly forgo some form of control over it, some form of hetero-direction. If newly constituted, such an agency would have to travel the same difficult path taken by central banks over the decades to assert the real technical independence, not only *de jure* but also *de facto*, that is indispensable to governing the financial system. The politicization of supervision would be a serious problem. The risk is not negligible even in such an established democracy as the United Kingdom or a socially cohesive one like Japan.

Even in countries where supervision is not shared out according to object and purpose, as it is in Italy, the differentiation we have referred to emerges. On the one hand there are spheres in which supervision consists mainly in checking, almost like a law enforcement body, that agents' conduct obeys detailed rules laid down by law. On the other, there are spheres in which supervision consists mainly in technical definition of agents' behaviour, thus providing a guide in the face of changing realities, and subsequently verifying their conformance.

Competition, efficiency, risk and stability are the parameters that most appropriately correspond, in supervision, to discretionary powers that resemble the classical powers of central banks more than those of the more recently created administrative authorities. The latter's independence is derivative. It stems from a suspension of their hierarchical subordination to the executive. It implies laws that govern the nexus between instruments and objectives in detail, for every type of situation. It allows less scope for secondary legislation. It envisages administrative procedures based on transparency and the participation of the parties affected. The independence of central banks, by contrast, is inherent in the function they perform. It leaves greater scope for secondary legislation.

Supervisors exert a constant pressure on the financial system in both moments, that is inviting certain conduct and checking compliance. The aim is to bring arrangements and conduct closer to those considered best by the legal order and, within the limits of their discretion, by the supervisory authorities. The latters' contribution to achieving observance of the principles of the legal system, reflecting the intensity, priorities and manner of their action, is potentially very great indeed. This is especially true when the legislative guidelines change. In these cases, the question is whether supervisory action helps or hinders the system's envisaged change.

Competition

Competition is 'the most energetic source of social dynamism' and 'a permanent threat to all those who are established'. No one has illustrated more vividly than Maffeo Pantaleoni the concept of competition, the difficulty of attaining it, the influence of initial positions on end positions.[33] Competition posits equal opportunity among those engaged in the selection, in the contest, in the market. It is the job of the rules and the referees who enforce them to seek, as far as they must, and to ensure, as far as they can, equality of starting conditions, a level playing field and the correctness of the encounter in the marketplace. A ruleless market is no market at all. For another towering figure in Italian economic thought, Luigi Einaudi, 'the battle against monopolies'[34] and legislative action were essential for the market to establish itself. He reaffirmed this viewpoint, unheeded, before the economic committee of Italy's Constitutional Convention:

> In our country, the law has created and is creating monopolies...At the very least, therefore, we must lay down the principle that the law

must not itself create monopolies. Where monopolies do exist independently of the action of law, they must be eliminated; and if we fail to eliminate them, we must require, in general, that appropriate methods be adopted to control them.[35]

Even in the absence of privilege, *laissez-faire* does not necessarily lead to competition. It can result in monopoly. This happens where the conditions handed down by history are adverse, where an industry is characterized by economies of scale, where outside the industry oligopolistic behaviour predominates, where transaction costs are high, and where entrepreneurs, new or old, are few. By the logic of the marketplace, the best producer, and only the best, should win out. He earns the reward of temporarily above normal profits. He must not abuse his power as long as he holds it. He must not prevent others from challenging him and proving themselves better than he. The environment must enable challengers to launch their challenge. All these 'musts' justify not only the defence but the active promotion of competition: a legal and economic policy of defending, fostering and imposing competition, one of the few unquestioned 'values' of all schools of political economy, classical, Marxian, neo-classical and Keynesian alike.

Openness to international trade and finance; number of actual and potential producers and purchasers; information; renegotiation; divisibility of transactions; cost of collusion; intersectoral mobility of resources, both static and, more important, dynamic; structure of the market, but also of behaviours; competition in quantity and quality, not just price; diverse forms of competition, licit and illicit, in different markets; the need for controls and controllers, but above all for promoters, 'imposers' of competition; second best; competitive markets, not just perfect markets[36] – these are but some of the key words that go with competition as a category of political economy and with economic and institutional policy designed to foster it.

The contribution of competition, relative to monopoly, to static allocative efficiency was long considered small though not negligible. With average long-term costs constant, monopoly prices 20 per cent higher than competitive prices, elasticity of demand schedules of 1.5 and an incidence of monopoly sectors equal to half the gross domestic product, the loss in total income is 'only' 1.5 per cent. Actually, empirical estimates range between very low values[37] and sharply higher ones.[38]

The picture changes, however, if we reject the canonical assumption that every producer, including the monopolist, minimizes costs and hews to the efficiency frontier; if, more realistically albeit still within a static framework, we admit that the average productivity of firms may fall far below that frontier. In the absence of competitive stimuli that oblige them and motivations that induce them to be efficient, firms produce with a high – but reducible – X-inefficiency:

> (a) contracts for labor are incomplete, (b) the production function is not completely specified or known, and (c) not all inputs are marketed or, if marketed, are not available on equal terms to all buyers...The level of unit cost depends in some measure on the degree of X-efficiency, which in turn depends on the degree of competitive pressure, as well as on other motivational factors. The responses to such pressures, whether in the nature of effort, search, or the utilization of new information, is a significant part of the residual in economic growth.[39]

Needless to say, in the economies that are now highly developed, the so-called 'residual' – forces other than the mere endowment of labour and capital – describes, *ex post*, somewhere between one-half and two-thirds of what is the crucial phenomenon, namely the increase in the wealth of nations.

If we move from the static to the fully dynamic vision – classical or Schumpeterian – competition becomes the lever of change, the essential propellent of growth. Only by virtue of competition can the accumulation of capital be turned to the more productive uses, levelling the rate of profit. Only by virtue of competition will the resistance of inefficient firms and declining industries, reluctant to give up the resources they still control, be overcome. Only by virtue of competition will there be a spur to innovation, breaking with routine and introducing new, better combinations of productive factors (Schumpeter's 'enterprise').[40] In this vision the benefits of competition, which are always substantial, cease to be limited by the static concept of efficiency. The benefits, however great, are no longer one-off; thanks to growth they become potentially enormous, with no upper bound.

These general considerations on competition, on its value, apply to the economy as a whole and to every component sector. Thus they also apply to the banking and financial industry. Yet in this case some qualifications and shades of emphasis are indispensable.

That both rules and policies to promote and safeguard competition are necessary is especially true for finance. In the long run, an uncompetitive financial system will be inefficient, relatively unprofitable, exposed to shocks, fragile, unstable. So competition is an essential element in supervisory action. At the same time, the competition engendered by the market at any given point in time must be accompanied by adequate prudential regulation. This is needed above all to make sure that competition bears on prices, costs, the quality of risk assessment and management and does not degenerate into irresponsible risk-taking, unhealthy banking practices, perilous speculation. Otherwise, we would have a sort of 'Gresham's law' of finance, with bad banks driving out good.[41] Prudential supervision is a condition for competition's generating stability. It solicits the sound and prudent management of financial institutions. It sets operational limits so that competitive pressures on profit margins do not prompt high-risk, speculative finance but rather stimulate efficiency and capital-strengthening. Thus there is no conflict between the aims of competition/efficiency and those of capital soundness and stability in the supervision of financial intermediaries and markets, and in particular banking supervision. On the contrary, these objectives are strictly complementary, as are the functions mandated to pursue them. This complementarity increasingly becomes a virtuous interaction, the greater the extent to which both prudential rules and actions for competition stem from a single vision and from the consistent exercise of the two functions by the banking and financial supervisory authority.

In the static vision of mere protection of consumers against monopoly pricing, the social benefit of antitrust legislation is even smaller in proportion to output when referred to the financial industry alone. The industry's value added in the developed economies is ordinarily around 5 per cent of the national total, rarely as much as 10 per cent, and a twentieth of 1.5 per cent of GDP is frankly unimpressive. Yet few industries, if any, have as many customers as the financial industry. Customers are often organized into consumer associations, precisely because of the delicacy of monetary, banking and financial services. If bank customers were not treated properly, and equally, then the overall reputation of the banking and financial industry would be compromised. If the supervisory authorities neglected these aspects then there could be serious, even systemic, repercussions.

The competitive pressure on firms and their managers is most intense when competition within their product market is flanked by the threat of takeovers, that is the contestability of corporate ownership and control, in forms that may range from a simple sale to a hostile takeover bid. Ownership structures, which are a key focus of supervisory activity, thus represent the intersection between guaranteeing sound and prudent management of intermediaries and safeguarding competition in banking and financial markets.

Various factors may impede competition in banking and finance: large economies of scale; information asymmetries; non-substitutability between loans based on customer relationships; 'exit' costs for customers; and network technology, which may create entry barriers. In the market for bank credit in particular the concept of competition that best fits reality is that of 'monopolistic competition', essentially because loans are heterogeneous goods with high information content, comparable to 'named commodities'.

Competition policy cannot be limited to a single market. It must extend to the general context, the entire economy; it must consider all the markets and their interaction. However, there is one market, one sector, whose condition is special, which determines the degree of competition in every other market and industry more than any other single factor. This is the credit market. Banks are unique in so far as they both allocate and create credit for all the other enterprises within the economy, in all industries. The entry of new enterprises into any market, contestability, the competitive spur for established firms, all depend crucially on access to credit. An entrepreneur who does not command sufficient resources but perceives an opening for competition and an opportunity for profit can seek to exploit them only if he can get credit. The exit of losing firms from the market, the entry of new ones, the success of the best, hinge on the criteria banks use in granting or withholding credit. Competition within the credit market, the separation of banking from industry, the banks' procedures for assessing firms' creditworthiness, their propensity for risk, their ability to cover and manage risk and their risk-control procedures are crucial. Information asymmetries and uncertainty are a reality. They call for intimate, lasting customer relationships between debtors and creditors. In certain circumstances they may require contracts between firms and banks such as to prevent competition between banks from impeding the supply of credit to new firms, blocking their creation and success.[42] Banking supervision, which concentrates on the credit market, necessarily and routinely considers all these aspects. Banking supervision and the safeguarding of competition between banks are strictly interrelated.

On the institutional plane, these considerations militate in favour of entrusting both the supervisory and antitrust functions for the banking industry to the same authority. This was the approach elected by the Italian parliament in 1990, when it assigned the Bank of Italy to safeguard and above all to promote competition in banking. In the United States, with its century-old antitrust tradition, the task of evaluating the anti-competitive effects of mergers and conduct potentially harmful to competition is assigned to the Federal Reserve and to the other supervisory agencies as regards the banks under their jurisdiction. In France bank mergers are not within the powers of the antitrust authorities, being placed under the jurisdiction of the banking supervisory authorities. In cases of agreements or abuse of dominant positions in banking, the Conseil de la Concurrence must ask the opinion of the Commission Bancaire and justify any decision not in accord with the latter.

There would thus appear to be a tendency, not unopposed but capable of spreading, to transfer formal antitrust powers to the banking supervisory authority. Even were this not so, however, banking supervision could never ignore the competitive dimension. The maintenance of a reasonable level of competition is a necessary, intermediate objective of prudential supervision. Only in this way can regulators pursue the competitiveness of intermediaries and hence long-run stability. A supervisory approach not centred on competition between banks, or that neglects competition or views it as an impediment to stability, would be in blatant contrast with the principles we have briefly recalled here. Such an approach would have every chance of failing to achieve its avowed aims.

Legislation lays down the principles and guidelines to which the financial system must adhere. The tax system must not conflict with those guidelines and principles and may reinforce them. Supervision is assigned to check and elicit compliance with the principles. And finally, it is the job of a regulated competitive market to press the financial institutions to respond and comply. Where the financial system is driven by law, by the tax system and by supervision towards new arrangements, the promotion of competition, which is the engine of change, is all the more crucial and complementary to the other constituent elements of the framework in which policy on financial structures unfolds. Of course, even competition can do nothing if market agents lack the entrepreneurship to perceive the signs and respond to stimuli, even the loudest and clearest. If it is empty of content, even the most elegant frame will not adorn.

The next four chapters recount the way in which government policy influenced the transformation of the Italian financial system in the last two decades of the twentieth century, working with the legal order, the tax system, the supervisory rules and the promotion of competition. The underlying assumption is that government action was important in working the change and therefore warrants description and analysis;

not that it was the sole or even the main factor, or that it was necessarily more important than international pressures, the needs of the economy or the ability of market agents to respond to stimulus. But to evaluate and quantify the relative importance of such diverse forces would be beyond the scope of this already lengthy work.

3
The Legal Order

Since 1980, provisions of Italian law in the financial field that prohibited or imposed have been attenuated or removed, provisions that permit and give guidance introduced, ambiguous rules clarified and completed, valid principles reiterated and new ones established. This overview of the legislative interventions seeks to bring out the underlying economic rationale of each measure. They are also grouped under seven headings with a linearity and symmetries that only the hindsight afforded by completion of the process permits. The outcome was the passage first of the Consolidated Law on Banking in 1993 and then of the Consolidated Law on Finance in 1998. These two laws gave the Italian banking and financial system a legal framework commensurate with its potential development.

In the first place it needs to be said that the Italian legal order conforms with the letter and the spirit of Community legislation in the three sectors of banking, non-banking intermediation and issuers. The conformity is not the result of a passive transposition of Community provisions but of autonomous innovations, interactions and complex time sequences.

Community banking law is based on the principles of minimum harmonization, mutual recognition and compliance with parameters. There are many banking directives, most of which are of a technical nature (own funds, solvency ratios, supervision on a consolidated basis, large exposures, annual accounts and deposit-guarantee schemes), but two stand out, known as the First Banking Directive (1977) and the Second Banking Directive (1989). They establish the principles and the rules for the taking up and pursuit of the business of credit institutions within the Community.

The First Banking Directive (77/780/EEC) served to give Community banks freedom of establishment in all member states. It established uniform objective parameters for granting authorizations to engage in banking business. It forbade any discrimination against credit institutions authorized in another member state. Although important, the steps taken with the First Directive went only part of the way. The harmonization process accelerated in 1985 with the approval of the Single European Act for the creation of a single market in Europe by 1 January 1993. The Act simplified the procedures for the adoption of the necessary measures.

The Second Banking Directive (89/646/EEC) introduced the principles of mutual recognition of authorizations (the single licence) and home country prudential supervision. Under its provisions credit institutions authorized by one member state can operate throughout the Community, either with branches or under the freedom to provide services, without having to apply to the host country for an authorization. The country that issues the authorization is also responsible for the prudential supervision of the credit institution's activities in other member states. The activities that Community banks can perform subject to mutual recognition are listed in the annex attached to the directive. The scope is vast. The directive sees credit institutions as multifunction entities. The condition for the issuance of the European licence is the minimum harmonization of the supervisory rules in a wide variety of fields: authorization to engage in banking business, the conditions for carrying it on, controls on upstream and downstream shareholdings. The prudential supervision of matters subject to minimum harmonization is the responsibility of the home country. Supervisory authorities are required to cooperate.

The Italian legislation applying to banks followed a path that was conditioned only in part by the various Community directives, although it naturally conforms with their provisions. The recognition of banks as enterprises, enshrined in the Civil Code, had long been the basic principle adopted by the Bank of Italy. One strand of court decisions, however, had considered banking as objectively having some of the characteristics of a public service. The fact that this view also clashed with the principles of Community law was one of the factors that led Parliament to reaffirm expressly the entrepreneurial nature of banking when it transposed the First Directive (Presidential Decree 350/1985). On the other hand, neither the main changes concerning the legal form and ownership of banks nor the principle of operational specialization derived from the directives. In Italy the scope for operations assigned to the various categories of credit institution was significantly broadened until a state of *de facto* despecialization was reached, although this was only given formal recognition in the legislation transposing the Second

Banking Directive (Legislative Decree 481/1992). The Italian legal system had long provided for the control of banks' ownership structures and restrictions on banks' shareholdings and holdings of banks' capital. Similar restrictions were subsequently imposed at Community level. Non-bank intermediaries are also subject to control in Italy, even though the Community has not yet adopted minimum harmonization rules in this field.

The Community rules on non-bank intermediation – albeit cumbersome and improvable – govern the investment services sector and, as regards collective portfolio management, open-end UCITS (mutual funds and SICAVs). The Investment Services Directive (the ISD – 93/22/EEC) is modelled on the Second Banking Directive and defines the minimum harmonization for investment services. It allows Community investment firms to operate throughout the European Union subject to mutual recognition, according to the principle of home country control and under the prudential supervision and capital adequacy rules of the home country. It contains a functional definition of investment firms as providers of one or more of the services listed in the directive where they involve financial instruments (ranging from universal banks to specialized investment houses and right through to individual broker-dealers). To avoid overlapping the banking directives, only some of the provisions of the ISD apply to banks, so as to ensure equal treatment with the other types of investment firm. European licences are granted for the performance of even one of the investment services listed. In the collective portfolio management field Community law (Directives 85/611/EEC and 88/220/EEC) provides for only open-end funds and SICAVs that invest in listed securities to be eligible for a European licence. Whereas the banking legislation and the ISD apply to intermediaries that engage in financial activities (banking, investment), the UCITS directive focuses on the product supplied. It is funds and not the management companies that are harmonized and can receive a European passport. The cross-border supply of other collective management products and services continues to be governed by the Treaty.

The ISD was issued after the approval of Law 1/1991, the first comprehensive law on securities intermediation in Italy. However, the lengthiness of the preparatory work leading to the adoption of both measures made it possible for the Italian law to take account of the Community orientations that were emerging. Since Law 1/1991 conformed basically with the provisions of Community law, most of the innovations introduced in 1996 in the decree transposing the ISD (Legislative Decree 415/1996) and subsequently embodied in the Consolidated Law on Finance served more to increase the competitiveness of the Italian legal system than to give effect to the directive. The following aspects were the direct result of the transposition of the directive: the removal of the restrictions imposed by Law 1/1991 on the supply of investment services in Italy by EU investment firms; the recognition of Italian banks' unqualified right of access to regulated markets; the easing of the requirement for transactions involving listed securities to be concentrated on regulated markets. Legislative Decree 415/1996 also introduced the changes needed to give effect to the directive on investor compensation schemes (97/9/EC), which were also taken over in the Consolidated Law on Finance. The similarly short interval between national and Community legislation on mutual funds made it possible for the Italian legislation in this field to be basically in line with Directive 85/611/EEC.

Lastly, between 1979 and 1994 the Community issued a series of directives on the information that issuers of listed securities must disclose to the public. The objective, pursued with growing intensity, was to provide investors in the various EU countries with uniform protection. The transparency requirements are set out in detail. The most important directives concerned: the conditions for the admission of securities to official stock exchange listing (79/279/EEC); the requirements for the drawing up, scrutiny and distribution of listing particulars (80/390/EEC); the information to be published on a regular basis by listed companies (82/121/EEC); the disclosure of major holdings (88/627/EEC); the drawing-up, scrutiny and distribution of the prospectus for the public offering of securities (89/298/EEC); and insider trading (89/592/EEC).

Italian legislation was always aligned with the principles these directives gradually affirmed. It differed in some minor details or owing to the absence of specific provisions needed for the recognition of foreign prospectuses. Insider trading was an exception in this respect. The rules on this matter were introduced into Italian law on the occasion of the transposition of Directive 89/592. At the time the debate on the desirability of countering the use of privileged information was in full swing in Italy. The transposition of the directive imposed a solution on the parties involved and swept aside some justified doubts. The result was a somewhat incoherent set of rules, which the provisions on insider trading of the Consolidated Law on Finance attempted to improve on. However, anomalies have continued to occur in the Italian share market. In 1999, on the day preceding the announcement of a tender offer, the shares of the target companies rose on average by 8 per cent and in the case of the sale of a controlling shareholding the shares of the companies involved rose on average by 10 per cent.

The amendments to the legal framework of banking and finance

Banking and commerce

The cardinal principle in this field, unchanged from the 1936 Banking Law to the 1993 Consolidated Law on Banking, is the separation between banking and commerce. The refusal to allow non-financial companies to own controlling equity interests in banks is one of the pillars of Italian banking legislation. From an unwritten norm underlying the 1936 Banking Law it was given explicit expression in article 19 of the 1993 Banking Law. The prohibition is attenuated in the case of a number of non-financial companies that control a bank through shareholders' agreements in which no one company plays a dominant role in the choice of the directors. Article 53 of the 1993 Banking Law provides for the Interministerial Committee for Credit and Savings and the Bank of Italy to regulate the acquisition of shareholdings by banks. The Supervisory Instructions issued by the Bank of Italy set limits on banks' holdings in non-financial companies in relation both to their own funds and to the capital of the investee company (not more than 15 per cent). Except in marginal cases, banks may not exercise control.

The First Banking Directive did not contain any provisions on shareholdings in banks. However, the Second Banking Directive granted supervisory authorities considerable discretion in assessing the suitability of the owners of banks with a view to ensuring their sound and prudent management. This directive also established prudential limits on banks' equity interests – which can also be controlling interests – in non-financial companies. Italian law expressly decrees the separation between banking and commerce. This position is deeply rooted and has many analogies with the US Bank Holding Company Act of 1956. It existed many decades before the corresponding Community provisions were enacted. It is one of the most rigorous in Europe. The commingling of banks and non-financial companies would risk augmenting the economy's static and dynamic inefficiency and its instability.

The relationships between prices and costs and – owing to the existence of X-inefficiency – the cost levels in the economy would tend to rise were the discipline that independent banks can impose even on large firms to disappear. But the separation between banking and commerce is also a necessary condition for dynamic efficiency in the economy. Only access to external finance allows firms with potential to translate this into performance. In particular, credit plays an irreplaceable allocative role, in a dynamic sense, as Schumpeter made clear. It is an essential condition for competition and contestability among firms operating in every sector of the economy, in every market, for products and factors of production.

Banks can create credit. They can therefore ensure the prompt reallocation of resources from one firm to another, not only when the resources are partially used but also when they are fully used. Lending relationships that penetrate the most intimate aspects of firms' activity are likely to result in banks possessing information that makes them especially well equipped to assess corporate creditworthiness. The independence of the assessment – the separation between banking and commerce – is the condition in the absence of which the whole allocative mechanism based on credit breaks down, with serious repercussions for the efficiency and stability of the economy. Among the firms competing to carry out an investment project, that deemed most creditworthy will be chosen. The contribution of finance to optimizing the use of resources extends to the discipline it imposes on firms by requiring them to honour the debts they contract to obtain the resources for production and investment. Continuous pressure is thus brought to bear on firms to minimize costs for given production objectives, or to maximize output with given inputs. The firms that are less able to service their debts, that are less efficient, will have fewer resources placed at their command.

The banking system, if it is diversified and open to competition, is the best mechanism known for selecting the most suitable firms – and managements – to carry out investment projects the market has indicated to be efficient and for forcing producers to comply with budget constraints. The stock exchange works alongside banks in the choice of firms, but only for those that are listed. Creditworthiness continues to be the criterion for making these delicate decisions. If it is to be applied correctly, the relationship between firms and banks must be a dialectical one. This will ensure the double scrutiny, internal and external, of corporate operations. One institutional requirement is that banks be independent in granting credit. Lending must be based on strictly financial parameters that are not corrupted by a priori preferences for specific uses, this or that company, this or that sector, or uses advocated by economic or social policy or politics pure and simple.

In Italian economic history extreme banking instability has often been linked, more or less closely but not exclusively, with violations of the principle of separation between banking and commerce. In the early 1890s this was the case of Credito Mobiliare and Banca Generale, marked by the abnormal size of the asset item 'shares and corporate bonds' and the concentration of loans to just a few firms. The collapse of Società Bancaria Italiana in 1907, with the volatility of its liabilities, was also due partly to the difficulties of a large firm (Fiat), to which the bank had made very substantial loans. The liquidation of Banca Italiana di Sconto in 1921 and the losses incurred by Banco di Roma (temporarily made good through the rescue put together in 1923) sprang from involvement in the Perrone-Ansaldo group. Similarly, Banca Agricola Italiana's problems in the early 1930s were due to its financing of the Gualino group. Banca Commerciale Italiana, Credito Italiano and yet again Banco di Roma were shaken at the height of the Great Depression by the commingling between banking and commerce ('Siamese twins', as Raffaele Mattioli put it).

Commingling between banking and commerce also tends to undermine stability indirectly, but no less dangerously. Banking supervision and monetary policy are joined together at the central bank through lending of last resort to the banking system. Failure to separate banking and commerce would raise the problem of making lending of last resort available to non-banks, to entities that are not subject to supervision and whose solvency is less certain. Lending of last resort is reserved to banks with liquidity problems; it is not available to those that are insolvent. Otherwise, by supporting or indirectly granting credit to individual large firms, the central bank would see its power to regulate the monetary base diminish. Stabilization policy would be deprived of the fundamental contribution that monetary management is called upon to make.

That this is not a purely abstract possibility is confirmed once more by Italian experience. In the early 1930s the Bank of Italy's exposure to banks and firms in difficulty was equal to half the value of the banknotes in circulation, to six times that of its capital, reserves and provisions, and to 7 per cent of GDP. The rehabilitation measures adopted between 1933 and 1936 – those implemented through IRI amounted to nearly 10 per cent of GDP – were also, perhaps primarily, intended to prevent the collapse of the Bank of Italy, to give the country back its central bank.

Moving beyond publicly controlled banks

In the 1970s it became clear that the dichotomy between the public-law framework in which banks were set as legal entities and the provisions of private law governing their activities had become a source of inefficiency, institutional confusion, unfairness and obstacles to competition. Court decisions sought to overcome the problem by putting the general interest before entrepreneurship, with a consequent tendency to see banking as a public service. Not that banks were necessarily inefficient because they were under public control. Well-managed and badly managed banks were to be found in both the public sector and the private sector. The extreme, pathological cases of bad management – Banca Privata Italiana and Banco Ambrosiano – occurred in the private sector. Well-managed public-sector banks – of international standing, such as Raffaele Mattioli's Comit and Enrico Cuccia's Mediobanca – were more efficient than the (few) well-managed private-sector banks.

The main problem was to create a level playing field. Public-sector banks needed to be seen as enterprises, not as institutional instruments of a public policy for the allocation of resources. Their capital could also be provided by the state. Those having the legal form of limited companies (*società per azioni*) could raise equity capital on the market, those that were public-law institutions could not.

The question of publicly controlled banks, which had already been raised in the Bank's Annual Reports in the late 1970s, was addressed in a Bank of Italy white paper drawn up by a group of economists and lawyers coordinated by Guido Cammarano and published in 1981. However, neither the Annual Reports nor the white paper openly advocated privatizing the public-sector banks, with the risk of returning to a pre-1930s banking system. Law 23/1981 on replenishing the capital of the southern public-sector banks required the ministerial decrees on the use of the resources granted 'to approve...guidelines...for harmonizing and rationalizing the banks' bylaws'. The ensuing Treasury Decree of 27 July 1981 laid down principles requiring operations to be more market-oriented. A start was thus made on the amendment of the public-sector banks' bylaws. Internal controls typical of profit-oriented enterprises were introduced. Procedures and structures that increased the decision-making responsibility of directors were put in place. These bylaw reforms also involved nearly all the savings banks.

Subsequently, Presidential Decree 350/1985 reaffirmed the entre-preneurial nature of banking – already prescribed by article 2195 of the Civil Code – 'regardless of the public or private nature of the entities involved' and the desirability of creating conditions of competitive equality among credit institutions.

The company limited by shares was the model that would minimize the disparities between Italian banks as legal entities and at the same time offer a better solution for the governance, efficiency and competitiveness of publicly controlled banks. In the wake of a second white paper on these matters published in 1988, Law 218/1990 expressly provided for public-sector banks to be allowed to become limited companies. The transformation was not made mandatory, but was nonetheless encouraged by tax incentives. It was entrusted to mechanisms (the contribution of banking businesses to newly created companies, changes in legal form, mergers) that were put in place by implementing decrees (notably Legislative Decree 356/1990). The original public-sector banking entity had to disappear, leaving in its place a publicly controlled bank in the form of a limited company. The link between the public entity contributing the banking business and the banking company was not to go beyond the exercise of the rights attaching to the shares held as a result of the contribution. The transformation of the various legal entities into limited companies proceeded rapidly under the stimulus of the incentives. By the end of 1992 nearly all the public-sector banks had already been turned into companies and the process was completed in 1995.

The start made on the privatization process in 1993 was basically in response to the need to curb the public debt, which was tending to rise to new peaks. There was nonetheless a growing body of opinion – which had been in a minority since the 1930s – that public-sector entities were by their nature less efficient than their counterparts in the private sector, as well as being exposed to collusion with the political sphere. Public-sector banks were included in this evaluation, although this was not justified by events in Italy, where the banking industry had been dominated by large and inefficient private-sector banks that had colluded not only with the political sphere but also with industry. The drive to privatize was extended to banks. The first important privatizations in this field – of Credito Italiano and Banca Commerciale Italiana – were carried out by the government headed by a former governor of the Bank of Italy, Carlo Azeglio Ciampi.

Legislative Decree 481/1992 implementing the Second Banking Directive of 1989 had introduced a mechanism that would allow Italy's banking foundations to give up control of their banking companies. Law 489/1993 made it mandatory for public-sector banks in which the state held an absolute or relative majority of the capital (Artigiancassa, Mediocredito Centrale) to become limited companies.

Although Law 218/1990 was an essential step in the evolution of the banking system, it had restricted the scope for privatizations. Only in specific circumstances and to promote the public interest (by strengthening the banking system or increasing banks' international presence or size) could the Council of Ministers authorize the waiving of the requirement for public entities to own, directly or indirectly, the majority of the capital of the banking companies hived off from foundations.

Another four years were to pass before the public control requirement was repealed, by Decree Law 332/1994, subsequently ratified by Law 474/1994. The privatization of the banking system benefited under this law from the power granted to the minister of the Treasury to establish 'criteria and procedures of a general nature for the sale of equity interests approved by the entities that held them'. With Enabling Law 461/1998 and Legislative Decree 153/1999 a time limit of six years was established for foundations to sell off the controlling interests they still held in banking companies.

Banking specialization as a choice

The other principle embodied in the 1936 legislation on banking was mandatory specialization: distinguishing not only between commercial banks, which operated primarily in the short term, and special credit institutions, which operated in the medium and long term, but also among the latter, according to the sector they were intended to finance (agriculture, building, public works, industry and the Mezzogiorno). The organizational constraints consequent on Alberto Beneduce's concept of long-term credit specialization nonetheless appeared to be increasingly unjustified as the historical – economic and hence legal – *raison d'être* of the special credit institutions gradually ceased to apply, especially in the case of industrial credit.

Among the special credit institutions, those for the financing of industry were seen from the inter-war years onwards as a way of accelerating the industrialization of an agricultural country. Given the technology available at the time, industrial investment projects were not only risky but also offered a deferred return. The maturity of the credit was taken as the criterion for entrusting medium-term banks with the task of assessing the firm involved in the project. These banks were meant to be especially qualified in technical as well as economic and financial terms. In the joint assessment of the firm and the investment project, the destiny of the firm came to depend crucially on the destiny of a single project. The creditworthiness of the firm could not be separated from the project that was to be financed. In an economy now industrialized, in a technological context that saw a reduction in the average life of industrial capital and its variance, there was no longer the same need as before. If anything, there was a need for more merchant banks, able to compete in securities placements and underwriting and advising on transactions involving corporate ownership and control. The first explicit invitation to develop merchant banking business was addressed to banks by the governor of the Bank of Italy in 1983. The slow pace at which such services became more widely available confirms the fact that banks' ability to offer advanced financial services must be matched by firms' ability to demand them.

In fact it was inside the special credit sector that the principle of mandatory specialization began to give way to that of voluntary specialization. The decrees implementing Law 218/1990 gave a push to the process. In the same year article 18 of Legislative Decree 356 established that the banks formed as limited companies resulting from the restructuring of public-sector banks could grant medium- and long-term credit in all the sectors provided for in their bylaws. The same decree removed the legislative barriers to geographical diversification for all the special credit institutions set up as limited companies.

Having thus made a start on overcoming the restrictions applying to special credit, there remained the fundamental distinction between special credit institutions and commercial banks. Many of the latter, in addition to expanding their business beyond the short term, had begun to engage directly in other financial activities. Legislative Decree 481/1992 introduced the all-purpose universal bank that could raise funds in any form and engage in all the activities subject to mutual recognition on the list attached to the Second Banking Directive (such as factoring, leasing, medium- and long-term credit, including industrial and mortgage loans, advisory services and merchant banking). The restrictions on the acquisition of industrial shareholders were also eased.

The Italian legal system did not comprise an autonomous body of law on groups of companies, but only defined subsidiaries and affiliates. The underlying mismatch between the economic reality (when a group is run on a unitary basis) and the legal form (necessarily involving more than one corporate body) was also present in the special legislation on banking. This did not regulate banking groups, even for supervisory purposes – a first shortcoming to be made good, in view of the many financial intermediaries organized in this way. It did introduce the universal bank model, but in a partial form and further restricted by administrative provisions. In the 1980s the easing of administrative constraints made it possible for banks to achieve product diversification by participating in companies specialized in new products, to be distributed through banks' branch networks.

In addition to laying the foundations for the reform of public-sector banks, Law 218/1990 and Legislative Decree 356/1990 introduced the notion of banking group into Italian law. This met the need to render supervision neutral with respect to the choice of performing banking-related activities under a single legal umbrella or through entities legally separate from the bank and as such previously excluded from the supervisory net. Law 114/1986 had opened groups to supervision for informational purposes without arriving at the more cogent regulation.

The new legislation laid down rules for the composition of banking groups, established their scope, required their entry in a special register, made parent companies the sole interlocutor of the supervisory authorities, and, exclusively for supervisory purposes, gave such companies powers of direction and guidance over their subsidiaries.

The body of primary legislation approved between 1990 and 1992 and brought together in the 1993 Consolidated Law on Banking allows banks to choose between three organizational models:

- the universal bank;
- the specialist bank;
- the banking group.

Rules and supervisory action in this field must be neutral. The issues are of a purely organizational nature. It was and still is a decision left to each bank, to the wisdom of the directors.

The main exception concerns the relationship between banking and insurance. The scope for synergy between the two activities, both of a financial nature, are considerable. They would justify every kind of link: ownership, participation, control. The differences between the types of risks incurred nonetheless made it appear undesirable to mix the two lines of business in a single company. Credit risk cannot be insured against; liquidity risk is also typical of banking. The supply of insurance services by banks can therefore best be pursued by keeping the two lines of business separate within a banking group. The notion of a banking group needed to be introduced into Italian law at least to allow the bank (the parent company) to exploit the scope for synergy with the insurance company, with each operating in its own field in view of the difference between the nature and risks of the two activities; on the other hand, insurance companies were given the right to control a bank or a banking group. An additional objective was to allow synergy between banks and collective portfolio management, while respecting the difference – in this case of degree and not of nature – between the two activities and the respective risks and ensuring the independence of fund managers' investment choices.

Non-bank credit intermediaries

In the last twenty years the Italian financial system, like those of the other industrial countries, has seen considerable growth in specialized forms of credit intermediation different from that traditionally performed by banks (leasing, factoring, consumer credit, etc.). The appearance of firms engaged in these activities dates back to the early 1960s. Initially their growth was modest. It began to accelerate towards the end of the 1970s. The ceiling on the growth in bank lending combined with economic actors' specialized technical requirements to foster the development of alternative forms of credit. Non-bank credit intermediaries were regulated by Laws 52/1991 and 197/1991 and subsequently by the Consolidated Law on Banking. The two laws of 1991 were promulgated at almost the same time, with the aim of regulating two separate but contiguous aspects of non-bank credit intermediation: Law 197, in addition to laying down the first set of provisions to counter money-laundering, required firms to choose whether to engage in financial or industrial activities and reserved the former to companies registered with the Ministry of the Treasury; Law 52 regulated the assignment of corporate claims by way of derogation from the provisions of the Civil Code and provided for a register of factoring companies, to be kept by the Bank of Italy. The requirements to qualify for entry in the two registers were not the same, however, so that there was disparity of treatment within the sector. The limited coordination between the two laws was rectified in 1993, when the regulation of non-bank credit intermediaries was included in the Consolidated Law on Banking. Apart from intermediaries engaged in leasing, factoring and consumer credit, the sector includes merchant banks, venture capitalists, providers of money transmission services and foreign exchange traders. In 1999 there were some 1,400 such firms, which have to satisfy certain requirements and be entered in a general list kept by the Ufficio Italiano dei Cambi. A subset of these entities, identified on the basis of objective criteria related to the activity performed, the size of the company and its capital are entered in a special list and are subject to supervision by the Bank of Italy. Of the 203 intermediaries entered in the special list (article 107 of the Consolidated Law on Banking), more than half are owned by banks, while about one-third are controlled by industrial and financial groups. Especially rapid growth has been achieved by those that disburse specialized types of loans using either funds obtained from banks or their own funds. The increase in the importance of the activity of these companies is attributable to factoring and leasing, where the expansion in lending has outpaced that in bank credit. There has been only meagre growth in the demand for venture capital.

Until the early 1990s the development of banking-related business also reflected the constraints that had been imposed on bank lending beyond the short term and the fact that it was not subject to supervision. There were, however, also advantages in terms of labour costs and economies deriving from technical specialization. The latter are particularly evident in the analysis of the risk of acquiring equity interests in new unlisted companies. In leasing, the valuation of the leased good is especially important for the forced recovery of claims. In factoring, the important aspects are the commercial nature of the claims involved and, in general, the presence of two independent debtors (the assignor and the assignor's customer). In consumer credit, special methods of customer scoring are used to select borrowers. Finance companies grant loans to riskier borrowers; this requires an organization able to monitor borrowers and special skills in appraising the security provided. There is also a tendency to take more vigorous action against defaulters in order to acquire a reputation for greater severity in enforcing claims. One feature of this type of business is to be found in the types of customers served: households (26 per cent of lending) and small businesses, for which access to bank credit is less easy. The demand for credit coming from small borrowers has led to the volumes intermediated by finance companies growing faster than bank loans. The growth in lending and the profitability of the sector are additional indirect confirmation of the validity of the organizational solution based on specialization.

Securities market intermediaries

As late as the beginning of the 1980s asset management coincided with the supply in Italy of units of foreign investment funds. There was a real risk that, if not the economy, at least the country's financial system would miss the boat as regards asset management, which was already present on a very large and growing scale in the Anglo-Saxon economies. There was no legal framework for collective investment schemes. Securities business was entrusted to stockbrokers (governed by Law 272/1913), trust companies, stock exchange commission dealers and banks. Apart from open-outcry trading, which was entrusted exclusively to stockbrokers, the law did not reserve securities business to any particular categories of intermediaries. Rather, in accordance with the principle of freedom to engage in mediation, it excluded each category from engaging in certain types of securities business.

Law 77/1983 regulated open-end securities investment funds and the companies managing them. The establishment of investment funds as a separate pool of assets with respect to those of the management companies, and therefore not exposed to actions brought by the latter's creditors, makes them basically analogous to the trusts provided for in Anglo-Saxon law. The greater protection of unit-holders – the traditional form of investment company did not permit investors' funds to be separated from the company's assets – explains why the Italian parliament initially focused on mutual funds (common funds managed by management companies). Fund managers are subject to risk-limitation rules. Investors can redeem their units at any time.

Law 1/1991 introduced the first comprehensive set of provisions on trading, the reception of orders, placement, advisory services and individual portfolio management. The law included door-to-door selling within its scope. It created a new category of intermediary known as Italian investment firms (*società di intermediazione mobiliare*). Banks were explicitly authorized to engage in securities business, albeit subject to a serious limitation in that they were not allowed to trade listed securities directly on the stock exchange, except for government securities. This forced them to set up their own investment firms in order to compete in this field.

In 1992 in transposing Directive 85/611/EEC rules were introduced: governing SICAVs, another form of collective investment vehicle; permitting the distribution in Italy of investment funds that satisfied the requirements of the directive (so-called harmonized funds); and establishing a procedure for the marketing of units of non-harmonized funds. In 1993 provision was made for closed-end securities investment funds and in 1994 for real-estate funds.

In 1996, with the transposition of the Investment Services Directive, the ban on banks trading directly on regulated markets was removed. Italian investment firms were allowed to engage in other activities, including the financing of customers in connection with investment services. The rules governing securities intermediation were modernized and the limitations applicable to Italian investment firms, banks and other credit intermediaries were eased. Following the promulgation of Legislative Decree 415/1996, the authorization of Italian investment firms has been granted on the basis of criteria similar to those adopted for the authorization of banks. The instruments for stability-oriented supervision and the handling of crises were brought closely into line with those provided for banks. The application of the various bankruptcy procedures provided for in the original legislation on Italian investment firms had proved unsatisfactory.

The Consolidated Law on Finance reformulated the legislation on asset management. The regulation of collective investment schemes ceased to be the preserve of primary legislation and was largely entrusted to the competent administrative authorities.

In addition to investment funds aimed at the general public, which remain subject to binding rules and rigorous controls, there are now funds aimed at institutional investors and wholesale markets, which are permitted greater scope for self-regulation. Controls can also be graduated in accordance with the need to protect investors to which the various investment products are directed.

The innovations introduced in the asset management field create the conditions for a level playing field on which to face foreign competitors, which are attracted by the high level of saving in Italy. The restrictions on management companies concerning the types of investment funds they can set up have been removed and they are now allowed to provide both individual and collective asset management services. In the latter case the Consolidated Law on Finance no longer reserves the management of funds to the companies that set them up and explicitly allows managers to delegate investment choices to others. Individual portfolio management services can also be provided by banks, investment firms, stockbrokers and trust companies. Management tasks can be delegated to third parties for all or part of the portfolios of customers, subject to the latter's consent.

The idea that stock exchange contracts – especially forward contracts – were an immoral and socially harmful form of gambling had led to the belief that they gave rise to natural, non-binding obligations. The law of 1913 had had to specify that forward contracts were 'commercial instruments' entailing legal obligations. In Law 1/1991 the principle of the unenforceability of the exception of gambling was reaffirmed for futures and options traded on regulated markets. In Legislative Decree 415/1996 and the Consolidated Law on Finance (article 23.5) the principle was extended to all derivative contracts concluded in connection with the provision of investment services. In the field of derivatives the law makes the effects binding on the parties while leaving them free to negotiate the content of the contracts, which is standardized in order to comply with the needs of trading such instruments on regulated markets.

The protection of investors is also achieved through the law of contract. Mandates and fiduciary relationships had proved to be inadequate. The laws on investment funds and securities intermediation have provided a standard basis for collective and individual asset management.

In traditional investment funds the contract (that is the fund rules) is drawn up by one party, the management company and unit-holders cannot negotiate its terms. The protection of investors consists: in their right to obtain the redemption of their units at any time (in the case of open-end funds) or in the obligation for the management company to apply for the listing of fund units (in the case of closed-end funds); in provisions concerning fund rules that specify their content and limit the assumption of risks; and in the supervisory authority's approval of fund rules and any amendments thereto.

In the provision of individual management services the imbalance between the intermediary and the investor is less pronounced. The activity is directed towards wealthier persons than those who invest in investment funds. The content of the contract is normally negotiated between the parties; the investor has the power to guide the choice of investments. The law accordingly leaves the parties more room for manoeuvre than in collective portfolio management. The relationship between intermediaries and their customers is subject to more specific provisions that govern the rights and obligations of the parties, while leaving them ample scope for waivers provided that customers give their informed consent.

Issuers and the solicitation of investors

The obligation for issuers to provide information was already present in some countries' financial legislation in the 1970s. The justification provided by economic analysis lies in information being considered a public good. The absence of the obligation would, it is claimed, entail the risk of underproduction, social waste, manipulation and the disclosure of information in a wide variety of forms. There would be a threat not only to efficiency but also to fairness and transparency in the contractual relationship between issuers and investors.

The doubt, to be found in the unravelling result put forward by economic theory itself, is that the mandatory disclosure of information is useless and distortionary. According to this view, all the verifiable information would be made available spontaneously, voluntarily; making it available is in the interest of the issuer. This would be true, however, only if information was not costly to produce, was comprehensible by recipients and was known to be controlled by the provider, and if markets punished those who did not provide enough by making capital more expensive. If the economic grounds for the obligation to provide information are open to question, even more so are the frequency, scope and manner of mandatory disclosure.

In the US system of securities regulation, mandatory disclosure has long been one of the four pillars of the framework, together with the scope and taxonomy of instruments and operators, the rules against fraud and insider trading, and the structures of markets and the practices permitted on them. The crucial point is the philosophy of the legal order that the disclosure obligations underscore: a philosophy based on *caveat emptor*, without any control of individual issues in the light of an evaluation of the merits of the securities and issuers involved.[1] There has been a tendency for the US approach to be imitated. A growing number of countries have followed this course in the context of the financial globalization and homogenization of the last 25 years.

In Italy until 1974 the disclosure requirements for listed companies were no different from those applicable to the general run of companies. The information to be disclosed to the local chamber of commerce – including the annual accounts of the last two financial years and any other information requested by the chamber of commerce – was concerned exclusively with the latter's powers to list and delist securities. In short, the information made available to the public in connection with listing referred to securities and not issuers.

Law 216/1974 introduced not only some rules on transparency but also an embryonic disclosure system limited to public offerings and tender offers involving shares and convertible bonds. The newly established authority charged with supervising the markets, the Companies and Stock Exchange Commission (Consob) was required to examine the adequacy of the disclosures provided for by law and request additional information where necessary. The disclosure requirements referred to the situation both before listing (the prospectus that it was Consob's practice to require) and after it (annual and half-yearly reports and significant corporate events). Consob was empowered to request the communication or disclosure of information and to carry out inspections on companies' premises.

Laws 77/1983 and 281/1985 enhanced the regulatory system. The new provisions on public offerings formalized the obligation, previously based merely on the practice followed by Consob, to publish a prospectus. They also broadened the scope of the rules to include all public offerings of securities, made all the actors involved in public offerings subject to specific disclosure requirements and the powers of Consob, and exempted banks' typical fund-raising transactions from the disclosure requirements.

The legislation approved after Law 1/1991 on securities intermediation and before the Consolidated Law on Finance strengthened the legal requirements regarding disclosure. Law 157/1991 on insider trading and the accompanying implementing regulation made it obligatory to disclose price-sensitive information. The traditional procedure involving the communication of information to Consob, verification and disclosure was supplemented by another involving the simultaneous communication to Consob and disclosure to the market of price-sensitive information. Law 149/1992 on public offerings of securities (sale of existing securities and/or subscription of new securities) and cash and exchange tender offers introduced additional rules with respect to the general legislation on the solicitation of investors. In the case of public offerings, the aim of transparency is supplemented by that of equal treatment for bidders and in the case of tender offers by that of equal economic opportunity for controlling and minority shareholders (mandatory tender offers).

The Consolidated Law on Finance introduced new rules for public offerings and issuers of securities listed on regulated markets.

The information requirements applicable to issuers of securities listed on regulated markets (or widely distributed among the public) call for the publication of a listing prospectus before the start of trading and continuing corporate disclosures after listing. The latter requirements are laid down in a general set of rules for issuers listed on the stock exchange and in special rules, based selectively on the general rules, for issuers of listed bonds, closed-end funds listed on the stock exchange, issuers of financial instruments listed on regulated markets other than the stock exchange, issuers of financial instruments widely distributed among the public, and foreign issuers.

The information to be made available to the public has to be transmitted to Consob as well, except for price-sensitive information, which has to be made available only to the public. The information requirements concern price-sensitive events (continuing disclosure), extraordinary corporate actions (episodic disclosure), financial reports (periodic disclosure), and the remuneration and equity holdings of the members of the board of directors and the board of auditors. Taken together, these requirements are no less rigorous than those in force in other industrial countries.

The tasks of Borsa Italiana S.p.A. range from the requirements to be met by securities and issuers for listing purposes to those designed to foster transparency. The verification of listing prospectuses may be delegated to Borsa Italiana, as may that of prospectuses for offerings made for listing purposes or for offerings of listed financial instruments. Borsa Italiana may also be entrusted with powers concerning the disclosure of price-sensitive information.

From the stock exchange under public control to privatized markets

From the law of 1913 on exchanges onwards and for nearly the whole of the last century the establishment, organization and supervision of financial markets were set entirely within a framework of public law. The stock exchange performed a public service under a monopoly. The authorities played an active part not only in regulation and supervision but also in the creation and operation of the markets. The Bank of Italy and Consob were *de jure* members of the Stock Exchange Council, set up by law in 1991, and the rules governing the market support systems – the central securities depository and the clearing house – provided for the authorities to play a major role.

The MTS screen-based market for government securities was regulated in 1987 by a ministerial decree set within the framework of the 1913 law. A series of subsequent measures extended its operations to include standardized forward contracts. The organization of the market was entrusted to a management committee consisting of representatives of market participants. Non-voting representatives of the Ministry of the Treasury, Consob and the Bank of Italy attended meetings of the committee.

The Monte Titoli S.p.A. central securities depository operated under a monopoly, except for the government securities handled by the central securities system run by the Bank of Italy. The provisions governing Monte Titoli were contained in Law 289/1986 and the implementing regulations issued by Consob and the Bank of Italy. The operating rules and fee schedules of Monte Titoli had to be approved by the regulatory authorities. By law, the latter also appointed persons to represent them on the company's board of directors and board of auditors. Participation in the company's share capital was basically restricted to intermediaries (banks, Italian investment firms and stockbrokers) and the Bank of Italy.

The Cassa di Compensazione e Garanzia S.p.A. clearing house, set up under Law 1/1991, was governed by the regulations issued by Consob and the Bank of Italy, which were also required to approve the company's bylaws and operating rules. Non-voting representatives of the Minister of the Treasury, Consob and the Bank of Italy attended meetings of the board of directors.

In the mid-1990s the public-sector regime in force in Italy came to differ increasingly from the private-sector solutions that were gaining ground abroad.

First Legislative Decree 415/1996 and then the Consolidated Law on Finance provided for the transfer of the markets and their support systems from the public sector to the private sector. The functions of regulation and supervision were separated from those of organization and operation, which in a competitive logic were entrusted to firms and intermediaries. Both the stock exchange and MTS were turned into limited companies. In contrast with Borsa Italiana S.p.A., foreign intermediaries hold a significant portion of the share capital of MTS S.p.A. The regulatory authorities are no longer represented on the two companies' boards of directors.

Borsa Italiana operates the Stock Exchange (the MTA electronic share market and the MOT bond market), the Nuovo Mercato (for small and medium-sized enterprises with high growth potential), the IDEM market (for derivatives based on shares and indices) and the MIF market (for futures on government securities). It is engaged in reorganizing its services so as to make it easier for operators to access international markets. It has concluded agreements with MATIF and MEFF, respectively French and Spanish derivative markets; it participates in the European circuit for small and medium-sized enterprises (Euro.NM); it has signed an agreement with the leading European stock exchanges to create a single market for blue chips.

MTS S.p.A. operates the screen-based market for government securities, the repo market and the coupon-stripping market. It has built up its international activity with the aim of establishing itself as the technological platform for the European market in government securities. To this end it has set up joint ventures in the Netherlands, Belgium and France. In London it has created Euro.MTS Ltd, which runs the circuit in which European countries' benchmark government securities are traded. The system that is emerging consists of a network of 'local' markets (national MTSs) linked by a common trading platform, in which Euro.MTS brings together (as interdealer broker) the major international investors present in the wholesale market.

In so far as it did not fall within the scope of the legislation on securities markets, the MID interbank deposit market was not set up as an institution under public control. It was thus the first market set up at the initiative of operators (albeit at the urging of the Bank of Italy) and self-regulated. The organization of the market was entrusted to an operator-appointed management committee, whose meetings were attended by representatives of the Bank of Italy. The MID management committee has set up a company (e-MID S.p.A.) to be entrusted with the running of the market. The aim of this company is to expand its business to the whole of the euro area by establishing direct links with the leading operators of the European money market, which are offered the possibility of settling their cross-border transactions through TARGET.

The Consolidated Law on Finance ended the monopoly that the law had previously granted to Monte Titoli S.p.A. and required the Bank of Italy to begin the sale of its 44 per cent interest in the company by 1 July 2000. The main changes have concerned the unification of the central depository functions where they were duplicated and the broadening of the range of the company's business to include not only the management of accounts but also securities settlement and other activities such as securities lending and the management of collateral.

Cassa di Compensazione e Garanzia S.p.A. is no longer governed directly by special statutory provisions and no longer operates under a monopoly. The Consolidated Law on Finance permits any company to provide clearing and guarantee services for transactions involving financial instruments, subject to the regulations issued by the Bank of Italy in agreement with Consob.

The affirmation of the entrepreneurial nature of the activity of central securities depositories and the latter's privatization were accompanied by legislation (Legislative Decree 213/1998) exempting financial instruments widely distributed among the public from the rules of the Civil Code governing credit instruments and providing for their dematerialization. This has helped to make the Italian legal system more efficient and competitive, and to eliminate the cost of printing certificates and the risk of forgery.

The business of the new entities resulting from privatization is beginning to be marked by closer integration of the activities of the companies operating the markets (Borsa Italiana, MTS and e-MID) and those of the companies providing support services (Monte Titoli and Cassa di Compensazione e Garanzia). In view of the role taken on by information and communication technology in the infrastructure of financial services, firms operating in this field are finding themselves integrated into the new system or architecture of the markets. The aim of the market operators is to bring together post-trading activities (central custody, clearing, settlement, collateral management), where substantial economies of scale are needed for their cost to be competitive within the euro area.

The legal system: an overview

Following a long period of intense legislative activity, the need to create an organic framework and, above all, to bring out clearly the principles and aims of the law governing the financial sector led to the approval of the two consolidated laws, in 1993 and 1998. In what follows the crucial aspects are summarized, with special reference to those that have not yet been adequately addressed.

The Consolidated Law on Banking

The combination of monetary liabilities and assets that are difficult to value makes banking a special activity. By its nature it is exposed to the effects of crises of confidence among depositors. Such crises can spread to the entire banking system with serious repercussions for the economy. Hence the confirmation of the decision, in common with other countries, to reserve banking to entities subject to special rules and to supervision. Special rules and a supervisory regime do not exclude entrepreneurship or competition among banks. On the contrary, they must foster these features.

The Consolidated Law on Banking is based on a notion of banking as the issue of monetary liabilities – fund-raising related to the issue or administration of generally spendable means of payment (article 11.5) – in conjunction with the granting of credit (article 10). The latter also reaffirms the entrepreneurial nature of banking.

Consistently with the forms of organization of private-sector businesses, the bylaw stating the object of a bank establishes the scope of its operations. Before they are cleared by the civil authorities, a bank's instrument of incorporation and bylaws are examined by the supervisory authority, both in their original formulation, when the authorization to engage in banking is granted, and when they are amended. The choice of entrepreneurial organization is monitored constantly by the supervisory authority to check that it complies with the principle of sound and prudent management (article 2329 of the Civil Code and article 56 of the Consolidated Law on Banking). Similar checks are made on amendments to the bylaws of the parent undertaking of a banking group (article 61.3). Secondary legislation specifies that such checks should verify that the amendments do not contain elements 'able to hinder the orderly performance of the company's business or create uncertainty in the public'.

Access to the banking market is subject to checks aimed exclusively at preventing the entry of incapable and dishonest operators. The law requires entrants to have the legal form of a limited company (*società per azioni*) or a cooperative. In addition, they must have a minimum capital and an initial programme of operations, their corporate officers must satisfy experience and integrity requirements and their shareholders with qualifying holdings must satisfy integrity requirements. It is also necessary to check, both at the start and on a continuing basis, that the ownership structure does not prejudice the bank's operations.

The law makes explicit reference to the entrepreneurial nature of banks, regardless of whether they are in the private sector or the public sector. It clarifies that profitability is a condition for the existence of banking businesses and a yardstick for their evaluation. It excludes, indeed prohibits, calling on banks to act as distributors of credit according to political and social criteria. The view of banks as entrepreneurial entities is accompanied by the belief of the legislator that competition is necessary for both the efficiency and the stability of the banking system. Competition is a general principle of the legal framework of banking and underlies the provisions of both the Consolidated Law on Banking and Italian antitrust legislation.

The Consolidated Law on Banking requires the disclosure and authorization of acquisitions of significant holdings in the capital of banks (article 19.5). In verifying that the conditions exist for the sound and prudent management of a bank, the supervisory authority examines not only the quality of the shareholders but also the business plan, when the transactions involve the transfer of control. The Bank of Italy, after informing the Interministerial Committee for Credit and Savings, has established that it must be notified 'at least 7 days before the convocation' of the board of directors to approve a planned acquisition or tender offer. In the case of a cash or exchange tender offer, 'the time limit for granting the authorization is reduced from 60 to 30 days'.

In the event of a crisis that has not compromised a bank's ability to continue operating, the management of the company is entrusted to one or more administrators appointed by the authorities (special administration). In more serious cases, in which the crisis appears irreversible, the company is wound up with the disposal of its assets (compulsory administrative liquidation). The sector-specific regime for banking crises is justified by the nature of the problems to which it is applicable: the risk of systemic crises, assets whose valuation is uncertain in determining whether the company is insolvent, activities whose value lies in the stock of information the bank has acquired. The shortcomings of the ordinary bankruptcy procedures would have serious repercussions were they applied in the banking industry. The administrative procedures the law provides for do not diminish the guarantees of the ordinary procedures. The actions taken by the credit authorities can be challenged in the administrative courts. The activity of the bodies involved in the administrative procedures is subject to actions brought in the ordinary courts.

The liquidation procedure can be applied in practice to safeguard the bank as a productive organization by separating its fate from that of owners and entrepreneurs, overwhelmed by the market. A ministerial decree issued on 27 September 1974 created a mechanism by means of which the Bank of Italy can use its resources to make good the losses incurred by banks that intervene in favour of the depositors of banks in compulsory administrative liquidation. The aim is twofold: to permit the crippled bank to be acquired by another and to provide complete protection for its depositors.

Subsequently, this system was supplemented by a private-sector safety net in the form of guarantee funds set up voluntarily by banks, including that established in 1987 following a 1986 Community recommendation. Pursuant to Directive 94/19, Legislative Decree 659/1996 made it compulsory for deposits to be covered by a guarantee system. The repayment of deposits (up to 200 million lire per depositor) requires the bank to have been placed in liquidation. The other banks are called upon to finance the intervention for the amount of deposits each insures, which is determined on the basis of a regressive criterion adjusted according to a series of business indicators. In this way the exit from the market of inefficient intermediaries is facilitated. Depending on the results of an evaluation of the situation, the intervention in favour of depositors can consist of contributions to cover the shortfall remaining after the transfer to another bank of the liquidated bank's assets and liabilities.

The Consolidated Law on Banking also governs merchant banks, venture capitalists and companies that grant loans in any form and those that provide payment or foreign exchange services. The rules are modelled in part on those applicable to banks, although the risk of instability associated with these activities is lower than those inherent in banking.

Awareness that transparency is a necessary condition for competition and fairness in the banking market permeates the legislation in the banking field. Title VI of the Consolidated Law on Banking is intended to reduce the costs borne by customers wishing to compare the conditions offered by different banks. The protection of the customers of Italian banks is more far-reaching than is required by the relevant Community directives. The goal of transparency is present in all the different aspects and moments of the relationship between banks and their customers. It is pursued through rules serving both to ensure compliance with the customer's intentions and by means of measures concerning the acceptable form and contents of contracts. The Bank of Italy is entrusted with powers to gather information and carry out inspections to verify banks' compliance with the rules on transparency (article 128 of the Consolidated Law on Banking).

The Consolidated Law on Finance

The Consolidated Law on Finance provides a comprehensive legal framework for securities market intermediaries, financial markets and issuers of financial instruments. The law's scope is very extensive and it provides rules intended to ensure fair and correct behaviour, adequate disclosure of information and the solidity of intermediaries. It complements the Consolidated Law on Banking. The underlying economic principles are the same: free enterprise, competition, international openness, efficiency, stability and transparency. Taken together, the two texts provide the legal framework within which to exploit the scope for synergy between banking and investment services, between banks and the stock exchange. Banks that provide investment services and those that are listed or whose securities are widely distributed among the public are subject to the rules of both the consolidated laws.

The rules governing securities market intermediaries are based on the notions of investment services and collective portfolio management. The former – rooted in Community law – include: dealing in securities for own and customer account; placement, with or without firm commitment underwriting or standby commitments to issuers; the reception and transmission of orders involving financial instruments and bringing together two or more investors; and individual portfolio management. These investment services can all be provided by both investment firms and banks. Some investment services can also be provided by non-bank credit intermediaries entered in the list referred to in article 107 of the Consolidated Law on Banking (dealing for own account in derivatives and placement), trust companies (individual portfolio management) and stockbrokers (nearly all the services in question except dealing for own account).

Collective portfolio management is reserved to asset management companies, which can also engage in individual portfolio management. Permitting the two forms of asset management to be provided by a single entity improves the performance of both. On the one hand, the cost savings deriving from economies of scale lower the threshold below which asset management services can be provided on an individual basis; on the other, by supplying both types of service, an intermediary can guide investors to the product best suited to their needs.

The rules governing access to the market are standardized for all intermediaries engaging in securities business and similar to those applicable to banks. The authorization procedure is intended to verify that the conditions exist for the sound and prudent management of applicant companies, in part by checking that financial and other shareholders with qualifying holdings satisfy the requirements.

The prudential rules and those regarding transparency and fair and correct behaviour differ according to the risk attaching to the various services, the types of investor involved and the scope for intermediaries to exercise discretion in their dealings with customers. When this is considerable, as in the case of collective portfolio management, the law envisages mechanisms to guarantee not only the stability of management companies but also consistency between funds' investment policies and the composition of their portfolios. Article 24 of the Consolidated Law on Finance gives customers the right to withdraw from an individual portfolio management contract at any time. The legal protection of customers is reinforced by the provision that reverses the normal burden of proof in actions for damages and requires the intermediary to prove that it has acted with due diligence.

As regards the handling of crises, the nature of investment firms' assets, both liquid and marked to market, makes it easier than it is for banks to establish whether firms are insolvent and to manage their exit from the market. The separation of assets – between those of customers and investment firms and between those of individual customers (or investment funds) – means that one of the most difficult aspects of liquidations can be dealt with on its own. Nonetheless, the compulsory administrative liquidation and special administration procedures are analogous to those for banks. Investment firms are required to be members of an investor compensation scheme.

Turning to the financial markets, the Consolidated Law on Finance completed the legal framework put in place in 1996 at the start of the single market in investment services by bringing central securities systems within its scope. It also confirmed the shift from a system of markets in the public sector to one based on their private-sector ownership and operation.

The law permits the creation of more than one regulated market for the trading of the same financial instruments where this is likely to be profitable given the foreseeable costs and volumes. The express reference in the Consolidated Law on Finance to over-the-counter markets points the way to competition among all the different alternative trading systems. Public intervention still plays a central role, however, not only in supervision but also in the regulation of the sectors in which the general good is involved. This is the case for the clearing and settlement of transactions, where there is a need to protect against systemic risk. The law makes provision for the handling of crises of market operators and central securities depositories.

The legislation on regulated markets is supplemented by all-important rules on the disclosure obligations of issuers.

The key provision in this respect is article 114 of the Consolidated Law on Finance concerning the disclosure obligations of listed issuers.

Article 116 extends these obligations to issuers of financial instruments that, although not listed on a regulated market in Italy, are widely distributed among the public. Such issuers are defined as having shareholders' equity of at least 10 billion lire and more than 200 shareholders or bondholders. The first paragraph of article 114 requires listed issuers and the persons that control them to inform the public of events occurring in their or their subsidiaries' sphere of activity that have not been made public and that if made public would be likely to have a significant effect on the price of the listed financial instruments. The means established by Consob for the disclosure of information to the market is the press release. The third paragraph of article 114 authorizes Consob to require the disclosure, on a general basis or otherwise and in the manner it establishes, of the information and documents needed to inform the public.

Article 114 is thus all-embracing. It concerns information companies already possess and that they must disclose if it is price-sensitive or if Consob orders them to do so. It also concerns information they do not possess and that they must generate or obtain for disclosure because Consob considers it necessary.

Issuers of financial instruments that are neither listed nor widely distributed among the public are only subject to the disclosure obligations specified by Consob in the regulation referred to in article 94.3 of the Consolidated Law on Finance when their securities are involved in the solicitation of investors in the form of a public offering or a tender offer. Public offering is defined as

> every offer, invitation to offer or promotional message, in whatsoever form addressed to the public, whose objective is the sale or subscription of financial products.

The notion of public has its basis in the fact that article 100.1b of the Consolidated Law on Finance enables Consob to establish a threshold for the number of persons an offer is aimed at below which the rules on public offerings do not apply (at present 200). In turn, tender offer is defined as

> every offer, invitation to offer or promotional message, in whatsoever form effected, whose objective is the purchase or exchange of financial products, addressed to a number of persons exceeding that indicated in the regulation referred to in article 100 and for a total

amount exceeding that indicated in the same regulation [at present respectively 200 and €5 million].

When public offerings are made, the offerors must draw up a prospectus for publication. Analogously, the rules on tender offers provide for the publication of an offer document containing the information needed for investors to reach a properly informed decision. In addition, the target company is required to issue a statement containing all the information serving to evaluate the offer, together with its own evaluation thereof (article 103.3 of the Consolidated Law on Finance).

The Consolidated Law on Finance has profoundly changed the rules governing tender offers, especially those of a mandatory nature. The earlier legislation – which had introduced the mandatory partial tender offer at the full price for the transfer of the control of a listed company – had revealed shortcomings that completely undermined the competitive threat: the real contribution of tender offers to the proper working of the market. The new law radically simplifies matters. It gives certainty to the legal framework. It reduces the number of different types of mandatory tender offer, intended to improve the protection of minority interests by preventing the imperfections of the market from encouraging potential bidders to build up positions gradually and silently rather than make a voluntary tender offer.[2] It transfers the rules on tender offer procedures from primary to secondary legislation, largely entrusted to Consob. It forbids the directors of target companies from taking action that may hinder the success of the offer unless authorized by the shareholders' meeting (the so-called passivity rule). The administrative courts ensure the conformity of the regulations issued with the prescriptions and principles of the primary legislation. This is confirmed by the orders issued by the Lazio Regional Administrative Tribunal and the Council of State (respectively on 21 and 29 October 1999) concerning the start of the applicability of the passivity rule. The protection of minority shareholders also benefits from the total-acquisition nature of mandatory tender offers. The efficiency of the market for corporate control gains from the fixing of a price that, taking into account market prices, is lower than that of the earlier regime. The introduction of a fixed threshold (30 per cent) overcomes the problems deriving from the difficulty of determining the existence of control on a case-by-case basis. Tender offers have thus become important in the allocation of corporate control. Including hostile bids, which had previously been unlikely, they have become a plausible means of fostering competition, a real threat to incumbent managements. They increase the efficiency of the market for corporate control.

The Consolidated Law on Finance is complemented by the provisions of company law on listed companies. The protection of minority interests – individual shareholders or groups of shareholders, including those represented by institutional investors – is considered as fostering the growth of the stock market, increasing the demand of investors for listed shares, and reducing the cost of equity capital for firms. The difference between the legal protection of minority interests in listed and unlisted companies is appropriately graduated. It does not reduce firms' propensity to go public, on the contrary. Nor does it imply a substantial difference in the protection provided to the two categories of minority shareholders, in so far as both benefit from the overall efficiency of the capital market. This is the most effective protection of every minority and in practice of every majority.

Sanctions

The most precious good in an advanced market economy is trust in the proper working of the market, in those who participate in it. Defences, including sanctions, must be put in place to protect against the loss of trust that follows from violation of the rules.

The legal system is intended to ensure the truthfulness of companies' financial reports, to safeguard their assets and equity capital and to protect the proper working of the governing bodies, especially against abuses by the directors. The Civil Code, the Penal Code and the laws applicable to the financial sector contemplate numerous offences, some of which are being reconsidered.

Legal scholarship has stressed the desirability of having a general criminal offence for breach of fiduciary duties that would also cover companies belonging to a group. Private corruption would be made an offence with a view to protecting companies' assets and sanctions would be imposed on companies for offences committed in their favour.

In the banking and financial sectors new criminal offences have recently been introduced with the aim of safeguarding supervision (correct notifications to the authorities) and markets (for the appropriate use of information and the efficient formation of prices), combating unauthorized activity, protecting investors' assets and ensuring the regularity of banking.

There is also a broad range of administrative sanctions. In this field the task of investigating the technical aspects and proposing sanctions is entrusted to the competent supervisory authority, whose knowledge of the market permits offences to be fully assessed. Sanctions are imposed rapidly, while the right to submit counter-evidence is respected.

In the 1990s, in parallel with the liberalization of capital movements, Parliament intensified the fight against persons who hide the illegal origin of the proceeds of crimes by investing them in legal activities. Italy has played its part in the search for supranational and concerted methods of countering money-laundering. It has also been committed to fighting usury and tax evasion. These three phenomena are market pathologies that distort competition and undermine business ethics and the reputation of the economy.

Intermediaries are subject to a two-pronged obligation: to keep a single computerized data base and to report suspect transactions to the UIC. This entity (which corresponds to the agencies of other countries) is charged with countering money-laundering and monitoring inter-mediaries together with the Bank of Italy. The Bank of Italy has published the so-called Decalogue, which contains the anomaly indicators for transactions. The implementing instructions issued by the UIC refer mainly to the electronic procedures which intermediaries are to use in transmitting reports so as to ensure the anonymity of the whistle-blowers. Circulars issued by trade associations such as the Italian Bankers' Association (ABI) have explained the significance of the obligations applying to their members.

The adequacy of the legal system

The Consolidated Law on Finance is the most recent, and a most important, advance in the rules governing intermediaries, issuers and financial markets. Together with the Consolidated Law on Banking, it provides a comprehensive framework. Both the laws are based on the following principles: banking and finance as entrepreneurial activities; a pluralistic system of private-sector markets; international openness; competition; self-regulation; and supervision that is not overly burden-some and designed to promote efficiency and stability on the one hand and disclosure, transparency and fairness on the other. They provide for a *regulated competitive market*, a prerequisite for the development of banks and financial intermediaries that are able to earn profits by offer-ing high-quality services at a low cost and direct and indirect protection of savings in accordance with article 47 of the Constitution.

With the adoption of the Consolidated Law on Finance, Italy's legal system moved to the van in Europe, especially as regards the rules on collective portfolio management. In several respects it anticipates the positions of the proposed Community law in this field; in particular, the proposed framework directive under discussion in the Commission would allow management companies to operate seamlessly throughout the asset management industry and broaden the range of collective investment undertakings that can be supplied cross-border.

This legal framework allows Italian intermediaries to operate in a context similar to or even more favourable than those in which their main foreign competitors operate.

Rules, supervision and sanctions are in line with those of the other EU countries. The provisions of Italian law on investment services, collective portfolio management and regulated markets are also basically equivalent to those in force in the United States and the other leading non-EU countries. The primary and secondary legislation for the protection of investors in the Italian financial markets is on a par with those of the most important foreign markets. In the United States there is still scope for the exercise of a structural control over the banking system. The supervisory authorities can invoke the absence of 'economic needs' as grounds for refusing banking authorization. Rules require individual banks to allocate a proportion of their lending to specific geographical areas under the Community Reinvestment Act of 1978. The ban on commercial banks engaging in investment banking, established by the Glass-Steagall Act of 1933, was removed only in 2000.

Community harmonization does not eliminate but rather highlights the fields in which differences remain between legal systems, especially in private and bankruptcy law and civil procedure. There are often openings for regulatory arbitrage as competition between jurisdictions intensifies. Less-advanced legal systems accordingly tend to be brought into line with the more modern ones. For instance, article 203 of the Consolidated Law on Finance introduces the principle of close-out netting in the event of bankruptcy; it also broadens the scope of article 76 of the Bankruptcy Law and provides for the use of netting contracts in financial transactions, thus transposing a principle present in other legal systems and widely adopted in standard contracts at international level.

An overall judgement of adequacy needs to be qualified. It refers to the principles, the content of the basic rules and the structure of legislation. Views may differ with regard to specific aspects, from both an economic and a legal standpoint. The legal system 'photographed' here at the end of the last century is already changing in some major respects. It will adapt to new needs. The formulation of new rules at European level will continue on the basis of the Action Plan for Financial Services approved in 1999, which refers, *inter alia*, to investment services, takeover bids and the European company. This will necessarily affect Italy's banking and financial legislation.

Among the fields in which new legislation has recently been approved, it is worth noting the provision made in Law 130/1999 for the securitization of assets. This technique increases the flexibility of intermediaries' risk management. It encourages the development of a secondary market in financial instruments representative of the underlying assets. Parliament is examining a serious of matters, including trust law. More generally, the search will continue for the most efficient balance between primary law and the secondary legislation issued by the Bank of Italy and the other regulatory authorities, and between mandatory and non-mandatory provisions. The rationale of regulatory decisions and individual administrative acts, the extent to which they can be known by all the interested parties, and the relationship between the discretion exercised by supervisors and the transparency of their actions are all aspects of a single, ever-present problem. Self-regulation by the companies that operate the money and financial markets is a recent innovation in Italy. Time will tell what use these (private) entities will make of this power, whether its scope will deserve to be extended and how it can best be tied in with (public) legislation.

Naturally, the prospect of arriving at perfect rules is necessarily tinged with well-founded pessimism:

> How will it ever be possible . . . for a clear and well-constructed law to be written in Italian and correctly interpreted by persons who do not have a familiarity with Cicero, Dante, Machiavelli, Galileo and Leopardi, together with a subtle logic and a mature understanding of the social context in which the law is to operate, with all its problems, values and expectations?[3]

While the legal framework provided for banking and finance by the two consolidated laws can be deemed adequate with the above qualifications, in other fields there is considerable room for improvement in the law governing the economy. The passage from a 'mixed' economy to a market economy with suitable rules has still to be completed on a wide front, extending well beyond the privatization of Italy's leading public enterprises. There needs to be a bias in favour of entrepreneurship – the real engine of growth, the 'residual of the residual' in growth accounting – in the legal rules governing the lives of Italian firms, which consist primarily of sole proprietorships and small and medium-sized enterprises, albeit often linked together in industrial districts. Were this to happen, the consolidated laws on banking and finance would be buttressed and strengthened.

The reforming drive should be directed towards the following – once again seven – aspects of the legal system governing the economy:

Company law. The Consolidated Law on Finance has brought the rules applicable to Italian listed companies closer into line with those in force in the other leading industrial countries. An even further-reaching reform of company law is urgently needed. There is a need for an innovative system suitable for the configuration of Italian firms – predominantly small and medium-sized and often organized in industrial districts – that would foster entrepreneurship, restrict the scope of mandatory rules and increase firms' freedom to regulate their affairs in their bylaws.

Bankruptcy law. Bankruptcy proceedings are slow and costly. They penalize ill-starred entrepreneurs. They discourage start-ups and entrepreneurial risk-taking. The inadequacy of the alternative restructuring procedures is demonstrated by the limited use made of them and prevents recourse to a range of graduated remedies for corporate crises. Limited changes were made in 1999 to the special procedure for restructuring medium-sized and large firms in difficulty. A comprehensive reform of bankruptcy law would be desirable, matching that of company law.

Labour law. Recent legislation has altered the types of employment available, both introducing new ones (temporary employment) and changing existing ones (fixed-term and part-time jobs). The regime governing the hiring of workers has been reformed. There is nonetheless room in the regime governing payroll employment to arrive at a better combination – through specific rules, such as indemnification or mandatory protection for workers who are dismissed without due cause – of labour mobility and workers' rights.

Enforcement. The changes made a few years ago in the field of civil procedure and those currently being prepared must remove the chronic inefficiencies affecting commercial justice. In addition to increased resources, there is a need for a judicial body with specific skills and procedures in keeping with the need for rapidity and certainty in settling disputes involving firms.

Legislative and administrative streamlining. Legislative simplification must be speeded up. It is necessary to advance further along the path of administrative simplification, by applying it in the areas selected and selecting new ones in which to lighten the burden of firms' dealings with government.

Tax administration. The recent reform[4] – the regional tax on productive activities (Irap), the dual income tax (DIT), the reduction in the number and level of tax rates, and the taxation of capital gains – has reshaped important parts of the tax system. It is necessary to act quickly to complete the work already initiated aimed at streamlining and improving the efficiency and rigorousness of the tax authorities.

Promotion of competition. The legal barriers hindering the market entry of new firms and the exit of loss-making ones need to be removed. Authorizations, certifications, licences, guilds and public monopolies segment markets. Legislation and antitrust action must unite in protecting consumers from oligopolistic prices and removing the obstacles to the transfer of resources that declining sectors and firms put in the way of those that are expanding. The neoclassical concept of static competition aimed merely at protecting consumers must be supplemented by the classical and Schumpeterian concept aimed at fostering growth. The competition that is important – apart from the interests of consumers – for the vitality of the economy, for economic growth, is entrusted to two separate but complementary mechanisms: the levelling of profit rates through a freer play of relative prices and the selection of borrowers by a banking system on which the action of the Bank of Italy will continue to impose competition.

An economy based on entrepreneurship in regulated competitive markets, an economy that is not held back but served and fostered by the law: this is the goal to pursue. Within the framework of Community law an original national approach to the complex relationship between the law and the economy – an economic policy implemented through the law – can make all the difference in international competition.[5]

The legal order and change

By tying in with the morphological developments in the financial system, the legislative innovations of the 1980s and 1990s have strengthened principles and rules that had shown themselves to be valid, removed legal obstacles to change and encouraged private enterprise in the financial industry.

Since some rules have been strengthened and others replaced with new ones deemed to be more suitable, the alterations to the fabric of the law cannot be considered deregulation. Rather, they have reshaped the legal framework in a way that subjected financial activities to regulation based on an interpretation of the public interest of which the starting-point was the definitive recognition of their entrepreneurial nature. The classification of provisions concerning the financial industry as an *'ordinamento sezionale'* was superseded. Introduced in the 1940s, this concept referred to the existence in the overall legal order of a part of the economy, the financial sector, placed under the control of a body capable of issuing internal rules, directives and orders, in view of the public nature of the sector's activity. The rationale was to be able to guide the financial system in any direction that conformed with the general good, which was to coincide with the objectives that the economic and social policy of the state chose to pursue at any given moment. The instrumental nature of regulation and the potential mutability of the ends were the hallmarks of the *ordinamento sezionale* for credit.

Today's legal order – the outcome of the interaction of legal scholarship, court decisions and legislation based on article 47 of the Constitution – has established a definition of the general good in the financial field that is less mutable, almost permanent. Competition, efficiency, stability, sound and prudent management: these objectives are now embodied in laws, to the benefit of savers, users of financial services and the correct operation of a market economy. The relationship between these objectives and regulation is still one of means to an end. It is nonetheless much less instrumental than that inherent in the 1936 legal order, which the financial authorities, wisely, used only in part and only in serious economic crises.

The notion of an *ordinamento sezionale* implied an idea of separation from the general order that the relationship between the new institutions of the financial system and the overall legal order has overcome. Today it is preferable to refer to a special legal order directed towards firms that satisfy the demand for financial services in an economically viable manner. It differs from the overall legal order in its rules on activities, not in the underlying evolution of the law. It considers the autonomy of private persons and the international circulation of standardized contracts to be the main forces of legal innovation. The reference is to the freedom granted to the parties by article 1322 of the Civil Code. They can choose the definition of their interests that suits them best. They can also pursue these interests, within the limits of legality, through 'types of contract that are not already regulated'. In this way a series of new types of contract have been introduced into the Italian financial system – leasing, franchising, swaps and other derivatives – in response to new needs.

All in all, the legal system made a considerable, perhaps decisive, contribution to the changes in the Italian financial system in the 1980s and 1990s. In at least two sectors – privatizations and derivatives – the results achieved would not have been possible without new rules. In the fields of intermediaries and taxation these created the conditions for the bulk of credit institutions to pass from the public sector to the private sector. The exclusion of derivative contracts from the general regime governing obligations – in Italy as in other countries – has permitted the development of the market for these new risk management mechanisms. But the other main structural nodes of the Italian financial system have also received a stimulus, or support, from the legal system.

4
Taxation

The relationship between Italy's tax system and the developments in the country's financial sector in the last two decades of the twentieth century can be examined from several different angles. Did the overall tax and tax-related burden on the financial sector change, and in what direction? Did the degree of neutrality in the taxation of each of the various types of finance change, and in what direction? Were the principal changes in the financial system helped or hindered by the tax system? Finally, how do we evaluate the adequacy of the tax regime for the Italian financial sector following the introduction of the euro?

The fiscal burden and tax neutrality for the financial sector

The overall fiscal burden on the Italian economy, measured by the ratio of taxes and social security contributions to GDP, grew dramatically between 1980 and 1999. Overall, the fiscal ratio rose from 31.3 to 43.3 per cent, but it had already reached 39.6 per cent in 1990. The increase was more pronounced than in any other European country. In 1999 Italy's ratio approached the average for the euro area, but reducing it has become harder since the country's public debt is the largest in the area in relation to national income (115 per cent). The general government debt remains under special surveillance in Europe in the light of Italy's participation in the monetary union and its consequent commitment to comply with the 60 per cent debt limit. For Italy this undertaking implies that every reduction in public expenditure must be used for debt reduction rather than for decreases in taxes and social security contributions, while the European countries with less public debt will have more leeway to seek to boost competitiveness by cutting taxes.

Over the 20-year span, and especially in the 1980s, the tax burden grew even faster than the overall fiscal burden, of which it is the main component: from 16.7 per cent of GDP in 1979 to 24.9 per cent in 1989 and 30.5 per cent in 1999, one of the highest levels in Europe. In the same period revenues from taxes on intermediaries and bank and financial instruments rose from 1.7 to 2.5 per cent of GDP, while their share of total revenues declined from 10 per cent in 1979 and 12 per cent in 1989 to 8 per cent in 1999 (Table 4.1). This is still larger than the financial

Table 4.1 Revenue from taxes on the financial sector in Italy (billions of lire)

	1979	*1989*	*1997*	*1998*	*1999*
Direct corporate taxes[a]	1162	7807	11846	17139	16901
banks[b]	1125	7341	7583	12271	11703
investment firms[b]	–	–	495	706	763
asset management companies[b]	–	90	410	662	784
insurance companies[b]	37	326	2763	2857	2920
other financial companies (leasing, factoring and consumer credit)[c]	–	50	595	643	731
Taxes on financial instruments	4149	27971	46947	30725	30869
flat-rate withholding tax on interest and capital gains[d]	3684	22719	36403	19409	22335
withholding tax on dividends[d]	100	2108	3467	3384	764
net worth tax on investment funds[b]	–	169	194	402	–
taxes on insurance companies charged to policyholders[b]	340	2925	6808	7450	7680
registry fee and stamp duty on financial contracts[c]	25	50	75	80	90
Total	5311	35779	58793	47864	47770
MEMORANDUM ITEMS					
As a percentage of total tax revenue	10.0	12.2	10.7	9.0	8.2
Total tax revenue as a percentage of GDP	17.4	24.6	27.7	25.8	28.0
Financial sector's percentage share of total value added at factor cost	4.5	5.9	5.8	5.9	5.9

[a] Corporate income tax, tax on net worth, regional tax on productive activities, and local income tax.
[b] Annual accounts data.
[c] Partly estimated.
[d] State budget receipts.
Sources: Banca d'Italia, *Relazione annuale*, for the annual accounts data for banks, asset management companies and investment firms and for State budget receipts; ANIA, *Annuario*, for the annual accounts data for insurance companies.

sector's share of national value added (5.9 per cent), but less so than at the end of the 1970s, when the financial sector accounted for 4.5 per cent of total value added.

That the tax and tax-related burden on the financial industry – on banking and financial services, on those that produce them and use them – has tended to grow less than the tax burden on the economy as a whole and less than in other productive sectors will be even more evident in the light of two observations.

Apart from the always questionable national-accounts estimates of the value added of the financial sector, the volume of activities that the sector performs and services it supplies has grown more rapidly than the output of the other economic sectors. Gross financial assets have grown by a factor of 9 since 1980; still greater has been the increase in monetary and financial transactions and services, such as payment services, consulting, risk management and hedging. This expansion has been more intense than that in both nominal tangible wealth (5 times) and GDP (6 times), if not in the tax revenue extracted from the financial sector (also 9 times).

Alongside the explicit taxation of the financial sector, we must also consider implicit taxation, which in the early 1980s was pervasive and stood at historically high levels. In 1980 the Italian financial system was subject to a vast array of direct statutory and administrative controls. Recourse to these instruments had prevailed in the 1970s in response to the dangerous combination of stagnation, inflation and external account deficits caused by rising international prices of raw materials, the explosive growth of monetary wages, the shortcomings of fiscal policy and the crisis of the mixed economy. Foreign exchange controls, ceilings on the growth in bank lending, securities investment requirements, compulsory reserves on bank deposits and banking supervision based on administrative authorization went together with the inflation tax on money. The latter was high, considering both an inflation rate of more than 21 per cent in 1980 and the extensive use of currency (equal to 6 per cent of GDP) and deposits (70 per cent of GDP) for making payments and holding wealth.

Since then, the implicit taxation of finance has virtually disappeared. The securities investment requirement for banks was eliminated in 1986, the ceiling on lending growth in 1988 and foreign exchange controls in 1990. The number of supervisory administrative authorizations declined from 17,000 in 1980 to less than 8,000 in 1985, 3,600 in 1990 and just a few hundred at the end of the decade. Calculated on monetary base alone, the inflation tax fell from 3 per cent of GDP in 1980 to 0.5 per cent in 1990 and subsequently to a minimal level. For the effectiveness of monetary policy in view of the Treasury's large and variable borrowing requirement, the reserve requirement on bank deposits remained highly onerous for a longer time. The compulsory reserves may be likened to a tax that lowers banks' net interest income, tying up an appreciable portion of their resources in investments that yield even less than the minimum market rates of return (short-term government securities). The greater the differential between market rates and the yield on deposits with the central bank, the greater the opportunity cost. On the basis of this analogy, the implicit charge imposed on Italian banks by the reserve requirement between 1982 and 1995 was equal to an average of 30 per cent of their gross profit, with a high of 60 per cent in 1982 and a low of 15 per cent in 1993. The implicit charge calculated with reference to the alternative minimum yield offered by Treasury bills stood at 25 per cent in 1995. Subsequently it diminished rapidly, falling to negligible levels in 1998 in anticipation of the launch of the euro.

Nowadays, therefore, the financial sector is less penalized than in the past in relative terms. Compared with 20 years ago, the tax and tax-related burden has decreased in relation to the much larger scale of services supplied by the sector. However, it is above all in comparison with the other sectors of the economy that the financial sector's tax disadvantages have lessened. This is particularly true if one considers that financial activities and services have grown faster than productive activities as a whole. The curbing of tax and tax-related charges has promoted the quantitative growth of finance in a sort of virtuous circle. The increase in the financial interrelations ratio stems in part from this.

Important progress was also made on the other front, that of the 'neutrality' of the tax and tax-related treatment of financial services on both the supply and demand sides. As regards the composition of supply, the decisive advance consisted in the phasing out of the system of administrative controls set up to cope with the crisis of the 1970s. Still fully operative at the start of the 1980s, by the late 1990s that system had ceased to exist. The process focused on the structure of the assets and liabilities and organizational arrangements of banks, in Italy far and away the leading suppliers of financial services. Initially, restrictions applied to virtually all of the essential items of banks' balance sheets: loans, securities, liquidity, foreign currency position, fund-raising, capital. In turn, the constraints imposed on their organizational arrangements are perhaps best exemplified by the rules allowing banks to operate in the stock market only through subsidiary companies and not directly. The removal of this set of restrictions marked a decisive change, though one whose effects are hard to quantify, in the direction of a constellation of prices and quantities of financial services expressed in the most neutral way by banks and other financial intermediaries.

Similarly, the evolution of the structure of taxation since 1980 displays a trend towards the general and uniform taxation of the different financial instruments, especially in the late 1990s. This holds both for the returns on financial assets for investors (households and firms) and for the costs of the financial liabilities issued by enterprises.

In contrast with the tax system of 1980, the system subsequently put in place offers no exemptions to firms or households for income from financial investment. In 1980 interest on government securities and bonds issued by special credit institutions, state holding companies and listed companies was tax-exempt. Capital gains realized by resident individual investors on financial transactions also enjoyed *de facto* exemption; they were taxed only if they arose from transactions entered into with a speculative intent, which was hard to ascertain. The tax-induced diversification of contractual forms for financial products having an identical economic content has diminished. An exemplary case was the development of zero-coupon securities in the 1980s; initially the issue discount, being considered a capital gain, was not subject to tax when the securities were owned by natural persons. At the opposite extreme, income from certain financial assets was subject to a 30 per cent tax.

The Visco reform of 1997 (enacted in Law 461/1997 and named after the finance minister of the day) reduced the bewildering jungle of rates to a mere two: 12.5 and 27 per cent (Table 4.2). The ultimate goal was to unify the tax rates at the lowest level that the difficult conditions of the public finances would allow. Final withholding tax in lieu of income tax was confirmed in the reform. In view of the proportionality this implies and the levels of the tax rates, over time it has limited the tax wedge on savings, reduced the technical difficulties of combating evasion and, by preserving anonymity, responded to the risk of migration of savings.

The system of concessionary credit, which subsidized firms and the banks financing them, commingled lending and subsidies, with a distortionary impact on the institutional and market mechanisms of allocation and corporate finance decisions. The system's excesses were evident at the end of the 1970s. Its relative growth slowed in the 1980s and its importance subsequently dwindled; concessionary loans declined from 10 to 5 per cent of total loans outstanding to the private sector between 1990 and 1998.

Table 4.2 Rates of taxation of the financial assets of natural persons resident in Italy (E = exempt; P = progressive)

	31.12.1980	31.12.1999
Interest		
on government securities and the like	E	12.5
on bonds and similar securities		
issued by banks and listed companies	E[a]	
issued by unlisted companies	20	12.5/27[b]
issued by non-residents	30	
on bank and post-office deposits and current accounts	20	27
on certificates of deposit and savings certificates	20	27
on other (atypical) securities	15[c]	27
Dividends		
on qualifying holdings	10[c]	P
other	10[c]/15[d]	12.5[e]
Capital gains		
on qualifying holdings		27
other (other equity interests and bonds, derivatives, gold and foreign currencies)	E/P[f]	12.5

[a] The exemption applied to bonds issued by medium- and long-term credit institutions and sections. Securities issued by the state holding companies were also exempt.

[b] For bonds and similar securities issued in Italy or abroad by whatsoever issuer, a rate of 12.5 or 27 per cent applies depending on whether the original maturity of the securities is or is not less than 18 months. For bonds issued by unlisted companies with a maturity of more than 18 months, the 12.5 per cent rate applies if the yield is in line with the statutory limits; otherwise, the rate is 27 per cent.

[c] Withholding tax on account.

[d] The flat-rate tax of 15 per cent applied to the dividends on savings shares.

[e] Taxpayers may opt for taxation under progressive personal income tax (Irpef), claiming the amount withheld as a tax credit.

[f] Progressive tax was supposed to be imposed on 'speculative transactions', but identifying these was difficult in the absence of objective criteria (holding period, equity stake in the company, etc.).

The exemption from taxation of government securities, together with the deductibility of the cost of borrowing, engendered distortions in firms' financial behaviour. Sometimes the constellation of market rates made it advantageous to use bank credit in order to purchase tax-exempt securities. Corrective measures to prevent arbitrage of this kind, followed by the complete abolition of the exemption of government securities, restored allocative efficiency to firms' decisions.

The interference of tax law in corporate financing was greater than in the other European countries. Substantial arbitrage opportunities arose from the support given to corporate borrowing. The deductibility of its cost, combined with the taxation of profits, favours debt over equity capital in all tax systems. In Italy, the high tax rates, inflation and the taxation of interest on a nominal basis distorted the taxation of real incomes to a greater degree; they amplified the tax discrimination among the different financing options, and resulted in corporate tax offering heavily indebted firms a subsidy that was not always counter-balanced by the effects on depreciation and the taxation of interest and dividends paid to savers. The subsidy for borrowing remained after the administrative restrictions on lending were ended; the idea that, rather than a deviation from neutrality, the 'government premium' for debt capital was a corrective for the inefficiencies of the credit market is without foundation.

Comparative studies generally found that 'very significant progress in reducing differences in tax rates among assets, industries, or both has been made by every country except Italy' during the 1980s.[1] At the beginning of the 1990s the corporate income tax wedge, estimated under assumptions on which the final result strictly depends, was still strongly negative for debt capital financing and positive for self-financing and new share issues (Table 4.3). The tax incentive to borrow and the penalization of equity capital were accentuated in 1992 by the tax on companies' net worth.

In the field of direct taxes, Italy was a high-tax jurisdiction, with one of the highest rates of taxation of investments in Europe. In 1997 corporate income tax rates were still among the highest in the European Union. While in the other EU countries statutory tax rates were reduced or at least held unchanged, in Italy they rose between 1990 and 1997 by 6 percentage points, from 46.4 to 53.2 per cent. In 1996 the average effective rate was 35.3 per cent, against an EU average of 26.9 per cent. Italy was one of the few remaining European countries where the tax wedge on investments abroad was smaller than that on domestic investments.

For corporate taxes, as in other domains, the reversal of trend came in 1997–8.[2] The abolition of local income tax cut the statutory tax rate on profits from 53.2 to 37 per cent; the reduction was offset only partly by the introduction of the regional tax on productive activities (Irap), at a normal rate of 4.25 per cent. This weakened the primary source of allocative distortions, limiting the preference accorded to debt capital and rebalancing the treatment of the sources of finance for the determination of profits for tax purposes. The introduction of Irap ended the total deductibility of interest payments (fully deductible for corporate income tax (Irpeg) but non-deductible for Irap). With the introduction of the dual income tax (DIT) the cost imputable to retained earnings,

Table 4.3 Effective marginal rates of corporate and personal tax[a]

	1980[b]			1985[b]			1990[b]			1991[c]			1998[d]		
	Debt finance	Equity	Profits	Debt finance	Equity	Profits	Debt finance	Equity	Profits	Debt finance	Equity	Profits	Debt finance	Equity	Profits
Australia	13.6	79.1	59.7	-6.1	64.3	45.6	21.7	31.2	59.0	37.5	12.3	12.3	33.3	33.3	34.2
Canada	21.4	50.5	49.3	27.1	50.9	49.8	33.7	60.3	49.6	39.8	52.8	43.2	21.9	53.3	48.5
France	43.7	75.9	85.0	40.1	104.8	87.4	34.3	93.1	67.5	-2.0	56.1	35.1	13.8	63.0	46.8
Germany	12.5	61.8	87.3	4.6	56.6	85.1	-1.4	50.6	76.3	12.3	24.2	19.4	20.6	15.3	21.9
Italy	-16.6	85.8	47.1	-30.2	78.9	50.1	-28.0	81.4	59.2	-19.0	36.7	47.4	10.7	33.3	30.6
Japan	-31.9	65.9	60.5	-39.4	67.7	65.5	-8.3	76.7	66.2	-19.0	61.2	45.1	-6.4	59.7	47.4
Sweden	0.3	68.9	49.9	9.9	71.6	58.7	16.0	46.2	43.3	10.7	41.2	41.9	16.7	40.5	32.4
United Kingdom	114.7	20.5	12.7	49.1	25.5	41.0	35.1	25.5	43.8	32.4	20.6	27.5	26.5	35.9	30.6
United States	-10.4	75.1	55.5	-18.8	68.2	50.2	8.8	64.1	53.3	15.3	53.7	42.5	25.4	53.3	28.6
Average	16.4	64.8	56.3	4.0	65.4	59.3	12.4	58.8	57.6	12.0	39.9	34.9	18.1	43.1	35.6
Difference vis-à-vis rate on debt finance (percentage points)		48.5	40.0		61.4	55.2		46.4	45.1		27.9	22.9		25.0	17.6
– for Italy		102.4	63.7		109.1	80.3		109.4	87.2		55.8	66.4		22.6	19.8

[a] Maximum marginal rates for personal tax.
[b] Assuming a real pre-tax rate of return of 10 per cent and a 5 per cent inflation rate (see Jorgenson and Landau, 1993).
[c] Assuming an after-tax rate of return of 5 per cent and an inflation rate equal to the actual rate of inflation in the individual country (see OECD, 1991).
[d] Assuming a real after-tax rate of return of 5 per cent and a 2 per cent inflation rate (see OECD, 2000).

Sources: D.W. Jorgenson and R. Landau (eds), Tax Reform and the Cost of Capital. An International Comparison, Brookings Institution, Washington, DC, 1993; OECD, Taxing Profits in a Global Economy: Domestic and International Issues, Paris, 1991; OECD, Economic Surveys: Spain, Paris, 2000.

their 'ordinary' remuneration, formally totally non-deductible, became partially deductible (18/37 deductibility for Irpeg, nil deductibility for Irap). This relief was not extended to the ordinary remuneration of the entire amount of a company's equity capital beyond its retained earnings, as was instead the case of the dual income tax applied in the Scandinavian countries. The abolition of the tax on net worth has not only lessened the tax burden on firms, but has also acted in the same direction by eliminating part of the discrimination against equity capital.

Indications of greater neutrality regarding firms' financing decisions can be derived from the calculation of the tax wedges. The burden on debt has increased and the disparity in the treatment of the different corporate liabilities has diminished. To highlight the changes introduced by the reform, it is advisable for the sake of simplicity to disregard the taxation of savings, assume neutrality in the tax treatment of amortization and depreciation and posit the absence of specific incentives and of inflation. The wedge is now positive for debt and is perceptibly smaller for the other sources of finance; the favourable treatment of debt, though not eliminated, has been noticeably attenuated (Table 4.3).

Taxation and the structure of the financial system

The principal changes that have renewed the structure of the Italian financial system since the end of the 1970s were influenced in different ways and to varying degrees by taxation. The large number of tax measures, their opposite sign, and the interactions of their repercussions on the channels of saving make it extremely difficult to offer a summary judgement on the consequences of taxation for the financial system. What follows is an overview of the effects of tax measures on: (1) the banking system and, specifically, its restructuring; (2) the development of the markets, financial innovation and new intermediaries; and (3) the international attractiveness of Italy's financial system from the standpoint of taxation.

The banking system

The influence of taxation was fundamental in at least one case: the privatization of the public banking system, which would have been far less easy without the tax relief provided by Law 218/1990. This law provided for the treatment of contributions of assets to be tax-neutral, permitted the transformation of public-sector banks into public limited companies and facilitated their consolidation to form larger enterprises. The scaling up of the system and strengthening of its capital base were aided by recognition of a special 'retained profits reserve' ('concentration premium') subject to ordinary taxation only if and when these profits were distributed. Between 1990 and 1998 the reserves established under Law 218/1990 for concentrations brought the banking system tax savings of 2.2 trillion lire, equal to 1.5 per cent of the gross profits of the system for the period.

The dual objective of privatization and consolidation of the banking system was also pursued in the legislation on the banking foundations, Law 461/1998 and Legislative Decree 153/1999. These used tax relief both for shareholders (the foundations that still held controlling interests in banks) and for banking groups by providing for reduced taxation in the case of concentrations. The relief applies to structural operations (mergers and spin-offs) but also to acquisitions of controlling interests, in order to ensure neutrality among organizational choices. The first two years the legislation was in force saw a drive for restructuring in the banking system. A total of 60 concentrations took place in 1998 and 1999 between bank intermediaries other than mutual banks, including large-scale transactions involving Italy's major banking groups.

By contrast, it is harder to determine whether the orientation towards a bank-based rather than a market-based system prevailed so long in Italy in part because it was induced or reinforced by tax law. On the one hand, tax law accorded favourable treatment (the deductibility of interest expense) to corporate debt (largely bank debt, as in other countries) and to special credit institution bond issues. On the other, bank intermediation was taxed heavily, being a tax base less subject than others to evasion or avoidance and more easily assessed. Whether the net outcome was more positive for intermediaries than markets, or vice versa, is an open question in the absence of counterfactual evidence, the complexity of whose construction we can only succinctly describe.

The less favourable treatment accorded to the alternatives to debt finance reinforced firms' dependence on the banks. The 1980–1 measures excluding interest on special credit institution bonds and certificates of deposit from personal, corporate and local income tax acted in the same direction. During the period of exemption special credit institutions' net issues of bonds and certificates of deposit (CDs) grew by nearly 80 per cent, from 4.6 trillion lire in 1979 to 8.2 trillion in 1982. A further benefit for the special credit institutions came with the 1988 exemption for their securities issued abroad. Alongside the direct and indirect tax advantages, there were public incentives for investment through the use of subsidized credit.

However, over the years a heavy tax burden was placed on the banking system, and it was long accompanied by the very heavy tax-related costs already mentioned. Thanks in part to Community legislation, in the course of time the banks won virtually universal exemption of their services from VAT, even though they paid VAT on their purchases, but direct taxes remained at high levels; in 1990 the average effective tax rate was equal to 96 per cent of the (high) statutory rate. A contributory factor was the inclusion of banks within the scope of measures aimed at curbing firms' propensity to borrow by making otherwise exempt interest income taxable through the non-deductibility of an amount equal to interest expense (Decree Law 791/1984, then Law 6/1985). As a consequence of the introduction in 1986 of withholding tax on government securities, the large banks came to have substantial tax credits whose reimbursement was protracted. Over the years a heavy tax burden also arose from banks' bad debts. The amount of expected loan losses that could be deducted each year was limited to a flat 0.5 per cent of the value of loan assets stated in the balance sheet; value adjustments in excess of that amount were non-deductible. This system squeezed banks' operating results. Recognition of the tax deductibility of loan losses (for the part in excess of the allowed provision) only when the losses were realized was an impediment to taking the actual risk of the loan portfolio into account. For many banks this entailed the improper recognition of taxable income. The distortion grew larger during recessions, when bad debts increased. Law 549/1995 allowed value adjustments to loans in the accounts to be fully deducted, but only in eight annual instalments. The tax weight of bad debts was alleviated further when the ceiling on deductible value adjustments was raised from 0.5 to 0.6 per cent of loan assets. However, the positive effect was curbed by the simultaneous lengthening of the deduction period to extend even further beyond that in which the bad debts were carried (that is before they turned into realized losses). The withholding tax on interest on bank deposits was increased from 20 per cent in 1980 to 25 per cent in 1983 and 30 per cent in 1988; it has stood at 27 per cent since June 1996; the repercussions on the banks of this heavy taxation increased with competition. The tax on net wealth also weighed on banks' accounts. During the period it was in force, from 1992 to 1997, it coincided with a strengthening of banks' capital adequacy ratios. It was not until 1996 that a specific legislative measure (Law 549/1995) exempted cash share issues, indivisible reserves and subordinated liabilities, so as not to deter recourse to equity finance.

Between 1987 and 1996 the direct taxes paid by banks (other than mutual banks) to the Inland Revenue Service grew by an average of 10 per cent a year, rising from 41 to 55 per cent of the banks' gross profits. In 1993 the tax burden on banks reached its peak: the average effective rate of taxation leapt by 10 percentage points to reach 63 per cent, with a record differential *vis-à-vis* non-bank enterprises. It weighed especially on the large banks, which were more exposed to international competition. According to estimates made by simulating the application of the tax laws of four European countries to a theoretical bank balance sheet, in 1995 the levy on Italian banks (57 per cent) was much higher than that on British and French banks (36 and 39 per cent respectively) and even higher than that on German banks (55 per cent).

One of the most controversial episodes of the two decades we are examining involved the banks. It regarded the levy of 6 per mille on bank deposits in July 1992. (The measure also applied to Post Office deposits, deposits with special credit institutions, including certificates of deposit and postal savings deposits; interbank deposits and postal savings certificates were excluded.) The tax hit those who happened to hold wealth in liquid form on 9 July of that year. Collected by banks and the Post Office in September, it brought in 5.3 trillion lire, or 0.3 per cent of GDP, in the context of a budget correction designed to reduce the state sector borrowing requirement by 30 trillion lire (2 per cent of GDP) in the final part of the year. The tax was equivalent to around one-tenth of the nominal annual flow of interest on deposits, or to all the real income deriving therefrom. It could only be expected that such a tax would weigh above all on the financial assets of the poorest households or those least astute in their portfolio choices. At the end of 1991 households with an annual income of less than 20 million lire (18.5 per cent of all households) held 82 per cent of their financial assets in the form of deposits, compared with 22 per cent for households whose annual income exceeded 80 million lire. While for the latter the levy amounted to 1.3 per mille of the value of their financial assets, for households with incomes of less than 20 million the incidence was 4.9 per mille. The effective tax rate amounted to 4.6 per mille of average household income for the richer households and 6.4 per mille for the poorer ones. It was the analogue of the 1869 'grist tax', in an economy no longer based on peasant farming but by now monetary in the Keynesian sense.

The capital markets

As regards the effects of taxation on the capital markets, an obstacle to the efficiency of the bond market lay in the withholding tax applied by the issuer. It implied trading on a net basis, while the prevailing practice in foreign markets was trading on a gross basis. The withholding tax on bonds issued by the government, banks and listed companies was repealed with effect from 1997 pursuant to Legislative Decree 239/1996, and a tax in lieu of income tax, withheld by intermediaries, was introduced for investors other than firms and non-residents. The measure increased the liquidity of the market.

A further, longstanding brake on the growth of the financial markets was the tax on stock exchange contracts. Until the end of 1997 it was levied on trades in shares and bonds at rates ranging from 0.09 to 1.4 per mille, with an effect inversely related to the duration and return of the investment. It influenced the development of some types of transaction and the regulated markets, requiring continual legislative corrections. Because the twofold application of the tax made repurchase agreements unprofitable, in 1988 the amount of the tax on each of the two contract notes was halved. In 1992, to stem the migration of trading in Italian government securities to London, the tax was waived for non-residents (both intermediaries and individual investors), even if the counterparty was a resident. In the same year a general exemption was introduced for trades in government securities on the regulated markets (MTS and MIF). The opening up of the electronic market in government securities to foreign intermediaries in 1994 would have been incompatible with taxation of the market's Italian intermediaries, as the latter would have incurred a higher tax bill as a consequence of their subsequent trades with customers. In 1996, to avoid disparities of treatment between Italian and foreign intermediaries, the exemption for non-resident members of MTS was repealed for off-market trades with residents. In 1996 securities lending transactions, essential for the smooth operation of the markets and for the changeover to 'delivery versus payment' settlement, were made exempt from the tax on stock exchange contracts. Since 1998 trades concluded in the regulated markets and all trades between banks, investment firms and investment funds have been tax-exempt.

Unlike other countries, Italy did not introduce tax incentives to support innovative products from the very outset; on the contrary, legislation tended to follow the market. The categorization of the new instruments for tax purposes arose from the contingent objective of eliminating pockets of tax avoidance. Atypical securities – at the end of 1981 the amount outstanding was estimated at 1.65 trillion lire, with annual flows of 600 billion lire – were penalized in 1983 with the application of an 18 per cent withholding tax, which was increased to 30 per cent in

1988 and then trimmed to 27 per cent in 1998. There were fears for the effectiveness of monetary policy, which at the time relied in part on administrative constraints. When they were not penalizing, as in the case of banker's acceptances and commercial paper, the tax rules were aimed only at removing obstacles without promoting innovation. An exception was that of life insurance policies. Over the years these were supported on both the investor side (deductibility of premiums and reduced taxation of the income) and the insurer side (the possibility for companies to set aside the income in their actuarial reserves and to deduct the withholding tax paid from corporate income tax).

Tax law on derivatives was likewise aimed at preventing distortions rather than encouraging wider use of the new instruments. The measures enacted in 1994 and the 1997 reform sought to bring the products of so-called financial innovation into the tax net. As far as individual investors were concerned, the absence of taxation before the reform may have had a beneficial effect on the allocation of savings. For intermediaries, up to 1994 valuation gains were not included in taxable income; since then, the components deriving from the valuation of off-balance-sheet items contribute like all the other components to the formation of taxable income. It is not easy to assess the extent to which the legislative gap, filled for the banks in 1994, assisted the spread of these instruments. For years derivatives were subject to legislative uncertainty, especially as regards indirect taxation. The absence of a specific rule on VAT gave rise to discordant practices among intermediaries. In 1995 the applicability of the exemption to derivative contracts was finally clarified by Legislative Decree 440/1995, ratified by Law 556/1996. Domestic legislation was harmonized with European law. The years of uncertainty were especially detrimental to the market in domestic currency swaps; the controversial treatment of the revenues from such transactions for VAT purposes provoked long-running disputes between intermediaries and the tax authorities.

Tax law also provided only partial support for the birth of new intermediaries. Venture capital and project financing did not benefit from tax incentives. The taxation of collective investment undertakings (open-end and closed-end securities investment funds and SICAVs) was designed not to hinder their growth. Before the 1997 reform, these vehicles were subject to the same withholding taxes as individual investors and to a tax on net assets that differed depending on the category of assets (bonds or shares) in a fund's portfolio. Fund-raising by collective investment undertakings benefited from the fact that from their inception they did not entail tax obligations for individual investors, whose income from the ownership of fund units was not subject to personal income tax. The 1997 reform gave impetus to the development of the asset management industry. The shift of household savings from government securities to managed products would have been seriously impeded had the tax bite been larger than that on investment in government securities. As far as individual portfolio management accounts are concerned, the new tax rules are advantageous for savers by comparison with direct investment, given the absence of tax formalities for the account holder and the ample scope for offsetting capital losses against investment income.

By contrast, tax impediments can be found for real-estate investment funds (instituted in 1994) and pension funds. The launch of the former was not assisted by the original arrangements, whereby tax was levied on the management company at the ordinary corporate and local income tax rates. Law 503/1995 sought to remedy the over-onerous burden by establishing a tax of 25 per cent in lieu of ordinary corporate and local income tax. The measures enacted in 1993 and 1995 were insufficient to promote the growth of pension funds. The subsequent reform of supplementary pension provision and life insurance policies established innovative rules which, in combination with the reform of the taxation of financial assets, redress the balance of comparative advantages and lay a better foundation for the sector's growth. The deductibility of life insurance premiums, potentially now doubled, together with the taxation only of that part of the benefits corresponding to the sum of the premiums to which the deduction applied, constitute a deferment of personal income tax until the time of entitlement to benefits. For supplementary pension funds, the non-applicability of personal income tax to the part of the benefits deriving from the return on the amount invested, which is subject to a tax at a slightly reduced rate levied on the fund, extends the system established for voluntary savings to such funds. It is a favourable tax treatment, and that of insurance policies providing retirement benefits has been aligned with it. There is still a tax credit for death-benefit-only and disability policies; the remaining policies, with features more like those of voluntary saving, are treated as such, losing the advantages they enjoyed. The new system is more internally consistent and neutral.

International relations

Here, tax law may have hindered the permanent establishment of branches of foreign banks in Italy. The withholding taxes applied to financial income (most notably interest income from securities) resulted in foreign branches having substantial claims on the Italian tax authorities. Like Italian banks, they were embroiled for years in the dispute on the so-called self-applied withholding tax on foreign bank deposits that they held in the capacity as banks 'authorized' under the foreign exchange legislation previously in force. This lasted until the constraint was removed by Law 30/1997.

Obstacles to equity investment in firms by non-residents may have arisen both from the taxation of non-residents' qualifying capital gains and dividends – the latter subject to a very high withholding tax (reduced from 32.4 to 27 per cent after the 1997 reform) – and from the time necessary to recover taxes paid in Italy. The lower withholding taxes that bilateral tax treaties establish for dividends on shares in central securities depositories are now applied immediately.

Refunds of withholding tax on government securities by the finance department under bilateral tax treaties were speeded up in the second half of the 1990s. Contributory factors were the introduction in 1994 of the automatic procedure whereby non-residents can obtain payment of the difference between ordinary withholdings and the more favourable treaty-rate withholdings within 60 days and the abolition in 1997 of withholding tax on public-sector bonds and the bonds of 'large issuers' (banks and listed companies) for non-resident investors. Capital gains on non-qualifying holdings of listed shares and those on securities traded in regulated markets were exempted in 1998 and 1999, respectively.

In 1993 Italy brought its legislation into line with European Directive 435/90/EEC, by exempting almost all (95 per cent) of the dividends paid to an Italian parent company by its foreign subsidiaries from inclusion in the parent company's taxable income. This rule has favoured the establishment of subsidiaries in low-tax jurisdictions, such as Luxembourg and Ireland. A specific brake on the banking system's financial exposure to emerging countries, where corporate financing requirements remain high, stems from the non-recognition of value adjustments to claims on bank counterparties. The country risk, prevalently assumed *vis-à-vis* local bank intermediaries, is not deductible for tax purposes.

A textbook case of the influence that taxation can exercise on the composition of gross financial wealth according to instrument is offered by the rise and decline of CDs in the 1990s. CDs, transferable securities representing deposits with a fixed maturity of between 3 months and 5 years, paying interest at a fixed or variable rate and generally not redeemable early, could be issued by nearly all the special credit institutions beginning in 1981 and by ordinary credit banks as of December 1982, the latter change being introduced with a view to curbing the replacement of bank deposits with government securities. With CDs the banks remunerated stable deposits at a higher rate of interest than current accounts, which served principally as means of payment. Back then, 46 per cent of the banks' deposit liabilities consisted of savings deposits and 54 per cent of current accounts. The spread of CDs was assisted by the favourable tax treatment they enjoyed compared with other deposits; in 1984 the withholding tax rate on CDs with a maturity of at least 18 months was made equal to that on bonds (12.5 per cent). In the following years CDs rapidly replaced other deposits and by the end of 1993 they accounted for 28 per cent of the banks' total funding, compared with 17 per cent for savings deposits and 55 per cent for current accounts. The preferred treatment of CDs ended in June 1996, when the withholding rate on interest was aligned with that for all other bank deposits at 27 per cent. From the middle of 1996 onwards the elimination of the tax benefits led to a radical shift in the composition of banks' medium- and long-term funding liabilities in favour of bonds. CDs with a maturity of at least 18 months plummeted from 56 per cent of total funding in 1995 to 15 per cent in 1998. Issues of CDs of all maturities were affected by the shift in savers' portfolios following the fall in interest rates across the board. By 1998 CDs were down to 11 per cent of total funding. Correspondingly, there was an increase in the proportion of bonds, immediately substitutable for CDs in view of their similar risk, liquidity and maturity.

The revised model

In the three years since the passage of the 1997 reform, Italy's tax system has become much more favourable to the growth and efficient operation of the financial sector.

The new system of taxation for the savings of natural persons and entities that do not engage in enterprise, introduced by Law 461/1997, is all-inclusive, more homogeneous, transparent and simple for the taxpayer. It increases the degree of neutrality of the taxation of investment income and reduces the margins for distortion and avoidance.

The 1997 reform confirmed the basic choice, made in 1973, in favour of imposing flat-rate taxes in lieu of income taxes on households' savings income. The basis of taxation was widened. Exemptions connected with specific types of financial instruments were excluded. The closing of loopholes ensures that taxation is general. Both savings income (bond and deposit interest, share dividends) and other investment income (capital gains) are taxed. Capital gains include those realized on bonds and government securities, foreign currency, gold and derivatives.

The model is based on the notion of income 'received' (the amount of resources a person can consume without denting his wealth), which in the field of personal taxation is a more advanced indicator of taxpaying capacity, rather than on that of income 'produced' (the sum of incomes deriving from participation in production). Consistently with this notion, capital gains on financial assets are taxed at the ordinary rate, regardless of whether or not there is a 'speculative' intent, and the tax is payable at the time they accrue. These gains are increasingly in the nature of income rather than transitory revenue, especially when they are achieved on managed savings.

The approach of taxing natural persons and equivalent entities 'always but at reduced rates' has not hurt the market. Compared with progressive income tax, the imposition of tax at a fixed rate in final settlement of liabilities is advantageous for savers, even those with low incomes. On the basis of the current personal income tax brackets, even the higher withholding tax rate of 27 per cent is favourable for taxpayers with more than 30 million lire a year of gross income.

A large role is assigned to intermediaries in tax collection. Banks, investment firms and other intermediaries calculate and pay the tax due on behalf of savers, unless the latter opt to manage their own compliance directly. This frees savers of their liability towards the tax authorities and preserves their anonymity. As a rule, intermediaries report the names of resident savers to the tax authorities only when the income received is not subject to withholding tax.

The system therefore encourages the growth of managed savings. It permits savers to benefit from professional portfolio management by intermediaries. Individual portfolio management accounts and the portfolios of collective investment undertakings are directly taxed on their 'net operating profit for the year'. The tax is applied by the manager – the bank, investment firm or fund – at a rate of 12.5 per cent.

In most cases non-resident natural persons and firms that invest in Italy are not subject to tax. For share dividends paid to non-residents, the onerous refund procedure has been replaced by the direct application by the intermediary of the lower rates established by bilateral treaties against double taxation. There are still distortions for non-residents that invest in units of Italian funds; the fact that they recover the amounts levied only at the time they receive income, not when taxes are paid upstream by the fund, reduces the advantageousness of the investment.

This is likely to hinder the Italian asset management industry's strategies for international diversification of its customer base. The non-taxation of the capital gains on all transactions by non-residents in regulated markets favours direct acquisition of securities over investment in Italian funds.

The solution of not taxing foreign investors is in line with the rules adopted in the other European countries. Tax competition has led to the virtually complete exemption of interest payments and capital gains for non-residents in the 15 countries of the European Union. By contrast, dividends paid to non-residents are subject only to with-holding tax in final settlement (except in the United Kingdom, Ireland, Greece and Luxembourg, when the dividends are distributed through holding companies). The prevailing withholding tax rates on dividends (25 per cent) are similar to that in Italy (27 per cent). The EU countries, including Italy, are linked by numerous bilateral trea-ties against double taxation that provide for reduced withholding rates.

In the 15 countries of the EU dividends paid to resident investors are generally subject to progressive personal taxation. In Denmark, Finland and Sweden they are subject to separate taxation. The withholding system is used throughout the EU except in France, the UK and Greece (dividends are exempt in the last). In the majority of EU countries interest payments to resident investors are also subject to personal progressive taxation, generally with tax withheld on account. However, there are many exceptions to the rule of the progressive taxation of interest income. In some countries income from certain types of securities is entirely tax-exempt, as in the United Kingdom and Ireland for government securities. In others – Germany, Luxembourg and the Netherlands – there is an exempt amount of interest income that taxpayers can enjoy regardless of their income bracket. There are broad areas of exemption in the field of capital gains. Only France, Finland, Sweden and Spain tax residents' capital gains on both shares and bonds. Germany, Luxembourg, Austria, Portugal and Belgium tax only gains on investments made with a 'speculative intent', presumably defined on the basis of the minimum holding period. In some cases the tax bite on gains is mitigated by exempt amounts.

As can be seen, there is a diversity of legislation on the tax treat-ment of households' savings in Europe. Compared with the other countries, households' savings are not heavily taxed in Italy. The modernity of the Italian system lies in the recognition it accords to the role of intermediaries in asset management. The interposition of intermediation severs the link between the instrument utilized (whose choice depends on the intermediary) and the nature of the investment on the part of the saver (who often entrusts his resources simply with the aim of diversifying his income sources). Different tax rates for different instruments and exemptions in connection with a 'non-speculative' intent no longer appear suitable for the taxation of savings in Europe, which are now largely managed by investment funds. The Italian model of taxation of the 'net accrued operating result' is unique in Europe. Some countries, such as Germany, France and Luxembourg, follow the 'no-veil' system based on the principle of transparency, with the taxes falling on the individual investors in the fund and not on the fund itself. In some cases funds enjoy benefits that derogate from the principle of tax neutrality between direct and indirect investment, for example the non-taxability of capital gains achieved by funds (Germany) or the deferment of tax (in France for dividend reinvestment funds).

Turning from the taxation of individual investors' savings to that of corporate finance, the present system, geared to a gradual reduction of the corporate tax burden through the dual income tax and a more balanced relationship between the taxes on debt and equity capital (as a combined effect of the dual income tax and Irap), is more favourable to the development of finance and the markets.

Share issues and self-financing are granted a tax break through the reduction of up to 10 percentage points in the average corporate income tax rate. Firms with a net worth of less than 500 billion lire that decide to go public can enjoy three years of taxation at a rate that is below the average corporate income tax rate by up to 17 percentage points. The advantageousness of recourse to debt capital is reduced by Irap, since interest payments are non-deductible from the regional tax base.

Income from financial investments and working capital fall within the scope of corporate income tax. The tax reduction is extended to them through the application of the dual income tax. The flexibility of the mechanism, deriving from the concessionary 'multiplier' of the income base, enables the benefits to be magnified. A large increase in capital and reserves is still required to reach the average rate of 27 per cent; with taxable income for the year amounting to 11 per cent of shareholders' equity, the required increase in the capital base is 166 per cent. The extension of the dual income tax to the return on the entire capital base can further reduce the differences in the taxation of the different sources of finance.

Under the legislation on corporate restructurings, capital gains on sales of shareholdings in subsidiary or related companies may be taxed on an optional basis at a flat rate of 27 per cent in lieu of ordinary corporate income tax (in the financial year or over five annual instalments if the company so chooses). The measures, now pending approval, to reduce this flat-rate tax from 27 to 19 per cent and permit the revaluation of corporate assets could facilitate the transformation of production and distribution made imperative by technological innovation and the globalization of markets. The reduction of the taxes imposed on major corporate actions will facilitate changes in the ownership structure of firms; the extension of the scope of the flat-rate tax to include sales of stakes in subsidiary and related companies through public offerings can facilitate the transition to a broad shareholder base and encourage firms to seek listing. The revaluation of corporate assets, which is optional and taxed, makes it easier to compare Italian firms with foreign ones by cleansing their balance sheets of the distortionary effects of inflation.

Since capital gains and income from derivative instruments are not included in value added, they are not subject to Irap for non-financial firms. The tax treatment of derivatives for non-financial firms is being brought into line with that for intermediaries. The components deriving from the valuation of off-balance-sheet items will be included in non-financial firms' taxable income for the year. Non-financial firms can count on a clearer legislative framework.

Albeit with the constraints imposed by the state of the public finances, the Italian system is moving in the direction taken since the early 1990s by the other countries of the European Union: cutting corporate tax rates and broadening the related tax base. The decision to make the cost of debt capital deductible is consistent with the rulebook of all the other EU countries. Like France and Finland, Italy is seeking to counter tax avoidance by limiting the deductibility of interest payments on bonds issued at higher-than-market rates. Belgium, Denmark, France, Germany, Portugal, the United Kingdom and Spain all have thin capitalization rules that limit the deductibility of interest when the ratio of debt capital to equity capital exceeds certain parameters.

In Europe firms' financial income is generally taxed like other income. In some countries provision is made, in specific cases, for the possibility of not taxing capital gains (Belgium, Denmark, Ireland, Luxembourg and the Netherlands), deferring such tax (Greece, Italy, the United Kingdom and Spain) or taxing capital gains at a reduced rate (France, Greece and Spain). Such benefits are granted with a view to creating poles of attraction for international finance. As is shown by the tiny number of measures alleged to be non-compliant with the European code of conduct against harmful tax competition, Italy does not deliberately offer tax incentives for the establishment of holding companies.

In 1998, the first year Irap was in force, the regional tax afforded the banking system alone tax savings of around 2000 billion lire, notwithstanding the higher tax rate for banks than for other firms. The difference in tax rates remained in force until 2002. Banks' high rate of self-financing allows them to extract benefits from the dual income tax mechanism.

The tax rules are less penalizing than in the past, but some problems remain open. Impetus to bank mergers and acquisitions can come from the reduced taxation of corporate restructurings envisaged for all firms. Benefits will come from the increase that will presumably occur in domestic demand for investment banking services; the development of corporate advisory activity caused by the increase in mergers and acquisitions will contribute to the growth of banks' income from services. The scope of the tax treatment of loan writedowns is limited to loans to private-sector customers, so that there are still disparities with banks' results for civil law purposes. Non-bank financial companies (asset management companies and investment, leasing and factoring firms) suffer from the same constraints.

An area in which further changes may be expected is that of the consolidated taxation of banking groups, in line with most of the other EU countries. The right to offset tax credits and liabilities, which has served primarily to alleviate the effects of the non-deductibility from corporate income tax of withholding tax paid on bonds and government securities, does not annul the disadvantage *vis-à-vis* other countries in this respect. A first step has been taken with VAT on a group basis; the exemption of services provided between units of the same banking or insurance group makes the treatment of VAT neutral in respect of the different models of corporate organization (corporate divisions versus groups).

Banks and insurance companies are subject to a nominal corporate income tax rate of 37 per cent, which is higher than the European average. However, the gap *vis-à-vis* the other European countries has narrowed in the last two years in terms of both explicit and implicit taxation. Differences are still to be found in the determination of the tax base for corporate taxes (in the treatment of losses, depreciation and amortization, and allocations to provisions).

Italian banks' accounts are also saddled with the compliance costs in respect of tax rules; gauging their actual effect is not easy, considering the economies the banking system enjoys as a result of the encouragement the tax system gives Italians to channel their savings into the financial circuit. The existence of a large fixed component of costs means that the impact is smaller for larger banks; in the medium term the impact is likely to lessen as the legislative framework stabilizes. In countries such as Germany and Luxembourg, these costs are negligible. By contrast, in France and the United Kingdom banks play a significant role in the performance of tax formalities.

Taxation and change

Tax law exercised a specific influence on developments in Italy's financial industry in the 1980s and 1990s.

The onerous tax and tax-related conditions under which the industry was operating at the start of the 1980s tended to be alleviated by comparison with developments in the rest of the economy. Albeit with stops and goes provoked by the critical conditions of the public finances, this contributed to the quantitative growth of financial assets and to the financial deepening of the Italian economy.

In a succession of steps of which the most recent was the fundamental reform of 1997, the tax system moved away from a complex of rates, tax bases and administrative procedures far removed not only from any reasonable concept of neutrality but also from any conscious, consistent pattern of distortion. Together with the attenuation of administrative restrictions, the movement of the tax system towards neutrality helped to reduce the excessive pressure on the financial choices of economic agents.

This also generated effects on the structure of finance, influencing its changes. Considered as a whole, these effects played a modest role in promoting financial innovation; as a factor of the reorientation of the system from credit intermediaries to markets, they are not easily calculated; in the transformation of banks into public limited companies and their privatization, they were decisive.

Following the 1997 reform, the tax regime for finance in Italy is in line with European arrangements and requirements. In some respects it is more advanced than that of other countries. It is a participant in the difficult quest now underway for a 'European' approach to the taxation of finance; in the drive against tax dumping in respect of savings in Europe; and in the effort to strike a balance between the necessity (or choice) of continuing to tax capital, not just labour, and the worldwide competition to attract savings that financial globalization implies.

5
Supervision

Supervision, formerly a one-dimensional activity, is now, in Italy as elsewhere, multifaceted. The system of controls is now articulated and organic, embracing every major segment of the financial industry: banking, securities, insurance and private pension schemes. Companies must obtain authorization to operate in these sectors and submit to supervision of such aspects as stability, transparency and correct conduct. The infrastructure serving the financial industry – markets and payment, clearing and settlement systems – is subject to control. Financial companies are required to comply with the rules of antitrust legislation.

Article 3A of the treaty instituting the European Union calls on the member states to conduct their activities 'in accordance with the principle of an open market economy with free competition'. In Italy, once the concept of a mixed or planned economy had been set aside, it was gradually supplanted by an open and competitive economic model, with different types of balance between the public and private sectors. The change took place without constitutional discontinuity, in accordance with the letter and spirit of a constitution that recognizes the market as a means not an end.

Banking and financial supervision is one aspect of the changed relationship between state and market. The market is still considered instrumental to the values pursued by society, in the knowledge of the limits of its contribution to their attainment. Now, however, the controls have become market-friendly, their purpose being to ensure its smooth operation, according to rules and principles that form an integral, constituent part of it. They respect the market itself, its logic, at least as long as it unconsciously reflects the needs of society and effectively serves the general interest. In areas the market cannot reach or where it produces undesirable, even perverse effects, action is no longer 'through a glass darkly, but face to face', designed to address the overriding objectives: economic policy measures and management of the economy to achieve results that the markets, even with their rules and supervisory controls, cannot attain.

Through the performance of functions involving a more direct relationship with the institutions supervised, the gathering of information and the design of controls to work for and not against the market, an institutional evolution has taken place, transforming the technical controlling bodies into 'authorities'. Some supervisory entities have acquired administrative powers previously vested in the executive branch of government, while others were newly created.

Sectoral regulations provide for the joint presence of technical supervisory authorities and government authorities. In recent years, however, there has been a marked tendency to extend the autonomy of the former. The Consolidated Law on Banking does not entrust the Treasury or the Interministerial Committee for Credit and Savings with a 'policy' function beyond verifying the conformity of banking regulations with legislation. All the banking authorities, even the governmental arm, are required to observe the general aims of supervision. The tasks of the executive are laid down by law, which precludes the exercise of any power to direct or supplant. Similar considerations apply to relations between the Bank of Italy, Consob and the ministry of the Treasury regarding the supervision of securities trading in accordance with the Consolidated Law on Finance. In this sector, too, the scope of ministerial action is expressly defined. In the insurance sector, the provisions of the 1998 Law vest power in the Minister for Industry, who is entrusted with specific functions; ISVAP, the Supervisory Authority for the Insurance Industry, operates in accordance with government guidelines. Only in respect of private pension schemes does the law grant the Minister of Labour the power to set general guidelines for supervision and provide for ministerial control over the activity of COVIP, the Pension Schemes Supervisory Authority.

Ministerial powers in the various financial sectors are similar. The first sphere of action relates to the regulatory function. Sectoral legislation states that certain regulations must be issued by the competent ministry, either on the proposal of the technical authority or subject to its opinion. In general, these rules affect the actual and potential rights of parties other than those subjected to supervision. The second sphere is penalties and sanctions. The order must be issued by the minister on the proposal of the technical authority. Sanctions are issued against people, not firms. In order to exercise the power to submit proposals to the minister the sectoral authority conducts investigations and makes evaluations. The ministry's tasks are to ascertain the legitimacy of the proposal and verify the underlying investigations and evaluations. The third sphere covers the collapse of financial companies. The extreme delicacy of the matter calls for a complex administrative procedure whereby the authority's proposal is transposed into a measure formally promulgated by the minister.

Articles 24 and 113 of the Constitution lay down that the regulations and single measures of authorities entrusted with administrative functions are subject to judicial controls. The administrative court's role is to rule on their legitimacy or illegitimacy, be it due to lack of jurisdiction, breach of the law or abuse of power. However, the administrative court cannot impugn the evaluation of merit made when the act was issued. A decision of annulment eliminates an unlawful act from juridical existence from the time of origin. The authority cannot issue another with the same defects. If the act that has been declared unlawful has caused 'wrongful damage' to a third party, the issuing authority is answerable to the injured party. The ordinary courts ascertain whether there are grounds for this liability and, if so, order the party responsible to pay compensation. Since 1998, however, the administrative court has sole and full jurisdiction in all disputes regarding such matters (Legislative Decree 80/1998).

Independent authorities

The Bank of Italy, which was instituted in 1893, was joined in the period under review by a number of technical authorities, which were defined as independent. Despite their recent creation they successfully established themselves, performing their functions with increasing efficiency. Today, they are fully operational entities, to be strengthened further. The plurality of authorities implies the need for links between them: while these never operate smoothly they, too, are in place. An institutional structure should be judged on its results rather than on the basis of abstract paradigms. It is no accident that major institutional changes have been introduced in countries that have experienced serious financial instability. Italy is not among them.

Consob

The national Companies and Stock Exchange Commission was instituted in 1974. Law 216 established it as an organ of central government, without legal personality and with limited autonomy and powers. Its regulatory acts were generally effective only if the minister of the Treasury issued an order incorporating them.

In 1983 steps were taken to regulate investment funds and the solicitation of public savings, and Consob's powers were increased and extended. In 1985 its institutional position was redefined; it was granted legal personality and organizational autonomy. Its ties with the Treasury were loosened and Consob acquired full regulatory powers. Subsequent legislation granted it an increasing range of competences relating to securities and the corporate sector.

The Consolidated Law on Finance of 1998 confirmed that Consob's role was to safeguard investors' interests by regulating the securities market and supervising the transparency and correctness of operators: intermediaries, issuers and market operating companies. The Consolidated Law on Finance de-emphasized primary legislation, empowering Consob to complete the legal framework by issuing secondary legislation. In the first two years after the Law's passage three major regulations were introduced, covering markets, intermediaries and issuers.

Supervisory activity has been stepped up in all sectors and with every available means, assisted by 364 experts who are part of a staff of 450; the board consists of 5 members. Consob's main tasks with respect to company disclosure requirements are checking balance sheets and public prospectuses, guaranteeing the transparency of ownership of listed companies and supervising auditing companies; with respect to intermediaries and financial salesmen, Consob handles authorizations, examines periodical reports and conducts inspections; with respect to regulated markets, it verifies their correct operation and the smooth conduct of trading, in the interests of investors, by monitoring the performance of securities to pinpoint sources of turbulence and cases of manipulation or unauthorized behaviour.

In 1999 Consob approved 14 takeover bids and more than 300 prospectuses drawn up as part of campaigns to attract public savings. It entered 12 new investment firms in the register and eliminated 20. It ordered 21 inspections of supervised intermediaries and submitted 2 proposals to the Ministry of the Treasury relating to the management of investment firms in difficulty. Thirty eight investigations were brought to a close and 30 reports on the abuse of confidential information and market manipulation were forwarded to the judicial authorities. Sanctions were issued against 51 investment firms, banks or exchange brokers and 7 listed companies. Reprimands, sanctions, suspension or expulsion orders were issued against 127 financial salesmen, out of a total of 42,800. In addition, 74 preventive measures were issued and more than 100 reports of alleged breaches of the law were forwarded to the courts.

ISVAP

Insurance companies fulfil an economic function in which income precedes expenditures. This makes it necessary to safeguard the interests of users (policyholders or savers and injured parties), which are associated with the management of the savings that insurance companies gather in the form of premiums.

The first general measures regulating the insurance industry date back to 1923. The Ministry of the Economy, later to become the Ministry for Industry, was given power over the sector, placing insurance companies in a position of subordination. ISVAP was instituted under the provisions of Law 576/1982. Its basic task was to evaluate the technical and financial management of insurance companies, and it answered to the Interministerial Committee for Economic Planning and the Ministry for Industry.

During the 1990s prudential-type regulations were extended, in line with European legislation and international guidelines, in a move to foster the stability and transparency of the insurance market. In 1991 new duties connected with the ownership of insurance companies were entrusted exclusively to ISVAP, and in 1994 all supervisory functions relating to the sector were transferred to it, with the Ministry for Industry retaining power to act in cases of financial collapse and to impose sanctions. Legislative Decree 373/1998 granted ISVAP full organizational, accounting and financial independence.

With the reinforcement of ISVAP the regulation and control of the insurance industry were strengthened. The main focus was on controls to verify the correctness of companies' technical, financial and capital management; the examination of ownership structures; the investigation of customer complaints against insurance companies; and research work, partly associated with the market regulatory function attributed to ISVAP by law.

ISVAP watches over 209 insurance companies and monitors insurance agents and brokers. It is run by a chairman and six board members and has a staff of approximately 300, for the most part inspectors. Inspections in fact account for around 80 per cent of costs. In 1999, 130 on-site inspections were carried out, some of a general nature and others ad hoc and designed to analyse operations or activities earmarked for special attention.

Previously, most controls focused on the management of the vehicle insurance branch. They have since spread to all the other sectors, as well as to the distribution network. As a result the supervisory teams must constantly update their skills since their work brings them into contact with irregularities that are increasingly difficult to detect.

In 1998 the authority's supervisory activities led to the compulsory administrative liquidation of 30 insurance companies. Similar measures were taken in the case of 48 brokers operating unlawfully. Approximately 2,000 procedures were instituted for breaches of rules. Customer complaints against insurance companies received by ISVAP increased considerably, amounting to some 24,000 in 1999.

ISVAP's tasks also include examining annual balance sheets and generally performing documentary checks. These activities have become an integral part of the broader job of monitoring the calculation of insurance companies' technical and actuarial reserves.

The Antitrust Authority

Antitrust legislation was introduced in Italy by Law 287/1990, before which the market behaviour of enterprises was subject only to European regulations. Reiterating the provisions of the Treaty of Rome, the Antitrust Law forbids the abuse of dominant positions and agreements designed to limit competition. It also makes provision for the *ex ante* control of concentrations, which can be prohibited if they create or strengthen a dominant position.

The Antitrust Authority was instituted to enforce these rules. It is run by a board of five members and its staff can number up to 200 people. The Authority has powers of investigation and assessment regarding infringements. By virtue of the former it can request information and carry out inspections, while the latter allow it to prohibit anti-competitive agreements, abuses of dominant position and concentrations.

Antitrust regulations apply to all firms in all sectors of the economy. In the case of banks, antitrust functions are performed by the Bank of Italy, which adopts measures relating to competition in the banking sector after hearing the opinion of the Antitrust Authority. In the insurance sector, the Antitrust Authority bases its action on the recommendations of ISVAP.

In the event of serious breaches of regulations on competition the Antitrust Authority imposes fines, which can amount to as much as 10 per cent of the annual sales of the firms concerned. Penalties are also imposed on firms that fail to give advance notification of a concentration and those that go ahead with such an operation notwithstanding a prohibition. In the case of completed concentrations investigated by the authority and found to be anti-competitive, an order to restore the original situation may be issued.

The Authority has the further task of preventing misleading advertising. It may counter the effects of such messages by ordering the publication of corrections.

Law 287/1990, at articles 21 and 22, also assigns reporting and advisory powers to the Authority, which can notify Parliament and the government of legislation or general administrative measures that limit competition. It can also issue advice on regulatory and legislative initiatives and on any argument relating to competition.

Between 1990 and the end of 1999 the Antitrust Authority concluded some 7000 proceedings. More than 4000 concerned potential breaches of antitrust legislation and over 2300 allegedly misleading advertisements. The Authority issued a ruling on 3451 concentrations, 342 alleged anti-competitive agreements, and 233 suspected abuses by firms in dominant positions. It conducted 17 sectoral investigations, one of them jointly with the Bank of Italy, and submitted 349 opinions to that institution as part of its advisory functions in the banking sector. Approximately 200 inquiries were opened as part of the Authority's antitrust proceedings; breaches of the law on concentrations were found in 5 cases (a further 17 operations received conditional authorization), on agreements in 76 cases and on the abuse of dominant positions in 40 cases. In 96 cases the Authority deemed that the infringements constituted serious breaches of the law, resulting in the imposition of fines. Appeals were made to the regional administrative tribunal of Lazio against about 95 per cent of the penalties. After the passage of the legislative decree on misleading advertising, 1561 infringements were ascertained. The number of reports laid before the Authority has increased constantly since it began operating.

Over the years antitrust interventions gradually spread, taking in a broad range of economic activities. More than a third concerned the manufacturing sector, although most were in the service sector, where forms of regulation and self-regulation are widespread. Important work was done to foster the liberalization of public services. In the transport sector and related activities, numerous violations were found in shipping and air transport, motorway management and harbour services. Abuses were also common in the telecommunications sector, where the Authority's response anticipated the progressive liberalization from public-sector monopoly. Here and in other sectors the Authority ensured that efforts to open up markets were not defeated by the conduct of the dominant enterprise. Retail and wholesale trade has been the object of particularly close scrutiny. Finally, as regards the reorganization of distribution networks for insurance products, in which the banking industry plays an increasingly large role, the Authority called for changes in exclusive agreements between insurance companies and banks; a prohibition was placed on horizontal agreements involving a large number of insurance companies.

An assessment of the Authority's role must take account of the results of its advisory function. In about a third of the cases its recommendations in favour of competition were taken up by Parliament and the competent authorities. In this advisory capacity the Authority has achieved its best results when dealing with subjects and issues on which European bodies have already taken action in the form of directives, resolutions, infringement proceedings or decisions of the Court of Justice, or when recommendations have been preceded and inspired by an inquiry.

COVIP

Of more recent institution is the supervisory authority for private pension schemes. These were first regulated in 1993, when the difficulties of the public pension system were officially recognized. Control over the newly created private system was entrusted to COVIP, which was initially set up within the Ministry of Labour but changed legal status in 1995, becoming a public law body.

In the private pension system, market failures carry a specific cost for the community: they affect the financial situation of workers and pensioners. This has led to a regulation of the sector that differs in some respects from that of other financial industries, with ties linking the supervisory body and the government. Thus the Ministry of Labour and the Ministry of the Treasury have a general power to establish guidelines and exercise control over COVIP.

As far as the methods of control are concerned, the law instituting the private pension system recalls the other forms of financial supervision. The powers of COVIP – to grant authorizations, enact regulations, make inquiries and impose penalties – are designed to ensure the growth and the soundness of the private system through the stability and correct management of the pension funds.

The dual nature of private pension schemes, as vehicles of social welfare and financial entities, prompted Parliament to make provision for forms of agreement regarding the authorization to set up and run open pension funds and the approval of arrangements for the financial management of occupational funds and, more generally, close cooperation between the various authorities.

A series of legislative provisions extended COVIP's duties, which include self-regulation, the issue of measures to complete the legislative framework, secondary regulation and the preparation of supervisory actions.

The private pension system is now regulated. The intention was to foster its growth in new areas and financial instruments, such as open funds, employing typical supervisory tools. COVIP has a 5-member board but its staff long numbered fewer than 20 and was only raised to 40 in 1999.

On 30 September 1999 the number of private pension schemes in Italy was 889. Those set up under the new regulations (that is, after 1995) numbered 115, of which 30 were occupational funds, the outcome of agreements between workers and employers, and 85 open funds, set up by banks, insurance companies and other operators. A total of 1,250,000 workers (out of a labour force of 23 million) were enrolled in these schemes: 635,000 in pre-existing funds and 615,000 in the new ones, 532,000 in occupational funds and 84,000 in open funds. The net worth of the new schemes – that is, the net assets allocated for benefits – amounted to around 1 trillion lire (823 billion for occupational funds and 199 billion for open). No homogeneous figure for total funds is available, as the alignment of the financial accounting procedures of earlier pension funds had not yet been completed.

The participation rate in the four oldest occupational pension funds was 28 per cent from a pool of approximately 1.5 million workers. Overall, the participation rate in funds actively soliciting contributors (some of them only recently) drops to 13 per cent. For all occupational funds together, the participation rate was just 5.3 per cent of around 10 million potential members. The reason participation in these funds was so low was the limited supply rather than lack of demand. In fact the parties instituting the funds have not always cooperated effectively to implement the underlying agreements.

Most open funds began to actively recruit enrolees in 1999. These increased steadily in number month by month, mainly in the areas of the country with the highest proportion of self-employed workers, who are encouraged to invest in forms of long-term saving because their illiquidity is offset by personal income tax relief. As with occupational funds, it appears that participation grew less than expected owing to problems of supply: inadequate sales networks for a new and complicated product and the failure of some banking groups, even large ones, to include open funds in their branch budgets. The obligation, under transparency rules, to quote the investor an all-inclusive commission (being the sum of the single fees that intermediaries can set without restriction) held down management costs and the earnings that go to pay the sales networks, which therefore continued to push close equivalents such as life insurance policies.

Participation in open funds, which address a non-specific group of investors, will depend, at least in the near future, on the coverage provided by the occupational funds for employees (in accordance with the provisions of article 9 of Legislative Decree 124/1993) and the ability of the promoters to understand that they are designed to supplement rather than replace other products.

The Bank of Italy: monetary management and supervision

The Bank of Italy was one of the first central banks to be entrusted, in 1926, with vast, formal duties of supervision over banks. As a result of this long experience, the law has formulated the Bank's supervisory role, by analogy with its monetary policy function, as addressing general interests, which the Bank safeguards by exercising a non-neutral discretionary power. Unlike the independent authorities, the Bank's assigned objectives and instruments preclude restriction of its activities to verifying compliance with rules designed to preserve a balance of interests laid down in detail, once and for all, by law.

The reason why the Bank of Italy does not conform to the model of the independent administrative authorities becomes clear if we consider its contribution to the management of the economy. The Bank of Italy is first and foremost a central bank. It is responsible for safeguarding the value of the currency. By ensuring the stability of prices it guarantees equal conditions for borrowers and lenders. It may have to decide how far this objective should take precedence over the short-term goals of economic growth and full employment. Its institutional autonomy, the guarantees enjoyed by its senior management and its freedom of action in organizational and financial matters clearly show the intention to entrust the discretionary use of monetary policy to a body outside the apparatus of the government.

The deeply rooted principle of the autonomy of the central bank is written into the provisions of the Treaty on European Union as regards the European System of Central Banks. Once price stability, the ESCB's primary duty, has been attained, its role is to support national economic policies. The Bank of Italy's position in the ESCB is that of participant, not subordinate. Within the Monetary Union the national central banks have the dual task of helping to make the system's decisions and ensuring they are implemented in each economy. They have broad decision-making powers. They must correspond to the mutability of the macroeconomic framework, the changing relationship – complementary or conflicting – between objectives, and the shifting links between objectives and constraints.

The Italian model differs from the others in the depth and breadth of the tasks the central bank is called upon to perform. Apart from monetary policy, the Bank of Italy has five separate but related supervisory responsibilities: oversight of the payments system, banks, non-bank intermediaries, the relevant markets for monetary policy, and competition in the banking sector (Table 5.1). The ultimate purpose of these tasks, their *reductio ad unum*, the reason they are entrusted to the central bank, is to safeguard competition, efficiency and the stability of the monetary and financial systems. As in monetary policy, in supervision achieving the right balance between means and ends entails complementary actions and trade-offs, decisions concerning timing and methods, prioritization: it is economic policy.

Table 5.1 The Bank of Italy's supervisory functions

	Type of supervision	*Source laws*
I	Banks and credit intermediaries	Art. 1.1a and Art. 5 Consolidated Law on Banking Art. 5 Legislative Decree CPS 691/1947
II	Securities market intermediaries	Art. 1.1r and Art. 5 Consolidated Law on Finance
III	Markets	
	• Screen-based secondary market in govt. securities and related management companies	Art. 76 Consolidated Law on Finance
	• Interbank deposit market	Art. 79 Consolidated Law on Finance
	• Central securities depositories	Art. 82 Consolidated Law on Finance
	• Clearing and settlement systems and guarantee systems for trades in financial instruments	Art. 77 Consolidated Law on Finance
	• Securities issues and offers of foreign securities in Italy	Art. 129 Consolidated Law on Banking
IV	Payment system	Art. 105.2 EC Treaty Art. 146 Consolidated Law on Banking
V	Safeguarding competition in the banking sector and the transparency of contract terms	Art. 20 Law 287/1990 Arts. 115 and 128 Consolidated Law on Banking

Control over the investment services sector in Italy is split according to its 'purpose'. Competences are divided between the Bank of Italy, which is responsible for capital adequacy and risk limitation, and Consob, which monitors integrity and transparency *vis-à-vis* investors. This is evidence that Parliament judged it appropriate to entrust the central bank with responsibility for ensuring not only price stability but also the stability of the financial system. The Bank of Italy has the task of safeguarding the value of money against inflation and deflation, as well as against the risk that deposits, its principal fiduciary component, may not be honoured by their issuers. The Bank of Italy has the task of strengthening the systemic soundness of the financial industry by promoting competition and internal efficiency. The Bank of Italy also has the task, in preventing and resolving crises, of distinguishing illiquidity from insolvency; preventing intermediaries that are merely illiquid but solvent from collapsing; ensuring the exit of inefficient and insolvent operators; and preventing, at the lowest cost in terms of moral hazard, the difficulties of individual operators from infecting the whole system, and undermining the value of the currency and confidence in it.

Monetary policy and oversight of the payments system are mutually reinforcing, in so far as the quantity of money and the velocity of its circulation are variables that belong to a single block of functional relations.

Monetary management – cash, but above all bank deposits – and stability of the financial system are closely bound to one another. Monetary policy has a direct effect on the profitability and hence the capital endowment of banks. The enforcement of solvency ratios in turn affects banks'lending and investment decisions, one of the channels through which monetary policy is transmitted.

The central bank's engagement necessarily extends to supervising the main markets in which the effects of monetary policy unfold, such as the screen-based secondary market for government securities and the interbank deposit market, and the structures designed to minimize systemic risk in the clearing and settlement of financial transactions.

Assigning the protection of competition in the credit market to the same institution that is responsible for prudential supervision produces cost savings, maximizes professional resources and achieves synergy of information. These practical and organizational aspects aside, competition in the banking sector is an instrumental objective that the supervisory authority is bound to pursue, and with absolute priority. Banks' assessments of the creditworthiness of firms and competition in the banking sector are closely connected. The great importance of banks within Italy's financial system adds a quantitative element to the specific commitment to encourage banks to evaluate borrowers' creditworthiness qualitatively and competitively. In this way, as well as by ensuring price stability, it is possible to safeguard competition throughout the economy. Inflation/deflation and a banking system unable to lend efficiently would both distort the play of competition at its very roots. The two mechanisms of resource allocation on which a market economy is founded – relative prices and businesses' creditworthiness – would be distorted and undermined.

The ability to form opinions based on technical merit as a prerequisite for measures directed at objectives of competition, efficiency and stability is a salient requirement for all five of the Bank's supervisory functions. These functions were entrusted to it in its capacity as central bank, whose institutional history, experience and tradition of research endow it with knowledge of the Italian economy, information, technical know-how, and the habit of discretionary decision-making on matters of judgement and in changing contexts. The Bank of Italy dedicates a large organization and considerable professional resources to its supervisory functions, which have also been augmented of late.

The banking and financial supervision function in Rome consists of four departments, as well as the technical secretariat of the Interministerial Committee for Credit and Savings. Their tasks cover prudential regulations and the protection of competition in the banking sector (Competition, Regulation and General Affairs Department), the supervision of banks (Banking Supervision Department), the supervision of financial inter-mediaries and securities issues (Financial Supervision Department) and inspections of entities subject to supervision (Supervision Inspectorate). Oversight of the payment system and the markets relevant to monetary policy is entrusted to two departments belonging to different sectors set up in 1999, one covering each function. The decision to articulate the activities between different departments and make them part of broader areas reconciled the need for a clear attribution of institutional respon-sibilities with linkage of the formal supervisory tasks to the overall experience of the central bank.

The Bank's five supervisory activities employ a staff of more than a thousand, half at the head office and half in the branches. The Bank's branches are responsible for maintaining close contacts with the banks supervised, monitoring the local market, and gathering and filtering information that would be difficult to obtain from a distance. Thirty one of the Bank's 99 branches have a special supervisory unit and 12 have units staffed by a number of analysts, who work closely with the research units charged with analysing the local economy. In 1999 these branch units conducted 124 inspections, 72 per cent of the total. In 2,000 sweeping reforms of the branch network were begun to step up decentralized supervisory activities and establish closer coordination with the central offices.

Highly qualified personnel are assigned to supervision: 370 managers and officers work almost exclusively in this field; there are over 300 banking and financial analysts; more than three-quarters of the staff in this sector have a university degree. The whole of the Bank, however – 8,700 employees in 1999, including 1,900 in the managerial career track – contributes directly and indirectly to the supervisory functions.

The Bank of Italy's supervisory activities

A more detailed description of how the Bank of Italy has interpreted its supervisory role in the past 20 years is warranted on two grounds. The Bank's extended responsibilities for monetary management and the regulation of the financial system make its role a crucial one; moreover, it has broad discretionary power to act. It is therefore particularly useful to analyse *how* it interprets the supervisory functions with which it has been entrusted.

Ensuring the sound and prudent management of banks

The stability of the financial system is the foundation and ultimate goal of the Bank of Italy's supervisory activity. The efficiency of banks and competition between them are both specific objectives to be pursued and essential conditions for overall financial stability.

The Bank of Italy itself sets the criteria for supervision. It is central to the process of regulatory production for the sector. It issues general measures (supervisory instructions) and specific provisions (authorizations). It draws up proposals for resolutions by the Interministerial Committee for Credit and Savings. Article 6 of the Consolidated Law on Banking requires the Bank of Italy to exercise its supervisory powers 'in harmony with the provisions of the European Community'. Article 4 of the Consolidated Law on Banking confirms the principle of transparency and accountability in respect of the tasks and responsibilities entrusted to the Bank. It obliges the Bank to publish an annual report on its supervisory activity.

The economic notion of sound and prudent management of banks is obviously a flexible one. Legally, it is one of Bentham's 'impossible and indispensable' concepts of law.[1] The task of imbuing it with content lies first and foremost with the managers of banks and other financial intermediaries, for whom the clause represents a rule of good management. The credit authorities – through principles, rules and action – add their voice to the market, calling on the banks to minimize costs and maximize profits without taking excessive risks.

Our point of departure, therefore, must be the structure, the methods and the practices by which sound and prudent management is effectively pursued. Basically, the Bank of Italy's supervision of the banking sector centres on the following steps:

- fixing prudential rules and standards for reliable and correct management;
- exercising powers of authorization over the crucial moments in the life of banks (establishment, change of ownership structure, mergers, acquisition of significant shareholdings);
- assessing the quality of bank management by obtaining and analysing information;
- intervention, proportionate to the anomalies involved;
- managing crises.

The regulations hinge on capital adequacy, risk containment, permissible shareholdings, business organization and internal controls. In addition, they establish, also on a consolidated basis, the minimum requirements and essential conditions to ensure that banking is conducted in a spirit of sound and prudent management; they put the criterion effectively into operation.

Admission to the market depends upon compliance with specific requirements: company form, minimum capital, integrity of shareholders, experience and integrity of directors, suitable articles of association, by-laws and initial business plan. The role of the supervisory authorities is not limited to certifying these attributes. The law itself lays down the broader task of evaluating whether, on the basis of the information provided, the applicant bank fulfils the conditions for sound and prudent management. The documents of incorporation and business plan are examined to verify that the technical and organizational means match the bank's objectives. The checks on shareholders and senior management are designed to verify that the project has a serious purpose. They aim to rule out any possibility that dubious characters may be hiding behind the application for authorization. Attention is therefore focused on the reputation, connections and business relations of directors, senior management and shareholders.

The activities involved in monitoring individual banks include off-site analysis and on-site inspections, authorizations for single acts of particular importance, and corrective intervention.

The banks are monitored continuously to assess whether they have the capital and the organizational and professional ability to cover risks and pursue their strategic objectives. The information used for this purpose is obtained from the regular reports submitted by the banks, their official balance sheets and documents of any other nature requested or received by the Bank of Italy. The most important aspects examined are the capital base, income and expenses, credit and market risks, liquidity and organization. The work of the corporate bodies, changes in the volume of business and services provided, market shares and business prospects are also taken into consideration.

The monitoring concludes with an evaluation of each bank, issued once a year at the end of an administrative process which, although allowing scope for the evaluator's opinion of qualitative aspects, guarantees documentability and fair treatment. Every specific aspect and the overall situation of each bank are given a score from 1 to 5, rising with the seriousness of the problem.

The evaluation starts with a verification of compliance with prudential requirements. More generally, though, the objective is to ascertain whether the bank is sufficiently well managed to ensure, within reason, its long-term viability. The techniques have been fine-tuned over the years to improve their ability to predict outcomes with a view to preventive action; increasing use is made of projections and scenarios to pinpoint possible weaknesses. Given each bank's type of business and choice of strategy and taking account of the quality of its human resources and risk control and management system, expected revenues must be proportionate to the capital invested, and the variability of expected revenue (risk) must be covered by capital. Credit risk is the specifically 'banking' aspect of a broader analysis. A single loan does not have a secondary market price. Its degree of risk varies with the portfolio of which it is part; it may be acceptable for a solidly capitalized bank, unacceptable for one lacking capital and reputation.

On-site inspections provide a close-up picture of individual banks every few years, but off-site analysis is a continuous and dynamic process. Because it simultaneously covers all the banks subject to supervision, it provides an easy means of comparing strategies and situations.

Each bank is inspected on average every five years. In the majority of cases the investigation is of a general nature, embracing all aspects of business. The duration varies. The inspection may last a long time if it is decided to conduct a thorough and far-reaching investigation. Starting in the middle of the 1980s these inspections were supplemented by regular meetings with the senior management of banks to discuss plans for the future, qualitative aspects and measures taken to rectify the shortcomings noted in the past.

The analysis may result in measures being taken. Their purpose is to enforce compliance with rules, improve efficiency and reliability, prevent deterioration of the technical situation and restore banks to sound conditions. A variety of tools may be used: general meetings, sectoral meetings, letters, provisions under article 53.3 of the Consolidated Law on Banking. Their type and degree differs. Interventions on banking groups may be taken *vis-à-vis* the parent company for the group as a whole or its individual components.

Sanctions are imposed when supervisory evaluations link infringements of rules to the effects on the technical situation of the bank. They indicate an adverse judgement of management methods or areas of business and are a spur to remedial action, failing which more serious measures become applicable. An administrative penalty, as opposed to a penal sanction, can place greater emphasis on the actual operation of the financial market as one of the tools to achieve the objectives of supervision. Criminal law serves as a last resort, necessary to punish fraud, not just imprudent or unfortunate conduct.

Promoting competition in the banking sector

Favouring competition, transparency, efficiency: these are the levels on which the Bank of Italy conducts its actions in the credit markets, not only in the prudential but also in the antitrust field.

The efficiency of a market implies that its operation must not be ruled by the behaviour of firms in a position of power; indirectly, by this means the interests of users are safeguarded. The aim of transparency is to enhance informed consent, to encourage comparison of services and products, so that the 'weaker party' to the contract is given the information needed to choose.

The fundamental economic concept behind antitrust oversight is 'market power'. In the prevailing interpretation this indicates the firm's ability to keep prices higher than its competitors, thereby earning larger profits. According to the case law developed by the European Court of Justice (United Brands *v.* the Commission), a dominant position

> concerns a position of economic power that gives a firm the power to prevent effective competition being maintained on the relevant market by allowing it to behave in a manner significantly independent of its competitors, customers and consumers.

Several factors are taken into account to measure market power: the size and constancy of market shares, the market shares of competitors, indices of supply concentration, competitive pressures from outside the market, economic entry barriers, the firm's conduct and performance. In order to make this assessment it is necessary to define the commodity classes and geographical limits of the relevant market for all the products that are the object of customer demand and are supplied by other producers, old and new alike.

The cross-elasticity of demand provides information about the real substitutability of other products for those analysed. The SSNIP test (small but significant and non-transitory increase in price) equates the relevant market with the smallest set of products for which a hypothetical monopolist can profitably make a significant and non-transitory increase in price. The analysis of the relationship between prices and degree of concentration checks the existence of a positive statistical correlation between market shares, prices and profit margins in each separate market and between neighbouring markets. The analysis of price changes over the fairly long term uses benchmarking techniques to eliminate spurious correlation. The analysis of exogenous shocks subjects the geographical and commodity ambit of a given market to a 'resistance test' by assessing the competitive impact of large and unexpected changes.

The difficulty of tracing limits of the market geographically and by product and the very concept of competition as a dynamic process suggest focusing on the possibilities of entering the market, on its contestability. Antitrust measures therefore target behaviour that may immediately damage the interests of competitors and users. The assessment of positions of economic power no longer considers only market shares or number of companies but also entry and exit costs and the relationship between the prices of the dominant firm and those of competitors.

Because of the nature of the service provided by banks and their expansion to exploit the economies of scale and scope offered by technological innovation, antitrust supervision in the sector has certain specific features. Regarding market boundaries, as the range of banks' business evolved they decided, partly in answer to a call from the Bank of Italy, to move into markets for products similar to their traditional ones through mergers or commercial agreements with insurance and asset management firms. The banks operate in a number of connected markets: lending, deposits, means of payment, securities trading, asset management, insurance, leasing, factoring, consumer credit and corporate finance. In the Italian system, the majority of operators in the quasi-banking sector belong to banking groups. For the financial markets as for banking, the Bank of Italy possesses a vast array of information and in-depth knowledge of mechanisms of operation.

More importantly, banking involves a large element of sunk costs. That element relates to the information embodied in the customer relationships that lie at the root of lending. The fiduciary nature of these relationships may discourage entry to the market. Because of the information asymmetry between debtors and creditors these relationships are not completely interchangeable. Local banks form particularly close relationships with their borrowers, giving them an advantage in terms of information. This explains the difficulty of directly penetrating new markets. Expanding indirectly by buying up banks or their branches often serves to overcome this barrier and enter a retail market where information is asymmetrical. On occasion the authorities need to encourage concentrations to allow inefficient operators to leave the market without the large loss of customer relations that liquidation might entail. The possibility for 'external' operators to acquire local banks lowers entry and exit barriers and reduces the likelihood of collusive arrangements. A well-functioning market for bank control and ownership is a very desirable condition for the overall efficiency of banking.

Law 287/1990 sets the boundaries of antitrust action and provides a range of instruments. Under present regulations, the Bank of Italy's antitrust functions are organized along the same lines as in the EU, covering the three areas of concentrations, agreements and abuses of dominant position.

Bank *concentrations* require prior approval and are objected to if there is a danger they may reduce competition. The Bank of Italy has not had to prohibit a concentration since 1990. However, on several occasions concentrations have been authorized on condition that the banks removed the threats to competition. After cross-elasticity analysis has defined the geographical and product limits of the relevant market, market shares are examined, special care being taken when they exceed given thresholds. Almost all the concentrations that took place in the 1990s were below the thresholds, which are not applied automatically. If they are exceeded, or if further investigation is deemed necessary, the market positions of the banks concerned before and after the concentration, the entry barriers, the presence of real or potential competition and the other effects of the operation, positive included, are examined.

Agreements are opposed, irrespective of the actual market power of the banks concerned, if they have objectives detrimental to competition, such as price-fixing, division of the market or limitation of production.

In the case of price-fixing agreements, the prohibition extends to both minimum and maximum prices, which may be used as point of reference to determine the behaviour of operators. Authorization can be granted in derogation to the rules if this is justified by the benefits for users or necessary to the stability of the monetary system (Law 287/1990, article 20.5). The Bank of Italy issues a harsher judgement if the damage to competition is effective, if it is 'substantial' and if it occurs where the colluding banks possess strong market power. Standardized customer contracts are not objected to as such, provided they are 'incomplete', in other words provided they allow scope for competition between the participating banks. Similarly, agreements on the dissemination of information among competitors are also permitted.

Abuse of a dominant position is determined after a position has been identified as such; the anti-competitive behaviour in which the abuse consists is observed and the justifications for it are evaluated. Typical examples of abuse include: temporary predatory pricing, that is setting prices below (variable) cost to eliminate a competitor or discourage a prospective entrant, then raising them well above costs; refusal to contract, particularly when the firm concerned has exclusive rights or manages infrastructure indispensable for the provision of a service; and attempts to extend a dominant position to neighbouring markets through connected contracts.

When the antitrust authority detects an anti-competitive agreement or an abuse of dominant position it sets a deadline for eliminating the infringement and warns the firms concerned against such activities. A fine may be imposed, depending on the duration and seriousness of the effects on the market and ranging between 1 and 10 per cent of turnover. Administrative case law lays down that 'the basis used to fix the amount of the fine must be the firm's total sales in the sector in which the market rule was infringed as a result of the agreement prohibited' (Decision no. 873 of the Administrative Court of Lazio, 15 April 1999).

The Bank of Italy pays very close attention to the credit market and is aware that its proper functioning is crucial to competition in all other markets, for goods or factors, and to the economy's growth potential. Competitive conditions must prevail in the credit market, as in other financial markets. Moreover, the banks' lending procedures must correspond to the necessities of competition and growth in the economy as a whole, in a synthesis that demands the closest attention of banking supervisors. The principles and conditions that must be observed in determining potential borrowers' creditworthiness and managing bank lending are evident. A fundamental requirement, connected with the separation of banking and commerce, is the bank's indifference to the ultimate purpose of the funds, in every respect save the return and risk of the loan. The bank must be neutral *ex ante* regarding allocation: it must not have prior, subjective or externally imposed preferences for models of development, economic sectors, projects or customers. The risk/return ratio must be the only basis for the decision to lend. The creditworthiness of the firm must retain its importance over and above the prospects of the specific investment project for which it seeks funding: a project that is good in itself should not be entrusted to a firm incapable of carrying it through. The assessment should take account of both the firm's track record and reputation and its probable future results. Similarly, the firm's expected profitability and cash flow must be taken into account.

Put into practice by banks and banking supervisors, these criteria can do much to promote the *entry* of firms into markets and industries that harbour oligopolistic niches. In addition to increasing the consumer's surplus they will foster a dynamic reallocation of resources in the economy and help to overcome the resistance of declining sectors and firms to new uses of productive capacity.

Transparency is an end in itself. It is important for competition. It is also relevant to the sound and prudent management of banks. Article 117 of the Consolidated Law on Banking ensures that customers will be able to compare financial products by vesting the Bank of Italy with the power to prescribe standardized content of contracts and securities designated by a particular name; those failing to comply and thus misusing the name can be voided. The Bank of Italy has made use of this power to determine the basic technical features of bonds, certificates of deposit and savings certificates issued by banks. Certificates of deposit and floating-rate certificates must use objective financial parameters. Similar requirements are imposed on commercial paper and investment certificates, which can also be issued by non-bank operators. Issuing banks must give the investor a copy of the rules and must allow access to specific information on the technical characteristics and risks of the transaction.

The Bank of Italy also encourages self-regulation in matters of transparency. Voluntary codes of behaviour, such as that drawn up in 1996 by the banking and financial sector at the suggestion of the Italian Bankers' Association, can contribute greatly to increasing trust between banks and their customers.

The ombudsman for the banking sector, instituted in 1993 to provide a private law out-of-court procedure for settling disputes between banks and their customers, is also an expression of self-regulation. Decisions must be reached in three months, and the customer retains the right to have recourse to the law before and after the Ombudsman's pronouncement. Customers are resorting more and more to this procedure, although for the time being it is limited to maximum potential damages of 10 million lire. Almost 3,000 complaints are now submitted and processed each year. The banks participate voluntarily for reasons of public image, but also because it is an efficient method of handling small-scale disputes. The decision is binding for the bank concerned; if it fails to comply a deadline is set, after which notice of non-fulfilment is published in the press.

Supervision of securities market intermediaries

The activities of securities market intermediaries can be separated into brokering, market-making, assistance and placement of issues and asset management services, in which the manager is entrusted with the saver's funds and invests them according to instructions. The first group comprises not only brokers but also intermediaries that trade securities with customers on their own account and are market-makers. All these services are provided by banks and investment firms (*società di investimento mobiliare* – SIM). The latter are restricted by law to specified types of business, principally on the liabilities side, since they are prohibited from performing any monetary function. Banks, investment firms and asset management companies (*società di gestione del risparmio* – SGR) are all allowed to manage individual portfolios, but only the last of these and open-ended investment companies (SICAVs) can manage savings on a collective basis. Asset management companies specialize in the management side (and are not allowed to engage in any other financial activity) but have a broad field of operation. They are the only intermediaries allowed to manage both collective and individual portfolios. The networks of financial salesmen, which are set up mainly by investment firms and specialized banks, perform a dual role: they inform savers about investment opportunities and they offer advice regarding the choice of asset management products.

The objective of the Bank of Italy's supervision of investment firms and asset management companies is to ensure stability and contain risk. As with banks, it fosters efficient risk management by intermediaries. In the case of securities firms, consideration is given to their ability not only to handle their own risks but more especially to control the risks entered into on behalf of their customers. The central bank places very strong emphasis on stability in its supervisory function. It could not be otherwise in a financial system in which nine-tenths of business is directly or indirectly in the hands of banks, and nine-tenths of that answers to 'banking groups'.

The prudential regulations governing investment firms provide for entry controls, the limitation of risk, adequate organization and accounting systems, and instruments of crisis management. Pre-authorization controls ensure that the intermediaries have a suitable organization and that they are controlled and run by professionally qualified people who can guarantee their sound and prudent management. The Bank of Italy not only takes part in the initial authorization procedure but must also give its approval for transfers of significant holdings of the capital of investment firms.

The rules on risk consist essentially in minimum capital requirements for investment firms and limits on the possession of shareholdings and concentration of risk *vis-à-vis* individual counterparties. The system of capital requirements for investment firms resembles that for banks. This complies with the international principle that any given business activity should always be regulated in the same fashion, irrespective of the entity engaged in it.

In order to limit the risk taken on behalf of customers, investment firms must keep the assets of individual customers held as part of a service separate from their own assets and those of other clients. The Bank of Italy's regulations on the deposit or sub-deposit of customers' assets are designed to allow each investor's assets to be identified and quantified at any time.

The Bank's guidelines for the organization of investment firms require that risk management procedures set limits on risk-taking and establish functions and responsibilities at various levels of decision-making. This is essential in order to monitor the financial risk of those investment firms that take risks on their own account; it is equally crucial to enable those that do not to calibrate the operational risks involved in, say, running a distribution network. The organization must provide for internal controls by special units that are independent from the operational divisions and report directly to senior management and the board of auditors.

The supervisory authority's reporting requirements range from the periodical notification of data to the submission of accounting documents and records of board meetings, notices concerning ownership and reports on the organizational structure. Also of importance are the meetings organized with senior management, which allow in-depth analysis of specific aspects and offer opportunities for discussion of corporate strategy. As for banks, the inspections, supplemented by off-site analysis, perform a crucial function.

The results of investigations and the severity of the problems detected determine the remedial measures ordered. When serious infringements are discovered, the boards are dissolved, a special administrator is appointed and the company is put into compulsory liquidation.

All the companies already managing open-end, closed-end or real-estate investment funds in 1998 were entered in the register of asset management companies instituted that year. They were later joined by companies created from the transformation of investment firms and by new houses set up in response to the sector's expansion. In 1999 the major groups underwent a substantial reorganization, as asset management companies merged together and with investment firms. Many companies originally specialized only in collective fund management moved into individual portfolio management as well.

The supervision of asset management companies resembles that of investment firms, both being subject to the same regulations as regards individual portfolios. The Consolidated Law on Finance grants the Bank of Italy powers (of authorization to engage in business and approval of mergers) previously vested in the Ministry of the Treasury. Differences occur in the manner of regulation of the organizational structure and product, that is investment funds.

Regarding the organizational structure, the supervisory authorities pay close attention to relations among the intermediaries that provide the service, jointly with the asset management companies. In collective investment funds, the quality and reliability of services to investors depend on the performance not only of the company setting up the fund but also of the management company (if different), the depository bank and the distribution network. As the majority of management companies belong to groups, they both provide and use services within it. An evaluation of the organization of the management service must take these interactions into account.

The main risk for management companies stems from their capital liability for business errors affecting the value of managed assets. The regulations therefore oblige them to have a minimum capital base commensurate with the assets.

In the case of investment funds, safeguards against the risks taken on behalf of investors are embodied not only in the company's organizational procedures but also in prudential limits on the fund's investments. Prudential measures apply to investment funds and not individual portfolios because holders of investment fund units have less control over the investments made. The restrictions on the activity of investment funds are designed to limit the leverage of fund portfolios and enforce risk diversification. They are more binding on open-end funds available to the general public than on funds reserved for qualified investors and almost negligible on hedge funds designed for the very rich.

The main aspect of product regulation relates to the rules governing the management of investment funds and to the by-laws of 'SICAVs'. Since the unit holder can only accept or reject the whole contract proposed by the asset management company, the law gives the Bank of Italy the task of laying down the minimum contents and criteria behind the wording.

The supervision of asset management companies is conducted in the same manner and with the same objectives as that of investment firms. Since the financial risks of an asset management company are typically smaller, both the examination of individual circumstances and supervisory action are designed to foster adequate organizational structures.

Since the regulations address both asset managers and products, the companies are monitored on two levels. On the one hand, their range of products and their management methods are analyzed in terms of the individual funds managed (focusing on portfolio performance, management styles and results). On the other hand, the company's organizational structure, the performance of total managed assets and its financial equilibrium are examined. Within the supervisory authorities' overall field of operation, a special place is occupied by the aspects relating to product regulation: compliance with the operational limits on investment funds – which is checked automatically from the supervisory returns or from reports sent in by the depository bank – and administrative activities associated with the approval of fund rules.

Payment system oversight

Italy's payment system has traditionally been based with the central bank as regards the services to intermediaries, the network and market support infrastructure and the role of the Interbank Convention on Automation (CIPA), the body responsible for cooperation within the system, which the Bank of Italy chairs and provides with secretarial services.

In the absence of a specific legal framework, in this field the Bank has worked to:

- modernize interbank payment procedures by encouraging settlements in monetary base;
- introduce a large-amount real-time gross settlement system to reduce the risks of clearing-based settlement;

- reorganize and strengthen the network infrastructure;
- improve the security of the most common instruments.

In recent years, with the improvement in payment system security and operator skills it has become possible to review the Bank's role in the production and/or direct management of the services to intermediaries.

Since the function was legally recognized and the Bank was granted regulatory powers, oversight of the payment system has more successfully reconciled public objectives with individual and collective initiatives by intermediaries.

A new regulatory framework was introduced with article 146 of the Consolidated Law on Banking, which transposes the provisions of article 105 of the Treaty of Maastricht and article 3 of the ESCB and ECB Statute annexed to the Treaty. It officially charges the Bank of Italy with control of the payment system, granting it the power to 'issue provisions designed to ensure efficient and reliable clearing and payment systems'. In May 1997 the Bank of Italy detailed the guidelines it follows in the first *White Paper on Payment System Oversight*.

Oversight is a form of administrative control and as such is subject to rules and principles. Although operators do not require authorization for their actions, oversight is exercised in respect of all the subjects and activities that make up the payment system. This has two main consequences. The field of application cannot be identified beforehand, once and for all, since it has to be verified constantly as innovations are introduced. Second, the criterion for identifying the constituent elements, and consequently the area of interest for supervision, is that the activities should be instrumental to the payment system's functioning.

Accordingly, the payment system consists of the operators, procedures, technological infrastructure and instruments used to transfer money. Not all the components must be subjected to equally close oversight. The areas and degrees of control depend on the structure and development of the various sections of the system, and on the importance of their shortcomings for the payment system as a whole.

To improve dependability and security the Bank of Italy had to pay closer attention to the efficiency of the payment services and technical infrastructure. With the reduction in financial market segmentation and the fading of the traditional link between the location of intermediaries, reference markets and infrastructure, the payment services sector becomes increasingly important for competition between financial systems. Owing to the influence on services to end-users, competition in the payment system has also gained importance. The new risks of fraud and counterfeit or of unlawful use of the most innovative means of payment also demand greater focus on the technological characteristics of payment instruments and services.

As a result of the changes in the payments industry, conditions have progressively evolved to allow the Bank of Italy, in its policy-making and supervisory role, to rely less on the direct production of services and more on cooperation with operators to design, build and manage efficient and reliable systems and infrastructure. This accords with the suggestion embodied in the law calling upon the Bank of Italy to 'foster' the smooth operation of the payment system. The dismantling of the central system for government securities (*gestione centralizzata dei titoli di Stato* – CAT), the Bank's decision not to continue participating in the capital of the Interbank Company for Automation (*Società interbancaria per l'automazione* – SIA) and the transfer to operators of all securities settlement procedures except for the 'cash leg', belong in this context.

Regulation is the tool that the oversight authorities can successfully use to reach areas of the payment system affected by systemic risks or in which intermediaries, individually or collectively, appear unable to guarantee adequate security and efficiency. The adoption of suitable and non-discriminatory access requirements to payment systems and technical infrastructure responds to the need to enhance the autonomy and management abilities of private entities while safeguarding the principles of competition.

The emphasis on the production and distribution of information about the conditions governing the supply of payment services responds to the need to foster competitive and efficient intermediaries and safeguard end-users. Transparency is a prerequisite for a market in which the more effective systems and intermediaries prevail; complete and clear information is also essential to allow users effective access to payment services, which tend to be technically very complex.

At the end of 1999 the Bank of Italy published a second White Paper, elaborating on the reference concepts and describing for operators the supervisory authorities' intended course of action as a prelude to a systematic and precise set of regulations implementing article 146 of the Consolidated Law on Banking.

Market oversight

The monitoring of the markets has always been associated with the duties of a central bank. The smooth operation of the money and bond markets is essential to correct price formation, to the transmission of monetary policy signals and to financial stability.

Traditionally, Italian legislation – from articles 2, 44 and 45 of the 1936 Banking Law to article 11 of Law 77/1983 – acknowledges the need for central bank control of securities issues. As a consequence of article 129 of the Consolidated Law on Banking, the system of administrative authorizations for issues was replaced in 1994 with a procedure for prior notification to the Bank of Italy. The intention is clearly not to scrutinize the creditworthiness of the issuing firms, for the procedure, which is fast and simple, is designed to ensure the 'stability of the securities market' as a whole. With exceptions – notably of shares and government securities – the Bank can defer or prohibit issues that would jeopardize the smooth operation of the market. The ultimate objective is the orderly development of the financial market, and especially the primary market for private bond issues.

In recent years securities issues have been very dynamic in both volumes and characteristics. Italy's private bond market has always been noteworthy for the role of the banks in the dual capacity of issuers and distributors of securities. In 1994 permission to issue bonds as a normal method of fund-raising was extended to all banks. In that year the banks issued 44 trillion lire's worth of bonds, 41 trillion of this by the former special credit institutes. Decree Law 323/1996, ratified as Law 425/1996, fixed a tax rate of 27 per cent on the yield on certificates of deposit and bank deposits, making it no longer profitable to issue medium- and long-term CDs. It also led banks, even small ones, to resort almost exclusively to bond issues. Instantly, gross issues of bank bonds jumped from 97 trillion lire in 1996 (already up from 28 trillion in 1995) to 148 trillion the following year. Their volume is now about half that of deposits.

The growth in the volume of bonds was accompanied by radical changes in their technical characteristics. Through the first half of the 1990s issues usually carried fixed interest rates or were indexed to traditional money and financial market parameters. The innovations included eliminating the amortization schedule (bullet bonds), using more frequent reopenings to increase secondary market depth and, above all, introducing so-called structured securities, which are a synthesis of one derivative component and one pure bond component (index bonds, corridor and barrier securities, fixed-reverse floaters, reverse convertible bonds, credit-linked bonds).

Over the years the Bank of Italy has been active in promoting organizational improvements in two markets that play a crucial role in monetary policy: the money market and the market for government securities. Legislative Decree 415/1996 and the Consolidated Law on

Finance in 1998 codified the Bank's supervision and support of both; the organization of trades in financial instruments is thus now privatized but regulated by the public authorities.

The separation of management and control embodied in the Consolidated Law on Finance applies to both phases of transactions in financial instruments, their organization and their execution. In trading, the price formation mechanism and the correctness of operators' conduct both towards investors and among themselves play a crucial role. Stability becomes important in relation to settlement. An operator's illiquidity or insolvency during this stage can be transmitted to direct counterparties (in gross settlement systems) and to the community of intermediaries (in securities and cash clearing systems). Difficulties may arise in the payment system, which is where the cash part of the transaction is settled, infecting the whole of the financial system.

The Treasury is charged with regulating the institutional aspects of the market for its own issues and is empowered to impose penalties on the market operating companies. It is the duty of Consob to prevent and eliminate dishonest or insufficiently transparent conduct by intermediaries *vis-à-vis* customers and to ensure access to information by all operators authorized to trade. The Bank of Italy's oversight of markets and settlement systems is associated, on the trading side, with monetary policy and, on the settlement side, with the preservation of financial stability.

The most important markets for monetary policy are wholesale markets, where the banks trade liquid assets directly (the interbank market) or indirectly (the market for Treasury paper). Interest rates must form in an orderly and efficient manner so that undistorted signals can be exchanged between the monetary authorities and operators.

The Bank of Italy, which continues to perform the clearing service, oversees the settlement system and the management of collateral for financial market transactions because of the systemic importance of limiting risk. This role is progressively taking the form of control of the settlement infrastructure – settlement procedures, central securities depository, central counterparties and clearing houses – and of its managers.

The Bank's oversight of trading systems is based on parameters of market efficiency recorded by observing and studying price non-alignment with the yield curve and noting persistently non-exploited arbitrage opportunities. A market's efficiency can also be calculated from the liquidity of trades and the cost to an operator of conducting two opposite-sign operations in the same security. In brokers' markets this cost is the sum of the fees due for the buy and sell transactions. In a market-makers' market, such as the screen-based (secondary) market in government securities (*mercato telematico secondario* – MTS), the cost is the bid-ask spread: the narrower the spread the more efficient the market. More generally, to monitor, safeguard and stimulate competition among market-makers is to pursue market efficiency.

The regulations governing the central securities system were written for the purpose of overseeing the settlement systems and associated securities depositories and collateral management systems. They set out the main accounting and administrative rules to be observed by managers. The central management company issues its own regulation regarding operational aspects and points of detail.

A similar technique is used to draft regulations on the clearing and guarantee of transactions in financial derivatives and on the management of the gross settlement system. The Bank of Italy and Consob have drawn up a set of general regulations for these services. The service providers are required to furnish the operational content for the outlines prepared by the authorities. Subsequently procedures will be put in place to collect and record information on the managers' activity, which is the basis for efficient control of the settlement systems.

Inspections

Bank of Italy supervisory inspections also date back to 1926. The Bank was one of the first central banks to conduct on-site inspections.

The original, dual motive for supervisory inspections remains: the legal motive of checking compliance with rules, and the economic motive of evaluating corporate efficiency and risk. The very possibility of inspection access acts as a deterrent to agents against evading rules, putting up barriers and distorting information.

Supervision, once focused on compliance with the rules, has progressively evolved towards control of merit and quality. The ultimate objective of an inspection is to evaluate the inspected company's ability to participate in the market.

Quantitative gaps in knowledge become less frequent with advances in data processing, the transparency fostered by market regulations, and the checks based on off-site supervision. Statistics are more reliable, although this is constantly verified during the course of inspections.

Qualitative aspects remain the hardest to capture. They reflect the complex, specific, changing interactions between the company (its corporate and organizational structure, business culture, human resources and technology) and the environment (consisting of rules, competitors and customers). Asymmetrical information in this area often creates a screen that can be pierced during inspections.

For the most part, on-site inspections follow an annual programme. They are conducted by teams of specialists, each with a designated head. The head signs the final report on the findings, which is also made available to the bank so that it can prepare its defence.

Inspections are programmed not only according to the need for periodical investigations but also on the basis of information processed by the Bank's Supervisory Department offices, which, assisted by its branch network, constantly monitor every bank. Inspections lasting several months but conducted at individual banks every few years are combined with specific, in-depth investigations of a narrower field, in the intervals between the general inspections. The continuity of monitoring is guaranteed by the array of reliable data collected for off-site supervision.

The general inspections cover the entire spectrum of a bank's activity, at the least by means of sample surveys. They extend to foreign affiliates and main subsidiaries (which may be the object of ad hoc visits if necessary) on a consolidated basis.

The areas examined by the inspector include strategic aspects (system of governance, group policies, decision-making and planning methods, market positioning), technical matters (capital base, financial situation and profitability) and product areas (banking, financial intermediation and services) from the viewpoint of the different types of risk (market, settlement, operational and, most importantly, credit risk). Organizational issues relating to the quality of IT systems, accounting procedures and internal auditing have become increasingly important over the years. Financial innovation entails brusque changes in risk profiles (derivatives, including credit derivatives, and securitization) and tends to shift the assessor's interest from contingent quantitative elements to the intermediary's ability to handle risk.

During the inspections a range of documents, usually covering the past two years, are analysed. Meetings are held with the directors, auditors and senior managers to examine questionable aspects, strategies, strengths and weaknesses of the bank.

The accounts are examined for congruency. The technical analysis of the situation – profitability, solvency and liquidity – is based on the relevant aggregates, adjusted, where necessary, according to the findings and evaluated in comparison with other banks, and performance indicators, such as return on assets, return on equity, and solvency ratio.

The bank's capacity to generate adequate flows of income on a lasting basis plays a primary role. The cost/benefit analysis tests the ability to tolerate even very small spreads between lending and deposit rates. Account is also taken of the profit margins on various product lines, of operating expenses, capital strengthening, and market disclosure. The solvency analysis assesses whether the capital base is intact and sufficient to comply with compulsory ratios and financial flexibility. Liquidity is appraised according to the mismatch of assets and liabilities and thus in relation to the resources available both in 'the normal course of business' and in the event of financial tensions. The quality of the loan portfolio is assessed according to concentration (by company size, economic sector and geographical area), mobility and likelihood of repayment of loans. A large proportion (between 20 and 60 per cent) of loans and clients are examined, including all the riskiest positions according to the scoring systems. The analysis covers loan processing, granting, pricing, performance review and monitoring, legal proceedings and methods of recovery. The bank's classifications are checked for conformity with those set by the supervisory authority: bad debts, non-performing loans, restructured loans or loans being restructured, forecast losses.

The inspections are progressively evolving from the traditional, basic, detailed analysis of balance-sheet values towards an overview of the bank's skill in managing all its credit and market risks and the interactions between them. This sort of assessment entails a fairly lengthy observation of the actual, day-to-day operation of the bank's organization and technical personnel, and their reaction to market stimuli. The inspector's report describes and comments on the aspects examined and evaluates them separately, summarizing the results in the final appraisal, with a score of 1 to 5.

The following entities may be subjected to inspection: banks and banking groups (articles 54 and 68 of the Consolidated Law on Banking), investment firms, collective investment undertakings and related groups (articles 10 and 12.5 of the Consolidated Law on Finance), and financial intermediaries included in the special register under article 107 of the Consolidated Law on Banking. The inspections of individual intermediaries can cover all the areas and activities that are subject to supervision by the Bank of Italy. Constant attention is paid to compliance with the other regulations bearing on the intermediary's reputation (money-laundering, contract transparency and anti-usury). There is close and continuous cooperation with the judicial authorities. Institutionally, this is not an integral part of the actual inspection work, but it represents a substantial technical contribution the Bank of Italy makes to the administration of justice.

Between 1997 and 1999, the Bank conducted 517 general inspections of intermediaries, representing 34 per cent of total banking activity.

Every year 400 employees of the Bank's head office and branches are involved in this work.

Supervision and change

This survey of financial supervision in Italy provides ample confirmation of two propositions. First, Italy complies with the most advanced international standards regarding the institutions, methods and resources dedicated to banking and financial supervision. A long-standing tradition has been strengthened over the past 20 years. From 1926 to 1936 it was based around the central bank. This structure has remained but other institutions have joined the Bank of Italy in the performance of controls. The tasks of supervision have been extended and augmented, preserving a correct relationship between the political authority and the independent administrative authorities. At the same time, by international standards, the controls in Italy do not appear particularly burdensome for the intermediaries concerned.

Second, the contribution that supervision has made to altering the morphology of the banking and financial system has been an important one. It has consisted in matching, and occasionally anticipating, changes in the legal system and consequently is closely related to and logically stems from changes in rules, laws and regulations. This contribution has not, in substance, involved directing events, either against or outside the law. Basically, it has involved enforcing new rules, as well as in offering a different interpretation and application of old ones. This is the primary, fundamental task of supervision: to observe and promote behaviour among market participants that conforms with the law in force. It may seem a static function, even an obstacle to change, if the laws do not change. But when there are profound innovations in the law, as has happened in Italy's financial sector since 1980, the main problem – compliance – also acquires a dynamic aspect. It is an indispensable condition if the changes shaped by the law are to take effect and become a reality in the market.

This action relating to the system's institutional structure and forms has been accompanied by care and effort on the part of the supervisory authorities to raise the performance of intermediaries and markets. The main objective of this attention, during a difficult time of restructuring of the Italian economy, was to ensure that the transformation of the old system and the transition to the new did not occur in conditions of instability. This requirement was respected.

6
Competition

We can identify two phases in the policy for the defence and promotion of competition in banking and finance since the 1950s, placing the turning-point in the late 1970s. During the first phase the Bank of Italy ensured the independence of banks from industrial groups, that is from non-financial firms. It also ensured that the banking system consisted of a suitable number of banks, grouped into various institutional categories and size classes. These two objectives were instrumental to the fundamental aim of countering industrial monopoly. Under the logic of 'second-best', competition *internal* to the banking system – competition between banks in setting interest rates – was sacrificed to that higher goal. At the same time, the backwardness of the money and financial markets and the restrictions on cross-border capital movements limited competition *external* to the banking system. The economic crisis of the 1970s marked a watershed in the central bank's action for competition. In keeping with the analysis of the nature of the crisis set out above, the Bank acted to promote competition on prices and in all other legitimate forms, within the banking system as well as externally. The low level of concentration in banking, the progress of the capital markets, the increasing popularity of government securities and the opening-up of the economy to international capital flows also worked to favour competition between banks and throughout the entire financial system. This policy, already practiced in the 1980s, and the tendencies that emerged then were strengthened in the 1990s. The Antitrust Law of 1990 provided institutional confirmation of this approach, together with the formal definition of the instruments, aims and limits of action to favour competition.

The initial conditions and the turning-point of the 1970s

The arrangements for competition, in industry as well as in banking, that had been put in place under Donato Menichella, governor of the Bank of Italy from 1948 to 1960, continued to condition the system through the mid-1970s. The symbiosis between big business and high finance had deprived the Italian economy of authentic competition, amplifying the crisis of the 1930s. Bank credit was removed from the oligopolistic control of the industrial groups with the creation of IRI in 1933, the public takeover of the leading banks and the passage of the 1936 Banking Law. One of the basic prerequisites for competition throughout the economy was thus re-established, albeit in traumatic fashion and in peculiar form. The line taken by Menichella, and not basically modified by his successor Guido Carli through 1975, consisted in preventing the return of industrial credit oligopoly, safeguarding free access to industry and guaranteeing two key necessities: banking pluralism and banks' independence in financing industry, both large and small. The presence of public banks and the articulation of the system, with numerous banks and a variety of institutional categories and size classes, were the prerequisites for good resource allocation. On this point, Menichella was perfectly clear: 'The multitude of credit institutions provides a guarantee of fair allocation of savings; in a word, it is the guarantee that all can freely enter the economic contest.'[1]

The number of banks had plummeted from nearly 5,000 in the 1920s to 1,200 after the Second World War, and there was a real risk of further diminution. It stabilized in the 1950s, while concentration in banking fell to historic lows. The Herfindahl Index of concentration – calculated for banks, not branches, and for all of Italy – was around 0.05 in the 1950s, less than half as high as in the 1920s and low by international standards as well. Menichella's approach sacrificed competition between banks to competition in the economy as a whole, to the diversification of the banking system and to safeguarding medium-sized and small banks. He was convinced that this was necessary to 'avoid a battle to corner deposits that would inevitably lead to the demise of the smaller banks, sharply reducing banking services to small and medium-sized enterprises.'[2] Local banks were protected by the administrative authorization process and the tools of structural supervision. They were also protected by Bank of Italy sanctions on banks that violated the Cartel deposit and lending rates – decided by the authorities, compulsory for all banks and in force until 1952 – and by the Bank's approval of voluntary agreements between banks. The Agreement of 1954 remained in effect until 1974.

Menichella's approach was widely endorsed. The cultural and political – liberal and Marxist – calls for action against private monopoly were also aimed mainly at big industry. Indeed, the very notion of public enterprise carried an anti-monopoly tinge, which embraced such developments as the reconfirmation of IRI, the growth of another great public corporation (ENI, the oil company) and the nationalization of electric power companies. With the creation of the National Electricity Authority, ENEL, in 1962, the clamour for an antitrust law subsided. A number of European countries had passed antimonopoly legislation in the 1950s; Italy had no such law until 1990. In any event, those European laws exempted the credit system, as did the last of the many Italian proposals to safeguard competition, the government bill presented in 1960. With exceptions – among them Luigi Einaudi, governor of the Bank of Italy from 1945 to 1948 – in the light of the experience of the 1930s, competition in banking was not considered a priority in academic and political circles or at the international level.

Though limited, banking competition was not non-existent. This is demonstrated by the difficulties encountered in enforcing the Cartel and the Agreement, which were repeatedly threatened by interest rate 'violations' on the part of the more aggressive banks, those which Raffaele Mattioli described as willing to 'howl with the wolves'. Competition was also evidenced by banks' inclination to maximize growth rather than earnings, sacrificing the latter to the former. Yet in the 1950s costs in some segments of the banking system rose to as much as 4 per cent of total assets, whereas in the 1920s, as now, they had amounted to around 2 per cent. This cost peak – twice the 'norm' – came despite the economies of scale connected with greater average bank size. In the 1950s and 1960s, years of low inflation, the spread between the lending and deposit rates of the largest, most efficient commercial bank remained stably between 6 and 7 percentage points, the spread *vis-à-vis* government securities in the vicinity of 3 points. Risk was limited by the excellent performance of the economy in the 'miracle' years, which together with the wide spreads helped ensure high earnings for banks.

Oligopoly and the relative lack of competition in banking were an established and broadly acknowledged fact. The Bank of Italy was well aware of the trade-off between the articulated structure of the banking system and industrial competition on the one hand and banking consolidation, competition and efficiency on the other. The empirical terms of this conflict formed the subject of analysis and technical discussion within the Bank, but the ultimate judgment was quite straightforward:

> Our banking system is extremely dispersed. And this costs. Operating costs could be reduced, but the number of banks would have to be greatly diminished; and this could produce a degree of concentration quite dangerous to freedom of enterprise on the part of citizens and would clash with deeply rooted traditions and customs.[3]

In the later 1970s, based on the analysis of the Italian crisis as the crisis of the mixed economy, the Bank of Italy changed its approach. It moved to intensify competition between banks within the financial system and thereby also in the economy as a whole. The power of authorization that the Bank had enjoyed since the 1920s as supervisory authority began to be exercised with a view to competition. Even a tool for structural supervision like article 28 of the 1936 Banking Law – authorization to open new branches – was now wielded not in order to limit competition but to heighten and equalize it. In his concluding remarks in May 1977, Governor Baffi was explicit: 'The supervisory authority has developed criteria which emphasize the need to increase the productivity of the system and, where necessary, to raise the degree of competition to a more uniform level.' This was done on the basis of work published in the early 1970s, which showed that 15 per cent of the 1500 local deposit markets into which the national territory could be divided had just one bank and another 25 per cent just two.[4] The branching plan for 1978 – like its successors right up to liberalization in 1990 – approved new branch openings above all in the areas where the concentration of lending and deposits was especially high.

In other words, long before it was given a formal antitrust mandate the Bank of Italy had put competition at the centre of its action to increase the efficiency and soundness of the banking and financial system. And it continued to act in this sense in the years that followed. With Law 287 of 1990, Parliament simply recognized an existing state of affairs and built upon it.

The Bank of Italy came to reject an idea that had gained widespread currency with the crisis of the 1930s, and not only among central bankers, namely that competition, or at any rate 'excessive' competition, was a cause of banking instability, antinomic to stability. In reality, though, especially given the international openness of the Italian economy in normal times, a banking system that was inefficient but profitable thanks to oligopoly would itself be doomed to systemic instability. More competition was thus a crucial intermediate objective, the linchpin of the Bank of Italy's monetary, exchange and supervisory policy. In the long run, without competition there is no efficiency; and without efficiency, in the long run there cannot be stability for the banking and financial industry. A final tenet, drawn from the economic theory on which antitrust principles are ultimately based, was that competition is not the same thing as *laissez-faire*, that the latter can negate the former, especially in an industry characterized by economies of scale; and that deregulation itself is more effective if undertaken as part of an economic and institutional policy to protect, promote and enforce competition on producers, who are not required to like it and will use all means to avoid it.

The assignment of the antitrust mandate in banking to the Bank of Italy was thus no break with the past and is not an anomaly that needs correction but rather the natural, institutional recognition of a state of affairs in being for decades. It sanctioned a principle that should be consolidated and extended. Prudential supervision and the safeguarding of competition do not conflict; they are complementary.

Up to 1990

These general principles were interpreted and put into practice during the 1980s in a series of statements of intent, strategic decisions and single acts that cannot all be listed here. What follows is a brief summary of the most important.

The crucial passage, at the start of the decade, was the reaffirmation of banks, whether private or public, as in essence enterprises. After the transposition of the EC's First Banking Directive in 1985, this solution was eventually ratified by a sentence of the Court of Cassation in 1989. This was followed by the introduction of the possibility of transforming public-sector banks into public limited companies, by means of Law 218/1990.

The quality, quantity and diffusion of banks' disclosure to customers and to the markets were increased. The Bank of Italy used its powers to direct banks in that sense. The turning-point had been marked in 1974 by the introduction of the computerized prudential report for banks. This replaced uncoordinated, paper-based reports with a single report by each bank to the Bank of Italy based on a set of checks of internal consistency that sustained data quality control. The format of the report was revised in 1989 and again in 1998. It hinges on a unified procedure (PUMA2, introduced in 1989) that is not only a software generating the reports but also a source of feedback and information on competitors for each bank. At the end of the 1980s the Bank of Italy launched an advanced information system of its own (PRISMA) based on a generalized infrastructure with control systems for validating at source the banking data that then go to the markets and to the public.

Since 1985, the Italian Bankers' Association has released the half-yearly financial statements of the leading Italian banks. At that time the law on banks' financial reports only determined the layout of the profit-and-loss account and the rules for its compilation. The initiative benefited from advances in the field of prudential reporting. Some completely new tables were introduced: the breakdown of assets and liabilities by residual maturity, the concentration of lending by sector and size of borrower, loan quality, breakdown of the profit and loss account (interest income and gross income, gross operating profit). The information content of the half-yearly report was subsequently recognized by Consob and, after revision in 1993, further refined with the incorporation of a series of changes in administrative rules on the accounts. The number of participating banks rose from the original 30 to 112 in 1992; the 131 banks now involved account for 95 per cent of total banking assets; 60 groups issue consolidated half-yearly financial statements.

Between 1985 and 1990, while the legislative changes that would eventually produce the Consolidated Law on Banking in 1993 were being prepared and passed, the possibility of establishing new commercial banks was reopened. Through the capital adequacy ratios, the expansion of banks was increasingly dependent on the amount of capital they could accumulate. In 1989, the requirements for operating a bank were limited to a minimum capital amount and to the professional experience and integrity of shareholders and corporate officers. Regulatory changes steadily eased the limits on the types of business in which banks could engage.

In his concluding remarks to the shareholders' meeting in 1986, Governor Ciampi could say:

> The instruments and procedures of banking supervision have been directed more to increasing competition and enhancing intermediaries' decision-making autonomy. This approach has been adopted in the Bank of Italy's supervisory activity regarding branches, geographical restrictions on operations, changes in statutes, the raising of capital in the markets and derogations from operational limits. Procedures have been streamlined.

By the end of 1988 the changeover from direct and administrative to indirect, market-based instruments for the conduct of monetary policy had been completed. The ceiling on the growth in bank lending, which had been in effect in various forms from 1973 to 1983, was suspended, temporarily reinstated in 1987 and abrogated definitively the following year.

Under the pressure of the growing volume of government debt securities to be placed with Italian investors, the development – indeed, the creation – of efficient money and bond markets was promoted. For the first time in decades the banking system as a whole faced the risk of disintermediation on the liabilities side, with deposits being crowded out by government paper.

Foreign exchange liberalization, begun in 1988 and completed in 1990, achieved full external convertibility of the currency for the first time in Italian history, with total opening to short-term and long-term capital movements. Cross-border capital flows in both directions increased immediately.

Together with the institutional groundwork for competition, structural conditions and conditions involving the business environment were also put in place. These developments and the action of the Bank of Italy had discernable effects. Many indicators reflect the increased degree of competition in the markets for various banking products in the course of the 1980s.

Between 1979 and 1989 the average number of banks per province rose from 20 to 27, although the overall number of banks remained broadly unchanged. The number of branches rose from 11,575 to 15,569. The concentration of market shares in provincial loan markets declined by 15 per cent, and by 20 per cent in the Centre and South of the country (Table 6.1). The decrease in concentration should be read in the light of the low elasticity found internationally of banks' profits with respect to concentration.[5] Yet by international standards the Italian banking system stood confirmed as having a structurally low degree of concentration. Domestic fund-raising and investment alternative to traditional banking channels grew in importance. The decline in the financial intermediation ratio (financial claims on banks in proportion to total financial assets) continued at a very rapid pace in the 1980s, as the ratio fell from 45 per cent in 1980 to 30 per cent in 1990. As the decade drew to a close, with the reopening of the foreign channel gross capital movements surged from 670 trillion lire in 1988 to 1180 trillion in 1990. This represented another potential source of competition for the Italian banking and financial system. To conclude, the 1980s were

Table 6.1   Banking concentration by geographical area[a]

	North-West	North-East	Centre	South	Islands	Italy
Loans: Herfindahl Index						
1983	17.18	15.91	18.11	20.01	18.63	17.94
1990	13.87	13.49	14.56	15.19	18.62	14.87
1999	13.64	12.15	14.57	14.89	24.63	15.01
Loans: Share of top three banks						
1983	57.3	57.4	62.0	61.5	63.9	60.1
1990	52.0	52.1	55.0	53.6	63.8	54.6
1999	51.6	50.3	52.2	52.3	66.7	53.5
Deposits: Herfindahl Index						
1983	19.77	20.05	20.62	21.03	24.02	20.87
1990	18.98	18.35	18.98	17.63	22.64	19.04
1999	19.04	16.91	17.63	15.92	24.38	18.28
Deposits: Share of top three banks						
1983	64.6	64.1	67.0	64.2	66.9	65.2
1990	63.2	61.2	65.3	57.8	64.9	62.2
1999	62.7	58.1	61.0	56.3	64.2	60.0

[a] Arithmetical means of provincial data. The data for 1983 and 1990 refer to ordinary credit banks only; those for 1999 refer to all banks. The Herfindahl Index of concentration, shown as a percentage, can range from 0 to 100 (the greatest possible concentration, with a single firm accounting for all output).

a decade of declining inflation and declining nominal interest rates, creating a framework in which a narrowing of the spread between lending and deposit rates was more likely, intensifying competition between banks.

The banks reacted to the institutional and structural alterations and changes in the economic environment with more aggressive lending policies to gain market shares. They increased the lines of credit offered to customers. Multiple-bank borrowing by firms itself helped to set banks in competition with one another, as those firms obtained finance on better terms, often in line with money market yields. The rapid growth of lending characterized the competitive climate of the later 1980s. It was fostered by the easing of the ceiling on the increase in lending and by the regulatory changes that extended the banks' possible range of business and reduced market segmentation. Bank loans rose steadily from 44 per cent of GDP in 1986 to 64 per cent in 1993.

The differential between the average interest rate on bank loans and the gross yield on Treasury bills narrowed from four percentage points in 1986 to just over one point in 1992. This differential can be seen as a mark-up that is correlated inversely with the degree of competition and directly with credit risk. The decline occurred while bad and doubtful debts held at higher levels. The decrease between 1986 and 1990 in the dispersion of lending rates, both by bank and by geographical location, in concomitance with the narrowing of the gap between the average lending rate and the Treasury bill yield, corroborates the competitive interpretation.

The banks accepted, or at most resisted irresolutely and unsuccessfully, the deposit disintermediation triggered by the competition from government securities sold to the general public and traded on increasingly efficient screen-based markets such as MTS. Foreign exchange liberalization in a setting of exchange rate stability enabled the banks to meet domestic credit demand by raising funds abroad as well as by reducing their holdings of government securities. The differential between Treasury bill and bank deposit rates widened by about 3 percentage points. The share of households' financial assets consisting of bank deposits fell from 53 per cent in 1979 to 34 per cent in 1990. Although the spread of competition in the deposit market was less rapid, the dispersion of deposit rates too was less at the end than at the beginning of the decade, and in any case the standard deviation was no more than 5 per cent of the average level of deposit rates.

From 1984 through 1990 there was an average annual shift in market shares (net of that due to mergers and acquisitions) of 2.6 per cent for deposits and 5.7 per cent for loans. The shift stemmed largely from interest rate competition.

Beginning in the mid-1980s the heating up of competition also influenced the provision of banking services other than deposits and loans. Fees for collection and payment services had been rising in proportion to transactions effected via customer current accounts (other than the crediting of interest) until 1986, but they fell sharply in the following years. The benefits of large-scale automation in the payment system were passed on rapidly to customers. The same pattern can be observed in the unit earnings on securities custody and management. The volume of third-party securities in custody rose from 23 per cent of total bank assets in 1975 to 80 per cent in 1993; fees on this service rose until 1986 (from 1.5 to 1.8 per mille) but then fell significantly to 0.9 per mille in 1990.

Banking and the stock exchange are strictly complementary. If competition in the stock market is limited, it is unlikely that competition will prevail in banking, or in finance as a whole. Within the Italian banking industry competition in the product market was intensifying, but the ownership and control of most banks was not yet contestable.

Few banks were under private control. In 1981 just eight banks were listed on the stock exchange, accounting for 15 per cent of banking system assets. Adding in the 24 banks listed on the Mercato Ristretto brings the share up to 23 per cent. In 1990 it was only moderately higher at just over 30 per cent.

The idea that a stock-exchange-based financial market, although not 'perfect', is almost inevitably competitive was questioned in the 1970s and 1980s with reference to markets, such as New York, that were more advanced than that of Milan.[6] In extreme versions, the doubt extended to the economic function of the stock market, its very *raison d'être*, when it is oligopolistic.[7]

Actually, at the time the Italian stock market combined an informational efficiency that was weak at best[8] with such evident features of imperfect competition as the brokers' monopoly, high minimum commissions and the fact that not all trading took place on-exchange. The small number of listed companies limited investors' scope for diversification. During upswings fund-raising, whether by new share issues or the listing of subsidiaries, was effected mainly by the industrial and financial groups already present in the market. From 1981 to 1993 nearly 80 per cent of issues of listed shares involved the top four private groups and public enterprises. Of 114 new listings of non-financial corporations on the Milan Stock Exchange between 1981 and 1993, more than a third consisted in the listing of companies that had been subsidiaries of already-listed groups. As late as 1993, with record fund-raising (16 trillion lire) on the Milan exchange, issues numbered fewer than thirty. The largest five, all for more than 1 trillion lire, accounted for two-thirds of the total amount.

After 1990

After the law instituting the Antitrust Authority assigned the antitrust function in the credit sector to the Bank of Italy, banking competition increased at an accelerating pace.

Impetus for competition arose both on the institutional front and from the economic context. Legislative reforms in the late 1980s and early 1990s, such as the 'European passport', were incorporated in the Consolidated Law on Banking in 1993. One basic principle laid down by the law (article 5) was that 'efficiency and competitiveness' were among the purposes of supervision of the financial system, competition being the prime prerequisite. The downward trend in the financial intermediation ratio continued in the 1990s. Cross-border capital flows increased many times over. Inflation and nominal long-term interest rates declined to historic lows of 1.5 and 4 per cent early in 1999.

Structurally, following the liberalization of branching authorizations by the Bank of Italy in 1990, the number of bank branches increased by more than 10,000, or 70 per cent, to the figure of 27,134 in 2000, while in the rest of Europe the number of branches declined. The average number of banks doing business in a province rose further, from 27 to 31, in the course of the decade. About 80 per cent of Italian citizens can now choose among at least three banks in their town of residence. Banking concentration indices have remained low by international standards (Table 6.2), although this level is slightly higher (19 rather than 15 per cent) if concentration in provincial loan markets is measured taking account of membership of banking groups. The foreign presence increased. In the 1990s the share of assets held by foreign bank branches or subsidiaries rose from 3 to 7 per cent, midway between the 12 per cent registered in France and Spain and the 4 per cent figure for Germany. The foreign share is higher in such segments as household credit, corporate financial services and government securities interme-diation. Foreign banks' equity interests in Italian banks are substantial.

Table 6.2 Banking concentration in 11 European countries[a]

	1990		1997	
	No. of banks covered	*Concentration index*	*No. of banks covered*	*Concentration index*
Finland	7	29	7	30
Switzerland	170	12	72	27
Denmark	31	21	16	19
Sweden	5	23	19	13
Austria	50	8	41	12
Belgium	42	13	39	12
Spain	125	4	98	7
United Kingdom	135	12	162	4
France	151	11	221	4
Italy	58	6	151	4
Germany	214	4	510	3

[a] The Herfindahl indices of concentration refer to the entire national territory. Those for 1990 are taken from L.G. Goldberg and A. Rai, 'The Structure-Performance Relationship for European Banking', *Journal of Banking and Finance*, 1996, table 1, p. 753; they refer to deposits with commercial banks and savings banks. The indices for 1997 are estimated on the basis of data from IBCA, *Bankscope Database*, Bureau Van Dijk, 1998; they refer to total assets of banks with assets of more than one billion dollars. Strictly speaking, therefore, the data for the two years are not comparable.

At the end of 1998, foreigners held more than 10 per cent of the equity in each of the top five Italian banking groups. In 1998 non-residents accounted for 8 per cent of total banking business. Lower figures were recorded in most of the other G-7 countries (5.5 per cent in Canada, 5.2 per cent in France, 3.7 per cent in the United States, 2.5 per cent in Germany, 0.5 per cent in Japan), a higher one in the United Kingdom (11.3 per cent). Values higher than 10 per cent were also found in Spain (12.4 per cent) and some smaller eastern European countries.

In the 1990s as a whole the differential between average lending rates and gross Treasury bill yields remained at approximately the level to which it had declined towards the end of the 1980s, despite the widenings that occurred when monetary policy was sharply tightened in 1992 and 1994–5. Further, partly owing to the poor shape of the economy, the decade saw a considerable increase in the average loan risk and a deterioration in the quality of banks' assets. The stable differential between lending rates and government securities yields thus confirms the intensification of competitive pressures in banking. Italian lending rates are now in line with those of the euro area. The launch of stage three of EMU has eliminated exchange rate risk, historically a major factor in the segmentation of European financial markets. At the end of 1999 the rates charged for current account overdrafts of between 1 and 5 billion lire averaged 6.5 per cent, compared with 7.5 per cent in Germany, whereas in early 1997 the Italian rate had been 3 percentage points higher than the German.

The difference between banks' lending rates in different parts of Italy also declined, after the peak recorded in the second half of 1994. For short-term lira loans the gap between North and South narrowed to two percentage points, entirely explained by the greater risk on loans in the South and the slower credit recovery process in that part of the country. In 1999 the ratio of bad debts to total lending was 22 per cent in the South, compared with 7 per cent in the Centre and North.

Looking at the years from 1995 to 1999 in comparison with 1990 and distinguishing the interest rates charged by banks with large and with small market shares, one finds that the tendency of the former to convert their market power into higher charges for customers was reduced, practically annulled. Despite the increase in concentration in a number of local markets owing to mergers and acquisitions, the interest-rate differential between the dominant and the other banks generally narrowed. The gap in corporate lending rates diminished sharply, especially in the South. The rates charged by the dominant banks did not diverge significantly from those of other banks in lending to small firms, that is those borrowing less than a billion lire, or producer households. The rate differentials in credit to consumer households were also perceptibly smaller than in the past.

The difference between the rate on medium- and long-term loans and the cost of bond funding – which together with long-term certificates of deposit finances 80 per cent of bank lending – averaged 3.4 percentage points in 1997. It fell below 2 points in 1999, considerably lower than the values that had been registered in the 1950s, when inflation rates had been comparable. For medium- and long-term loans to households, consisting largely of mortgage lending, the contraction of the spread over the same years was more pronounced, from 4.8 to 2.1 percentage points.

Sharper competition was a factor in a substantial redistribution of loan market shares. After the redistribution that followed the lifting of the ceiling on bank lending, the yearly variation in market shares remained large. In the course of the 1990s on average 5.6 per cent of the loan market changed hands each year, apart from the transfers due to mergers. The concentration of loan market shares diminished.

The advance of competition in the provision of services continued in the 1990s. Fees for payment services were lowered further, and in 1999 were less than a third as high as they had been in 1990. Unit earnings on securities custody and placement held at their 1990 levels until 1996. The rise registered in the next two years came in concomitance with the sharp growth in professional asset management, demand for which had originally been rigid; this expansion altered the qualitative characteristics of supply.

As the decade proceeded, the heightened competition also involved the deposit market, which it had just barely touched towards the end of the 1980s. The gap between Treasury bill yields and the average deposit rate (CDs and other deposits) narrowed by about a percentage point. The concentration of deposits among the banks present at provincial level lost the importance it had had at the start of the 1990s in lowering deposit rates. Freedom of market entry and the possibility of substituting other financial assets for bank deposits became decisive in determining yields. The dispersion of deposit rates continued to diminish or remained very low. In this setting, in the deposit as in the loan market the tendency towards a single price for the same product indicates competitive collision, not oligopolistic collusion. Such a measure of dispersion as the coefficient of variation (the ratio between standard deviation and mean) did not exceed 5 per cent, which is lower than those for primary products, manufactures and non-financial services, including mass consumption products. The decline in deposits as a share of households' financial assets continued (from 34 to 23 per cent), but less rapidly than in the 1980s. The average annual shift in deposit market shares rose to 3.5 per cent, with a peak of 6.6 per cent, higher than that in the loan market, in 1998.

The differential between short-term lending and deposit rates fell from 7 percentage points in 1990 to 4 points in 1999, the ratio between the two holding constant. The difference – the level of which reflects not only competition but also the amount and structure of costs – is at about the euro-area median.

A growing number of banks succumbed in the competition and were driven out of the market, with no repercussions on the financial industry's systemic stability. In the 1990s, 510 banks, or nearly half of those in business in 1989, left the market or were taken over by groups. The number of banks dropped sharply (by 25 per cent), although less sharply than in Spain (45 per cent), France (40 per cent) and Germany (30 per cent). Most important, the decade saw an increase in both the absolute value and the relative importance of the banks with anomalous balance-sheet situations that were taken over by others or subjected to supervisory measures. This category rose from 1.5 per cent of all banks in 1990 to 4.3 per cent in 1996–7, and their share of total assets from 0.2 to nearly 6 per cent. Crisis measures, taken when a bank still has positive net worth, sought market solutions and reduced the burden on the deposit guarantee system or the public finances. The number of banks eventually liquidated nevertheless rose from 6 per cent of all those subject to reorganization in 1990 to 16 per cent in 1997. The assets of the banks liquidated rose from just a few per cent of those of all banks in difficulty at the start of the decade to 11 per cent in 1997.

In the 1990s the reorganization of the banking system came principally in the form of mergers (324 operations); there was also a significant number of takeovers that resulted in legally independent subsidiaries (137). These operations, even where they did not reduce operating costs, resulted in more efficient use of capital, tax benefits, increased income from services and an improvement in the loan portfolio of the acquired bank.

Ultimately, consolidations should produce benefits for customers. The law recognizes that a high degree of concentration is a threat to competition. However, the prejudice against consolidation has been attenuated in view of the possible positive effects. The reasoning by comparative statics of the 1980s, which postulated that 'More concentration means less competition,' was supplanted by the dynamic postulate, 'More competition means more consolidations.' As a rule, mergers and acquisitions have brought a review of the 'target' bank's loan portfolio, an increase in the number of assets classed as bad debts and a sharp decrease in the number of borrowers. However, the contraction in the amount of credit offered in the short run was less pronounced *vis-à-vis* small and medium-sized enterprises. And the best customers, most especially, enjoyed greater availability of funds.

The assumption, long since corroborated by the Bank of Italy's analytical work, was that within the Italian banking system – traditionally little concentrated, with small banks and a large number of branches – there was, together with significant niches for small banks, a great deal of room for economies of scale and scope. In the end, under the pressure of an intensifying competition accepted and solicited by the Bank, this potential was realized.

The prospect of contestability opened up by privatization was confirmed by the legal changes finalized or introduced by the Consolidated Law on Finance. The new rules gave impetus to disclosure, greater efficiency in the stock exchange and other financial markets, and the contestability of ownership of listed companies, in part thanks to the new procedure for takeover bids. Banking legislation and supervisory practice allow for takeovers, including hostile ones, under procedures made final in 1999.

By comparison with other enterprises, banks carry on a business activity – taking and investing fiduciary resources – whose import reaches far beyond the interests of their shareholders. The enormous volume of deposits and bonds by comparison with the banks' capital and reserves is such that the macroeconomic effects of banking concentrations on credit and deposits are significant indeed. The general law on takeovers is designed to protect minority shareholders, not depositors whose funds are a multiple of the bank's capital. This requires special attention to the reallocation of ownership in banking. The vetting of the underlying business plan is needed. The costs of inefficient transfers of control must be avoided.

These are the considerations that preside over the rules governing concentrations in banking. They justify the requirement for the Bank of Italy's authorization and its rigorous procedures. But this in no way diminishes the value of market discipline of takeovers. The prior screening of takeovers by the Bank of Italy can increase the contestability of control, making the operation more credible. Supervisory clearance amounts to ratification of the consistency of the business plan and recognition that the financial commitment is commensurate with the post-takeover development plan. This is all the more true in the case of a hostile takeover bid for a bank. Prior screening of the operation and of the bidder's plan increases the market's confidence in the success of the transaction, without prejudice to the target bank's ability to take every legitimate defensive measure.

Under the 1990 Antitrust Law the Bank of Italy has the institutional task of safeguarding competition in the credit sector. It has done so on the three fronts envisaged by the law: screening concentrations, imposing sanctions for understandings that restrict competition and combating abuse of dominant positions.

Between 1990 and 1999 the Bank of Italy evaluated 450 proposed concentrations for antitrust purposes. Over the years, the transactions came to involve larger and larger banks. The proportion of total bank capital changing hands in Italy was one of the highest found internationally. From 1996 through 1999 the banks involved each year accounted for an average of 8 per cent of total bank assets. Concentrations were especially significant in the South of Italy, owing partly to the acquisition of control of troubled local institutions by central and northern banks. In 17 cases the Bank of Italy conducted an inquiry to determine whether the proposed transaction would create or strengthen a dominant position, materially damaging competition. In 10 cases approval was made subject to compensatory measures (sale of branches to other banks in a position to provide effective competition, ban on opening new branches) to maintain the competitive tone of the reference market (notably the provincial deposit markets).

Of the 13 inquiries which looked into agreements potentially harmful to competition, 8 reached a finding of harmfulness, resulting in a modification of the agreement between banks. Especially important were the inquiries into uniform banking rules, into unduly high charges for foreign exchange transactions, into the uniformity of charges for transactions in currencies belonging to the euro area, and that into the so-called 'friends of banking'. In this latter case, in January 2000 the Bank of Italy imposed sanctions for violations that had substantial, durable effects on fees and charges.

Five investigations for abuse of dominant position were conducted. In four cases the bank was accused of abusing its monopoly on tax collection services for improper competitive advantages in the adjacent loan markets. In the fifth, the Bank of Italy intervened to prevent the dominant bank from abusing its position to expand its branch network excessively and prevent the entry or strengthening of competitors. These typical investigations were flanked, in 1996, by an inquiry into the purported coordination of banks' pricing policies, but such coordination was not found. In 1997 a general study of corporate financial services was conducted in accord with the general Antitrust Authority.

The quantum leap in competition in the 1990s, the unfolding effects of the seeds of competition planted in the 1980s, depended on a precise development, though one that is hard to date. Competition spread from the banking product markets – loans, deposits, services – to ownership and control. It was in the early 1990s that this crucial market, until then practically non-existent, first emerged. The process involved the transformation of banks into limited companies, the stock exchange listing of a growing number of banks, and privatization.

The transformation into public limited companies was completed in 1992. Privatizations began in earnest in 1993. By 2000, 40 banks were listed on the stock exchange; with their unlisted subsidiaries, they accounted for 67 per cent of total banking assets in Italy. Another 6 banks were listed on the Mercato Ristretto. Bank shares represented a quarter of the entire Italian stock exchange, compared with between 10 and 15 per cent in the other main countries. The situation of the 1980s had been radically transformed. As late as 1991 listed banks accounted for no more than a third of total banking assets.

An essential, prime channel of competition may be mergers and acquisitions. The existence of an efficient market for corporate control, the possibility of hostile takeovers, has beneficial effects on competition. Of the 234 changes of control in banks in the United States between 1987 and 1992, only 4 were hostile takeovers. But the mere existence of the hostile takeover, the effective possibility of its occurring, has pro-competitive effects. Significant positive externalities derive from the incentives for efficient operation by the directors and controlling shareholders of potential targets. Especially when share ownership is diffuse, they know that if a hostile takeover bid is successful they will be replaced. They therefore try to run the company efficiently, to realize the objective function of the controlling shareholders, and to keep the share price from falling so low as to make a hostile takeover worthwhile.

The key changes in the share market came in 1991 with the launch of the screen-based continuous auction, together with block trading. Modernization continued with the introduction of the guarantee fund for the monthly settlement procedure (1992), the futures market (1994) and the options market (1995), and the changeover to cash settlement (completed in 1996). The 1992 laws on takeover bids and on insider trading – later reinforced by the Consolidated Law on Finance – plus the revision of proxy voting in shareholders' meetings and the new rules governing shareholders' agreements in the Consolidated Law all worked to increase the contestability of listed companies and enhance the ability of minority shareholders to defend their rights.

Market liquidity, transparency and speed of execution were all improved by the abrogation of the stockbrokers' monopoly, the liberalization of fees and the obligation to trade on-market. Since the reorganization of trading, transaction costs – the spread between the best limit buy and sell orders in the continuous auction – have been comparable to those on other European stock exchanges, and lower than the bid-ask spread on Italian securities on SEAQ International in London. British dealers, who in the late 1980s had attracted a considerable part of the stock exchange business previously done in Italy, now do part of their own trading on the Italian exchange. As a consequence the turnover in Italian securities on SEAQ, which in 1992 had equalled and in some months exceeded that on the Milan Stock Exchange, declined steadily to less than a fifth of that on the Italian market.

The reform of the government securities market in 1994, introducing the new figure of 'specialist in government securities', sharply narrowed the bid-ask spread on MTS to less than 4 basis points in 1999, and less than 3 for the most heavily traded issues. Over the same period turnover nearly quadrupled and market concentration diminished significantly. The number of active market-makers rose from the initial 7 to 28. The market share of the top 5 traders fell from 85 to 30 per cent. The Herfindahl Index of securities traded fell from 25 to 8 per cent.

Concentration in the asset management industry has diminished steadily and is now comparable to that in the United States. The Herfindahl Index stood at 4 per cent in 1997. The downtrend ceased only recently, with the onset of consolidations between major banks. Competition from foreign intermediaries is aggressive today. About half of the products supplied by the industry are offered by non-resident entities. Thanks in part to economies of scale and scope, since the end of the 1980s the operating costs of investment funds have fallen from 0.6 to 0.12 per cent of assets. Thanks to widespread competition, the reduction of costs has been largely passed on to investors in the form of lower subscription fees. These charges have fallen from 4 per cent of gross subscriptions in 1988 to 0.3 per cent, while management fees have held roughly stable at just over 1 per cent of the funds' net assets.

Competition and change

Figure 6.1 shows that between the 1980s and the 1990s there was an uninterrupted increase in competition in banking, which – given the pivotal role of the banks – is the prerequisite for competition in the financial system as a whole. Between 1981 and 1999 labour productivity in the banking industry (that is, total assets per employee at constant prices) rose by 70 per cent. Labour costs per employee (also at constant prices), which are structurally high, rose until 1992 but then held constant until 1996. In 1999 they were 9 per cent higher than in 1981. Nevertheless, the rate of profit fell from 11 per cent in the first half of the 1980s almost to zero in 1993–7.

This is the simple, incontrovertible portrait of an industry that began in conditions of inefficiency but great profitability, thanks to the lack of competition. Later this same industry, although it greatly reduced inefficiency, saw its profits trimmed by the intensification of competition both internally and externally. In particular, profits declined in the mid-1990s, even though the acceleration in productivity growth was combined with stable real labour costs.

Profits – and/or costs – would have declined earlier had they not been temporarily bolstered in the 1980s, as competition tended to drive

Figure 6.1 Productivity, labour costs and profitability in the Italian banking industry

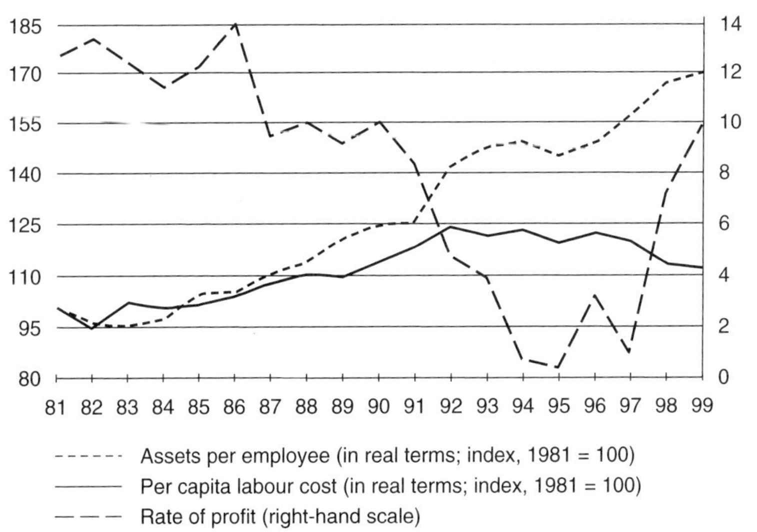

- - - - - - Assets per employee (in real terms; index, 1981 = 100)
———— Per capita labour cost (in real terms; index, 1981 = 100)
— — — Rate of profit (right-hand scale)

Source: Bank of Italy.

them down, by the substitution in bank asset portfolios of loans – more profitable but riskier – for government securities. If this were taken into account, the indicators of competition based on profitability would show a sharper drop in the 1980s and a more gradual decline in the 1990s. Above all, the competitive pressure to cut costs would have been stronger and would have come earlier had bankers not taken a temporary increase in profits to be permanent, leading them to postpone cost-cutting.

The classical, specific measure of the deviation of a market from pure competition – the difference between price and marginal cost – is the Lerner Index, that is the complement to one of the ratio of marginal cost to price. In competitive markets the index is near zero. The Lerner Index is commonly used in studies of industrial organization. The difficulty of calculating it derives from the fact that while the price of a good can be observed, to get the marginal cost one must estimate the production function or the cost function. For the banking market there are additional problems of method connected with the concept of banking product and its empirical correlatives. In banking, the Lerner Index, and indicators based on profitability in general, may depend not only on the degree of competition in the market but also on the earnings impact of general economic developments. For example, the increase in loan risk in Italy may have been a factor in the decline in earnings indices after the 1993 recession.

Figure 6.2 traces the Lerner Index for the Italian banking industry from 1984 to 1997. The curve assumes that 'product' can be proxied by total balance sheet assets and that deposits are a production input, traded in a perfectly competitive market. The price of the product coincides with the sum of total interest income and income from services, in proportion to total assets. Starting in 1993 the index shows a significant decline in market power.

The elements reviewed here indicate a clear, sharp *increase* in competition in banking and finance. The evaluations of the *level* of competition, which are less precise, show Lerner values that are now relatively low, almost always lower than those for banking and other industries in other countries. In particular, for the Italian banking system these index numbers rule out monopoly, show an appreciable degree of competition (0.2 to 0.3 on a scale running from 0, no market power, to 1, monopoly), and do not reject, statistically, the hypothesis of perfect competition.[9]

The Bank of Italy's objective over these two decades was very largely achieved: more competition, together with a good number of

Figure 6.2   Competition in the Italian banking market (Lerner Index)[a]

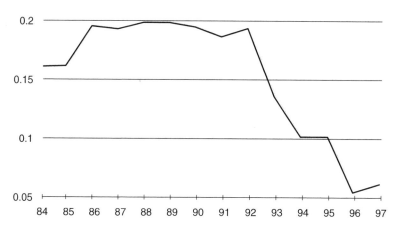

[a] Simple mean of the indices for banks operating nationwide, in the North-West, North-East, Centre and South, obtained by regression (see P. Angelini and N. Cetorelli, *Bank Competition and Regulatory Reform. The Case of the Italian Banking Industry,* Working Paper no. *32,* Federal Reserve Bank of Chicago, 1999).

concentrations and the start of a reorganization that could potentially produce greater efficiency. Competition was imposed upon a banking industry that until not too many years earlier had been largely recalcitrant. It definitely worked its effects on prices in banking, holding them down and equalizing them. However, competition must be free to unfold fully. The forces for competition continue to operate. The effects of technological innovation in telecommunications have only just begun to be felt. Privatization and the reduced availability of public support also work for more efficient arrangements. The integration of banks and markets can increase.

Through competition, the Bank of Italy aims at system efficiency. However, it cannot ensure it: producers may have insufficient capacity to respond to the competitive stimulus by cutting costs and improving products. The Bank's resolution is to proceed along the chosen path. And this not only because the rules of the Single Market require governments to act 'in accordance with the principle of an open market economy with free competition', not only because Italian law requires the simultaneous pursuit of complementary objectives, but also in the conviction that the road travelled so far is the right way to foster the progress of finance within the Italian economy.

On a more general plane, the increase in competition contributed decisively to the transformation of the Italian financial structure between 1980 and 2000. The pressure on producers that only a competitive market can exert prompted banking and financial intermediaries to adapt to the evolution of the Italian economy and international finance. However, the pressure also derived from the public policy stance, embodied in a series of laws, regulations and tax measures and in the actions of the supervisory authorities. Competition, far from constituting an obstacle to this stance, actually facilitated it. It was the legacy of lack of competition that prevailed at first, not the heightening of competition during the period, that acted as a deadweight brake on the process of change. If the initial conditions in '1980' had involved more competition, if competition itself had not been, necessarily, an intermediate policy objective, then public policy would have achieved its goals much sooner, with prompter response on the part of the financial structure – notably, even sharper price cuts – to the pressure from market demand and public action.

7
Performance

The changes in the Italian financial system whose causes and basic outcomes we have examined were structural and so mark an important advance. The old forms were incompatible with the new international trends. Above all, they corresponded to the *modus operandi* of a mixed economy undergoing a slow, contradictory but irreversible process of dissolution. But more advanced morphological arrangements, though positive *per se*, can operate with different degrees of efficiency and prove to be more or less functional to the economy. In our discussion these three levels – forms, efficiency and economic effects – are treated sequentially and separately. With this approach, our analysis can lay a better foundation for a concluding judgment and, if not predictions, at least some suggestions of the shape of things to come.

Our discussion of efficiency from the turn of the 1980s onwards, like the treatment of structures and structural change, considers Italian finance as an 'industry'. That the financial system consists of competing enterprises engaged in producing services that are mutually substitutable to a greater extent than they are with respect to other goods and services might not be sufficient for finance to be defined as an industry according to at least one of the meanings attributed to the term in economic theory.[1] Yet it will not have escaped the reader that we have used the term regularly. We have done so to signal our focus on the aspects of finance that can be assessed by considering it a separate activity, distinguishable from other sectors, independently of its interactions with the rest of the economy.

We shall therefore assess the performance of Italy's changing financial sector with the same criteria as those used to analyse the performance of any other industry: services supplied, productivity, costs, profits, organization, soundness of the capital base, exit of firms from the market.

We shall underscore the quantitative and qualitative advances achieved, but also the remaining problems and the delays in tackling them. We shall consider the two basic constituent components of the financial industry, first banks and then institutional investors and markets. The links between the financial sector and the performance of the Italian economy will be examined in the subsequent chapters.

Banks

The Italian banking system produces much more today than at the turn of the 1980s. Between 1980 and 1999 total banking assets grew six times over at current prices, nearly doubled at constant prices and rose from 116 to 136 per cent of GDP (Table 7.1). The expansion of banking activity was even greater considering that the growth in bank services outstripped that in total assets, as income from services rose from 0.26 to 0.76 per cent of assets.

Productivity has progressed along with the quantity and range of services. Since 1981 assets per employee have grown by 70 per cent at constant prices. The gain in labour productivity was particularly pronounced in the 1990s. At constant prices, assets per employee increased by 4.4 per cent per year in 1992–6 and by 4.8 per cent per year in 1996–9. The productivity increments are even greater if output is calculated including the supply of financial services, which, though not figuring among balance sheet assets, require a substantial utilization of resources. The gain came both from an advance of the efficiency frontier and from a decrease in X-inefficiency, a smaller gap between efficient production and actual production with given inputs. Recent comparative studies show that in the 5 years 1993–7 Italian banks' X-inefficiency was reduced from 24 to 14 per cent, by more than the European average, to stand at one of the lowest levels among the 15 EU national banking systems.[2]

Unit operating costs have trended downwards. As a percentage of total assets – that is not including services in output – operating expenses fell from 2.66 per cent in 1980 to 2.16 per cent in 1999. The reduction was accounted for by staff costs, which declined from 1.87 to 1.28 per cent of assets. The drive for cost savings concentrated on shrinking staff size more than on reducing costs per employee. By the end of 1999 the number of bank staff was down by 28,000, or 8.5 per cent, from its 1993 peak of 335,500 (compared with 278,200 in 1980). Incentives for the early departure of employees near retirement age cost banks 2.2 trillion lire between 1997 and 1999.

Table 7.1 Profit and loss accounts and total assets of Italian banks

Main items of profit and loss accounts (as a percentage of total assets)

	Net interest income	Net non-interest income			Gross income	Operating expenses		Operating profit	Value adjustments and provisions		Profit		Return on equity	Total assets		
		Total	Trading	Services		Total	Staff costs		Total	On loans	Gross	Net		Billions of current lire	q Billions of 1995 lire q	As a % of GDP
1980	3.43	0.85	0.45	0.26	4.28	2.66	1.87	1.63	1.16	0.47	0.47	0.22	9.40	450 332	1 455 454	116.5
1981	3.60	1.07	0.57	0.33	4.68	2.66	1.84	2.02	1.38	0.50	0.64	0.33	12.70	526 637	1 427 007	113.9
1982	3.42	1.12	0.61	0.31	4.54	2.72	1.78	1.82	1.02	0.56	0.81	0.38	13.50	613 029	1 427 375	112.7
1983	3.56	1.05	0.51	0.31	4.61	2.95	2.02	1.66	0.82	0.48	0.84	0.40	12.50	707 756	1 433 836	111.7
1984	3.42	1.12	0.57	0.31	4.54	2.85	1.92	1.69	0.81	0.43	0.87	0.43	11.46	808 985	1 481 875	111.5
1985	3.22	1.18	0.60	0.34	4.40	2.76	1.86	1.64	0.67	0.33	0.96	0.49	12.36	945 159	1 594 048	116.1
1986	3.42	1.29	0.66	0.38	4.71	2.84	1.83	1.87	0.56	0.39	1.30	0.64	13.90	1 022 014	1 624 126	113.5
1987	3.21	1.09	0.48	0.32	4.29	2.83	1.81	1.46	0.50	0.37	0.96	0.52	9.68	1 129 593	1 716 498	114.7
1988	3.28	1.07	0.50	0.30	4.35	2.75	1.78	1.60	0.55	0.19	1.05	0.56	9.93	1 240 803	1 796 079	113.5
1989	3.24	0.95	0.41	0.25	4.19	2.62	1.73	1.57	0.56	0.52	1.01	0.50	9.05	1 397 449	1 898 063	116.8
1990	3.29	1.02	0.52	0.18	4.31	2.67	1.75	1.64	0.59	0.55	1.05	0.57	9.96	1 547 585	1 981 061	117.2
1991	3.22	0.99	0.50	0.14	4.22	2.73	1.78	1.48	0.49	0.52	0.99	0.51	8.37	1 707 573	2 053 136	118.5
1992	3.20	0.70	0.24	0.10	3.90	2.57	1.64	1.33	0.57	0.49	0.76	0.33	4.82	2 035 715	2 323 080	134.1
1993	2.89	1.15	0.63	0.23	4.04	2.46	1.54	1.58	0.70	0.73	0.87	0.24	3.64	2 249 923	2 463 186	143.9
1994	2.54	0.89	0.26	0.30	3.44	2.36	1.53	1.08	0.83	0.51	0.28	0.05	0.73	2 365 680	2 491 789	143.1
1995	2.69	0.86	0.25	0.27	3.55	2.42	1.54	1.14	0.78	0.68	0.36	0.03	0.39	2 410 102	2 409 138	134.8
1996	2.54	1.04	0.38	0.30	3.58	2.39	1.54	1.19	0.69	0.49	0.50	0.18	3.17	2 538 141	2 443 339	133.4
1997	2.26	1.09	0.29	0.42	3.35	2.31	1.44	1.05	0.72	0.59	0.33	0.04	1.04	2 685 298	2 539 529	135.4
1998	2.12	1.42	0.32	0.63	3.54	2.14	1.31	1.40	0.49	0.47	0.90	0.46	7.37	2 819 345	2 621 184	136.4
1999	1.95	1.64	0.16	0.76	3.59	2.16	1.28	1.43	0.40	0.42	1.03	0.62	9.95	2 887 092	2 641 197	135.7

Source: Bank of Italy.

Despite the notable progress that Italian banks made in boosting output and productivity and curbing unit labour costs, they suffered a fall in gross and net profit. The decline in the indicators of profitability was especially sharp in the 1990s. In the first half of the 1980s banks had managed to increase their profits thanks to limited losses on their loan and securities portfolios; the rate of growth in both assets and operating profit was low. Subsequently, the maintenance of profitability was made possible by the expansion in lending, albeit with decreasing average returns, and by lower average funding costs.

The evaluations assigned by the Bank of Italy to the banks under its supervision deteriorated perceptibly between 1990 and 1993. The share of total assets attributable to banks receiving a positive evaluation fell from 70 to 40 per cent. In 1995–7 it fell further, to 34 per cent, before rebounding to 45 per cent in 1998–9. Banks receiving unfavourable supervisory evaluations accounted for 8 per cent of total assets in 1990, 18 per cent in 1993 and between 19 and 24 per cent in 1995–9. More and more, the banks where marked anomalies were found during the 1990s left the market. In 1999 supervisory evaluations registered a sharp improvement from the preceding year, owing mainly to the better earnings posted by several large groups. The share of total assets attributable to banks with a favourable supervisory rating rose from 40 to 51 per cent, that of banks with unfavourable ratings dipped to 22 per cent; the number of banks (other than mutual banks) classified as anomalous declined from 77 to 64, one-third of which belonged to banking groups with a positive technical situation. The changes in evaluation scores in the last two years of the decade showed that an important part of the system was returning to high levels of soundness and stability. In parallel, there was a sharper differentiation between the banks that had achieved progress and the mostly small institutions that had not made the strategic and organizational changes needed to face competition.

Between the 1980s and the 1990s, banks' gross operating result fell on average from 1.7 to 1.3 per cent of total assets; gross profit and net profit declined respectively from 0.9 to 0.7 and from 0.5 to 0.2 per cent of total assets. The return on equity, after fluctuating around 12 per cent between 1980 and 1986, plunged to just above 1 per cent in the four years from 1994 to 1997. In 1998–9, in connection with the rapid growth of asset management services and capital gains, it bounced back to almost 10 per cent. This brought it more into line with the level of that in the other main banking systems of continental Europe. Higher rates of return are found in the Anglo-Saxon countries (25 per cent for the top ten British banks in 1994–2000). These benefit from a faster-growing economy and from belonging to highly developed financial systems with ramifications throughout the world. In addition, they take larger risks.

The erosion of bank profitability in the 1990s was due to loan losses, which rose to 0.6 per cent of total assets, from 0.4 per cent in the 1980s. Following the performance of the economy with variable lags, bad debts were relatively high at the start of the 1990s (5 per cent of the stock of outstanding loans). They rose rapidly following the recession of 1993 to reach 10 per cent in 1996, the peak for the two decades under review. Their ensuing decline brought the ratio of risk on the loan portfolio back to normal values. However, the main factor eroding profits was the downward pressure of mounting competition on the prices of banking products and services. The sharper competition, a closer confrontation with foreign banks operating on a larger scale, and narrower spreads significantly reduced the contribution of traditional banking business to profits. The decline in net interest income, underway for years and intensified by the introduction of the euro, was not entirely offset by increased income from innovative activities: financial advisory services and assistance for firms, asset administration and management for households, securities operations in the international markets.

The hammer of competition, as it were, crushed profits against the anvil of operating expenses, notably wages and social security contributions, which were not curbed expeditiously owing to the rigidity of labour law, the resistance offered by the trade unions and the insufficient propensity of bank managements to overcome them. Banks' labour costs per employee rose from 35 million lire in 1981 to 100 million in 1992, or by 21 per cent at constant prices. Since then, they have remained high in real terms. The ineffectiveness of the measures in containing labour costs per employee in the 1980s as competition began to intensify is at least partly explained by the fact that bank profitability was temporarily sustained by the substitution of loans for bonds in a context of rising bond prices (declining interest rates). Partly as a consequence of the ceiling on the growth in bank lending, the ratio of securities portfolios to the aggregate of securities portfolios and lending peaked at 37 per cent in 1983. Thereafter it declined swiftly to 21 per cent in 1991. Other conditions being equal, this change in the composition of assets, through the higher return on lending than on securities and the dealing profits and capital gains on securities portfolios, is estimated to have increased the return on equity of the banking system by around 3 percentage points on average for the period.

Labour costs per employee, calculated using the irrevocable conversion rates of national currencies into euros, were equal to €61 100 in 1996, 30 per cent higher than the average for France, Germany and Spain

(€55,000, €43,300 and €41,500 respectively). In 1998 they fell to €59,000, with some €3,400 of the decrease due to the abolition of national health service contributions, which were incorporated into the regional tax on productive activities (Irap). The disadvantage *vis-à-vis* the average of the other three main banking systems in the euro area narrowed to 17 per cent (€60,200 in France, €46,800 in Germany and €44 300 in Spain); 7 percentage points of this reduction came from the abolition of health service contributions. In November 1999 the new national labour contract for the banking industry took effect (the old contract had expired in 1997). The new settlement provided for a 2.5 per cent wage increase over 2000 and 2001 and for measures designed to curb automatic increments and to make the use of labour more flexible.

Compared with their counterparts in the other European countries, Italian banks' profits are squeezed by a congeries of external diseconomies that are beyond their control and whose repercussions they can only seek to limit. Special costs arise from the tax and social contributions system, from labour law and from specific features of the local business environment, the latter notably in connection with enforcement proceedings, bankruptcy revocations, the demands of security, and the tax agency activity and anti-crime procedures. By one estimate, these reduced banks' return on equity by as much as 5 percentage points in 1998.[3] Irap, less overstaffing and the new labour contract may reduce the tax and labour-law handicap. The costs relating to the business environment are perhaps less high, but also less easily reduced. The problem exists; its importance cannot be denied.

Nevertheless, the average ratio of capital to risk assets has risen to 13 per cent, well above the 8 per cent minimum envisaged by the Basel Capital Accord. Only a few banks have solvency ratios lower than 8 per cent and the capital shortfalls are modest, totalling around 500 billion lire. This strengthening of banks' capital base has been achieved at the urging of the Bank of Italy, despite the fall in profits, through greater recourse to equity capital. The annual amount of equity funds raised by banks was 4.3 trillion lire in 1990–3, 4.5 trillion in 1994–6 and 8.7 trillion in 1997–9. New issues by listed banks were accompanied by initial public offerings, with the number of listed banks virtually doubling in the course of the decade. Cumulatively, 41 trillion lire of the increase in banks' capital in 1990–9 came from self-financing and 57 trillion from recourse to the market and to private- and public-sector shareholders.

The competitive pressures, declining gross income, financial innovation and the repercussions of the 1993 recession required a response from intermediaries. This response was fashioned on three interrelated fronts that were carefully monitored by the Bank of Italy: the strengthening of strategies for market penetration, the revision of organizational structures and control systems, and the improvement of risk management.

The integrated supply of services aims at higher, more stable profits. A close relationship with firms is a competitive, commercial and informational must. The development of relationship banking and corporate banking demands segmentation of the customer base to identify higher-value-added segments, the measurement of performance according to product and customer, and a judicious pricing policy.

Organizational change was directed towards streamlining central management, coordinating the different channels of distribution and differentiating production processes according to customer segment. Credit committees were established at bank headquarters, to increase internal discussion and enhance the role of the technical element in lending decisions. Special units were set up for the review and evaluation of credit relationships for large firms, groups, small and medium-sized enterprises, and households.

Credit disbursement is being separated from risk control. The major banks are creating risk management units entrusted with default forecasting techniques, loan screening, performance measurement, and the risk-adjusted pricing of loans. More sophisticated computer procedures are being introduced for the use of data on borrowers, to forestall possible non-performing positions. The aim of risk management at portfolio level is served by the establishment of goals for lending growth by sector or area that take account of their respective contributions to overall risk and profitability. The spread of methods such as internal ratings and the use of risk management techniques such as credit derivatives and securitization can further this end.

The last-mentioned process is still at a very early stage, according to a Basel Committee survey of the major international banks, including the largest Italian institutions. In Italian banks the rating reflects the evaluation of the counterparty, consistently with the findings of the survey. The type of transaction plays a role in loss quantification. About half the banks use a single system for all firms, while the others consider at least two types of portfolios (large corporate and middle market). Rating systems are being introduced for retail and small business customers, a field where the lesser complexity of transactions permits greater use of statistical techniques for predicting defaults. The share of loans covered by rating systems is also growing as a consequence of the progress made by individual banks on specific portions of the portfolio. All in all, the number of risk classes for the stratification of the portfolio is consistent with that reported by the international survey. The banks need to step up the creation of archives permitting them to estimate the portion of the exposure at risk of loss by type of transaction and guarantee on the basis of historical experience. In some banks rating systems are used to determine credit limits; they are still rarely used to decide pricing and provisioning policies and the allocation of capital among operating units.

Evaluation of borrowers' creditworthiness, lending criteria and risk control: these are banks' classic functions and they remain crucial for finance and for the entire economy. How banks perform them was the subject of a wide-ranging special survey that the Bank of Italy conducted in 1982–3, making use of comparative methods and field studies, among other techniques. The conclusion the survey reached was that

> the lending policy of Italian banks tends to be guided by valid general criteria . . . In many cases financial intermediaries are carrying out or preparing significant corporate programmes with a view to making loan evaluation and management more rational and efficient.[4]

This judgment was benevolently shaded and meant to solicit future progress. Since then, albeit unevenly across the system, with some banks well advanced and others lagging behind, there has been a substantial strengthening in the resources, instruments and organization of the apparatus with which Italian banks manage loans and seek the desired balance between expected return and risk.

Most of the bank mergers carried out between 1985 and 1996 involved small and medium institutions and were aimed at expanding the supply of services through the branch networks and the relationships of the acquired institutions. Thanks to more efficient use of capital and a reduction in tax liabilities, the banks involved registered a higher return on equity, albeit without an improvement in their return on assets. Income from services grew, compensating for higher labour costs.

By contrast, the more recent concentrations have involved larger banks. The earnings results are encouraging. The rise in bank shares shows that the market has priced in the benefits these operations are expected to bring.

Italian banks have shown their ability to compete with other intermediaries within Italy. So far they have preserved their role in savings intermediation by supplying new services. The bulk of investment funds and individual portfolio management accounts are attributable to them, directly or through subsidiaries. The bank is the chosen form for the supply of high value-added services both on the part of newly formed intermediaries and by existing intermediaries that decide to continue their activity by transforming themselves into banks. However, Italian banks' strategic repositioning and organizational overhaul has not yet been sufficient to bring them into line with the operating conditions and levels of profitability prevailing in the euro area.

The need to recoup profitability spurred Italian banks in the 1990s to adopt new group arrangements patterned on two models: 'federal' and 'multi-specialist'. The federal model, an extreme version of the multi-function group, separates production from distribution and seeks to exploit the particular strengths of the companies of the conglomerate and their links with local customers. Federal groups are generally structured as follows: a bank holding company responsible for group governance and direct management of business areas (international, treasury and finance, large customers); a number of legally independent units, specialized by product, channel (telephone bank, financial salesmen) and territorial market (subsidiary commercial banks); and one or more companies providing centralized instrumental services to all the units of the conglomerate (information systems, purchasing and logistics, low-value-added procedures, back office, credit recovery). By contrast, in the multi-specialist model, closer to that of the universal bank, the activities of the acquired companies are incorporated directly into the acquiring bank. Within the same legal entity separate divisions are created according to customer or product segment, although the match is not one-for-one. The two models also have some features in common: centralization of production processes with economies of scale; orientation of the networks to achieve commercial objectives; definition of the business units' operating scope and goals; decentralization into operating areas and evaluation of the results (return on allocated capital).

The ascendancy of the group models and the all-purpose bank does not mean there are no longer banks that choose to pursue a specialized mission. The continuing importance of specialization is attested by the birth of banks operating in niche markets (leasing, consumer credit, home mortgage lending, securities intermediation, distribution through networks of financial salesmen, internet and telephone banking). Many of these institutions are former financial companies that acquire a banking licence for the advantages in terms of reputation, image and access to the interbank market. In addition, some smaller traditional banks that remained independent have become niche players in regional markets.

The composition of the leading European banking groups has changed as a consequence of the wave of mergers. Of the top 15 euro-area commercial banks with total banking assets of more than €140 million at the end of 1998, 4 were German, 3 French, 3 Italian, 2 Dutch, 2 Spanish and 1 Belgian. Their return on equity that year averaged 11.9 per cent (10.4 per cent for the three Italian institutions). However, not one of the three Italian banks received a top rating from the main rating agencies in the first four months of 2000. In the market's view, therefore, an Italian bank that ranks at the top of the international scale has yet to emerge.

The accentuation of competition has hit the system's weak links, the relatively inefficient banks or those established in the 'less fertile lands' within Italy's historically dualistic economy, thereby increasing the disparities of performance across banks. An examination of several performance indicators of the sample of more than 100 banks that sent 10-day reports to the Bank of Italy in the 1990s confirms this. On average, operating costs in relation to gross income fell from a mid-decade peak of 68 per cent to 60 per cent in 1999, similar to the low registered in 1986. In 1994–9 the ratio of staff costs to gross income followed a similar trend. The ratio of net interest income to total assets fell from 3.3 per cent in the early 1990s to 1.9 per cent in 1999, while that of gross income diminished by less than 1 percentage point. Operating profit amounted to 1.22 per cent of total assets in 1999, slightly above the low levels touched between 1994 and 1997. After peaking at 1.4 per cent in 1993, the ratio of loan losses to total lending fell to 0.8 per cent at the end of the decade. The rate of return on equity, which had fallen to very low levels between 1994 and 1997, rebounded in the last two years of the decade; however, at 9.4 per cent in 1999, it was still far short of the 13–14 per cent range it had attained in the second half of the 1980s.

For this same sample of banks the distribution by quartiles reveals the increasing importance of the overall activities of the banks in the second and third quartiles for the ratio of gross income to total assets. The importance of the banks in the lowest quartile for gross income diminished. The ratio of loan losses to total lending is marked by high dispersion. Between 1993 and 1999 the banks of the first quartile, whose loan loss rate was half the system-wide average in 1993 (0.7 per cent against 1.4 per cent), saw this rate fall further in relative terms. However, their total assets declined from 34 to 27 per cent of the aggregate. The banks of the second quartile exhibited a similar trend. The loan loss rate of the banks of third quartile decreased by more than a percentage point, approaching the system-wide average, while their share of system-wide assets rose by more than 20 percentage points to stand at 40 per cent at the end of 1999. Lastly, the banks with the highest ratios of loan losses to total lending recorded a declining share of system-wide assets, especially in the final year.

Most of the banks that experienced the largest increase in defaults operated primarily in the South, whose economy was going through a phase of renewed, pronounced weakness. In the 1990s the annual rate of economic growth in the South fell to 0.9 per cent. The crisis of public and private construction, together with the reduction of state subsidies, weighed heaviest on the southern economy. In 1996 the ratio of bad debts to total loans reached 24 per cent in the South, compared with just 7 per cent in the rest of Italy. At the end of that year the bad debt ratio of banks based in the Centre and North on loans made in the South was one-fifth, lower than that of the southern banks but far higher than their default rates in their home markets. However, the lesser ability of the southern banks to select borrowers is also shown by the high incidence of loss assets on their lending in the Centre and North (a bad debt ratio of 10 per cent).

When the Bank of Italy arranges for a troubled bank to be taken over by another institution, its financial intervention involves a transfer of resources to the acquiring bank as compensation for the costs incurred.

These criteria were followed in dealing with the crises of southern banks, including large institutions with an ancient heritage. Systemic crisis of the kind other countries have experienced was averted. The solutions adopted safeguarded the banking business or part of the business, not the businessman. They led to the loss of equity capital, modification of ownership structures, changes of top management and derivative actions. Where ownership of a troubled bank was transferred, the acquiring bank was chosen from among those that had expressed interest in taking over the whole of the business, to which they attributed a positive operational value. For the banks with goodwill worth less than the shortfall of assets, the transfers were made possible by the support of the deposit-guarantee systems.

Public intervention was necessary in the failure of two major banks that could not be handled by the private guarantee systems. In one case, the Ministerial Decree of 27 September 1974 was applied under a specific statutory provision (article 3 of Law 588/1996). This permitted the instrument to be used without opening the procedure for the compulsory administrative liquidation of the bank, in the context of a detailed plan for restructuring, rehabilitation and privatization. In the second case, the 'restorative' measures were ordered by the Bank of Italy on the basis of straightforward application of the Ministerial Decree. A resolution of the Interministerial Committee for Credit and Savings confirmed that the general good was at stake, a prerequisite for public intervention. The solution of the crisis entailed the compulsory administrative liquidation of the bank and the transfer of assets and liabilities. The European Commission imposed compensating measures in both of these cases.

The series of interventions produced a radical change in the owner-ship structure of the southern banking system. At the end of 1997 banks based in the Centre and North held 73 per cent of deposits and 80 per cent of loans in the South, directly or by means of their control of southern banks.

The southern banking crisis coincided with difficulties for the banking systems of other industrial countries. In some cases these involved sys-temic disequilibria; in others the weaknesses were limited to individual banks, including some very large ones. The repercussions on economic activity and government budgets were heavy at times. Thanks in part to the preventive supervisory action taken by the Bank of Italy according to the criteria and with the instruments described in Chapter 5, the cost of public intervention to prevent systemic repercussions due to crisis of individual intermediaries was much lower in Italy than in other countries in the 1990s. The cost to the Italian public finances was less than 1 per cent of one year's economic output (1999), compared with approximately 2 per cent in France and Norway, 3 per cent in Japan, 5 per cent in Sweden and 9 per cent in Finland. Bank failures, not limited to the savings and loans, cost the US government 5 per cent of GDP in the 1980s. In the same decade the burden placed by bank instability on the public finances exceeded 15 per cent of one year's output in Spain.

Institutional investors and markets

The high cost of directly administering a multitude of relatively small individual portfolios whose aggregate amount is gigantic make it more advantageous for resources to be entrusted to professional investors for management. The ability of institutional investors to spread the fixed costs of running a securities portfolio over a wide base and to use sophisticated techniques gives savers access to portfolio management more efficient than direct investment.

The supply of asset management products has been expanding rapidly since the mid-1980s. In 1999 the 2,200 investment funds marketed in Italy and the more than 200 intermediaries offering individual port-folio management services (typically with more than one product line) administered assets worth nearly 1.5 trillion lire. As in other countries, the number of products has grown faster than the number of operators. The average manager of an investment fund or SICAV offers more than 20 funds or sub-funds. The variety of the content of asset management services makes the intermediary similar to a multi-product firm, continually introducing elements of differentiation in its supply. This has not impeded a gradual diminution in costs as a percentage of assets under management. Nevertheless, the costs borne by Italian savers are still higher than those in the other main European countries, albeit by a small margin.

Between 1994 and 1997 subscription fees fell from 4.05 to 0.34 per cent of gross funds raised. Management fees fluctuated in a narrow range of between 1.22 and 1.26 per cent of net assets, 0.2 percentage points above the European average. In a ranking embracing 19 European countries and 5 international financial centres, the average management fees charged by funds in Italy were lower only than those in Spain. The frequency distribution of Italian funds' management fees was more highly concentrated, with a standard deviation of 0.3 per cent. The extra cost with respect to the European average was slightly higher for equity funds (1.54 against 1.30 per cent). It is significant for the more standardized products such as money-market funds (0.92 against 0.73 per cent).

The sector's expansion and international opening-up are the keys to the convergence of Italian managers' costs with those found abroad. There is scope for further reduction, in part through economies of scale. The net assets managed by the average management company grew from €1.9 billion to €8.8 billion between 1995 and 1999.

On a risk-adjusted basis the average yield achieved by Italian managers and passed on to savers is in line with that achievable by investing in a well-diversified portfolio of financial instruments. The value added of management service lies not in the ability of managers to beat the market, risks being equal, but in offering savers the opportunity to achieve the desired portfolio diversification at less expense. The increasing popularity in the United States of passively managed and indexed products, with low management expenses, is evidence that the demand for diversification is an important component of the service savers request from intermediaries.

The transparency of fees is high, especially when investment funds are compared with other forms of investment. To improve it further, provision has been made for the inclusion of more detailed information in prospectuses. In compliance with Consob regulations, since 1999 investment fund prospectuses have contained a benchmark shedding additional light on the fund's choices and performance.

The growth in activity on the part of institutional investors has been paralleled by the development of the financial markets. The reforms aimed at better management of the public debt and more effective implementation of monetary policy based on the use of indirect instruments have enhanced the functionality of the government securities and money markets. In the equity market, the important changes of the 1990s were prompted by heightened competition among Europe's stock exchanges. The growing use of derivatives has contributed to the efficiency of the markets. The effort over the years to build and reorganize the Italian financial marketplace has succeeded in giving it modern arrangements, in keeping with the size of the Italian economy. The birth of Euro.MTS, the first European-wide market for euro-area government bond trading, and the enlargement of the MID interbank deposit market (extended to derivatives) to include the operators of the euro area, testify to the international competitiveness acquired in a few short years by Italy's trading infrastructure.

The progress of the secondary market in government securities has been accompanied by important innovations in placement techniques on the primary market: the abolition of the floor price for short-term issues (1988) and medium- and long-term issues (1992), recourse to the 'reopening' of auctions, the undertaking by the Treasury to maintain a regular flow of medium- and long-term fixed-rate securities, the tendency to limit the range of issues to a few standard types.

In contrast with the MTS electronic government securities market, after a brilliant start the MIF and MTO markets in derivatives based on Italian government securities have steadily lost ground to their counterpart in London (LIFFE). In 1991 the latter, together with France's MATIF, had created the first futures contract on 10-year Italian government bonds. The initiative came just a few years after the issue of 10-year bonds by the Treasury, which had ceased issuing fixed-term securities of such long maturity at the end of the 1960s. Unlike MTS, which had no foreign rivals when it was launched and whose subsequent growth was essentially uncontested, the MIF futures market faced the competition of LIFFE (set up in 1982 by the City's leading operators) and MATIF (created in 1985), both of them well established among international dealers. By 1999 MIF's market share, initially equal to that of LIFFE, had fallen below one-fifth. The Italian market's lack of success has been due partly to the particular comparative advantage enjoyed by the London market: the wide range of listed contracts on the leading bond issues and interest rates of the world financial market. The latter feature is especially appreciated by the participants most active in the derivative market, who operate on a global scale. Consequently, MIF has been confined to satisfying a minor segment of demand, that of less internationally active Italian operators.

By contrast, MTS is in the van internationally for its organization and efficiency. Average daily turnover rose from around 300 billion lire in 1988 to more than 18 trillion in 1999. The bid-ask spread is very narrow; in 1999 it averaged less than 4 basis points. Repos have been traded on MTS since the end of 1997 in the form of general collateral contracts and special repos (on specific securities). Average daily turnover exceeds 38 trillion lire. The market's operating efficiency and its privatization have favoured its opening-up internationally. More than 200 Italian and foreign intermediaries are members of the market, 22 of them operating also by remote access with a 25 per cent market share. Prominent among the most active dealers are the 16 'specialists', who account for 65 per cent of total trading. The Italian 'specialists' are the leaders in terms of their trading volume and contribution to the liquidity of the market (bid-ask spread and number of securities handled).

The composition of the stock exchange official list has improved. Many of the private companies that have gone public are industrial firms and not members of already-listed groups. 56 of the 74 companies that made IPOs in 1995–9 were independent; 46 had a market value of less than €200 million at the time of listing. The average age of newly listed companies has diminished. Fund-raising in the market is increasingly intended to finance new investments with capital increases. In 1999 the ratio of turnover to the market's capitalization was close to 1.5.

The growth of derivative products has contributed. In 1999 the Italian market in stock futures ranked second in Europe by trading volume. Foreign investors hold more than 8 per cent of the shares listed. They are more active in the derivatives market, accounting for one-third of all trades.

Non-financial enterprises are less important in the stock exchange in Italy than in other countries. They account for 63 per cent of total market capitalization, compared with 70 per cent in Germany, 75 per cent in the United Kingdom and 85 per cent in France.

Between 1992 and 1999 the Italian stock exchange's turnover ratio (value of trades/capitalization) rose from 30 to 150 per cent, in line with the level of the most advanced markets. Stock market capitalization has also increased considerably, from its low for the decade in 1992 to 65 per cent of GDP. However, the number of listed companies, their size and the extent to which they represent the economy as a whole remain smaller than in the other main industrial countries. The choices available to investors are further restricted by two specific factors. The high concentration of ownership limits diversification and reduces the actual size of the float, and the vast majority of listed securities continue to have very scant liquidity. In fact, three-quarters of all trades are in the 30 securities comprising the MIB30 index.

At the end of 1999 the proportion of the value of shares held by the market (holdings of less than 2 per cent of a company's share capital) had fallen to 48 per cent of total stock market capitalization. In the more recent privatizations the market judged the widespread ownership model to be inefficient and promoted initiatives to concentrate control. The proportion of market capitalization owned by listed companies rose from 19 per cent in 1998 to 25 per cent in 1999 as a consequence of the growth of controlling shareholdings. As a result of the spread of alliances, many listed companies are part of a web of cross-holdings.

Where institutional investors are lacking, ownership is more concentrated. The widely held company is a sustainable model if there is substantial investment in equities on the part of operators such as pension funds and insurance companies, which are more effective in exercising a function of stimulus and control on the management. Their absence favours corporate governance systems in which independent directors are few and the holding of multiple directorships common. In Italy, directors of listed companies who sit on the boards of more than one company not belonging to the same group are numerous. The boards of 175 companies are involved. Directors who sit on more than one board hold about a third of the directorships of those companies. This does little to foster aggressive policies of marketing and acquisitions, even if executed in less than brilliant fashion. The market for control is less lively, the ownership model based on large shareholders self-perpetuating.

On the whole, however, intensified competition and market participants' greater internal efficiency have contributed to the sharp operational and informational improvement of Italy's financial markets. The configuration and organization of the securities markets underpin the substantial gains of the financial system in operating efficiency. By international standards, the Italian system's functionality is state-of-the-art. The low cost of trading, the possibility of continuous trading throughout the day and the ability to contribute decisively to the price discovery function, characteristic of the different market segments, are all well documented.

As regards informational efficiency, the ability of securities prices to incorporate the information contained in past prices – weak-form efficiency – was pointed up by studies made beginning in the 1970s. Since then, the improvements achieved in the working of the markets with the growth of institutional investors, the introduction of rules for correct and transparent corporate disclosure and the entry of highly professional foreign intermediaries have enabled the share and bond markets to attain ever-greater efficiency. Recent studies show the ability of securities prices to incorporate both information disseminated among the public (semi-strong-form efficiency) and information developed by specialized operators such as investment funds (strong-form efficiency).

Since the end of 1994 the introduction of new derivatives markets (futures and options) has helped to reduce the volatility of the spot market. The portion of spot-market yield variance explained by the behaviour of futures contracts has increased over time. The gain in informational efficiency is also shown by the consolidation of a significant negative correlation between the volumes traded on the futures market and the variability of prices on the spot market. Similar indications are provided by econometric studies of intraday data. The impulses originating from the derivatives market are swiftly transmitted. A very close correspondence is established within just one minute between the changes in the price of stock index futures and that of the underlying basket of securities.

Following the reforms, the indicators based on the public trading data distributed to market participants have become less effective in predicting the daily performance of the market. For the most heavily traded securities their efficacy is negligible, while for the less liquid shares informational efficiency can still improve. The findings of recent empirical studies of the forecasting power of the indicators of market sentiment, such as the discount implicit in the market valuation of holding companies,[5] suggest the persistence of imperfections in informational efficiency.

The financial industry: advances and lags

The Italian banking system has expanded its volume and range of intermediation and services, raised productivity and reduced unit costs, strengthened its capital base, improved loan and risk management, eliminated inefficient companies without upsets, carried out mergers and organizational restructurings, and seen the emergence of several large groups, three of which rank among the largest in Europe.

However, bad debts have increased, per capita labour costs remain among the highest in Europe, there is still scope for improving the quality and profitability of some services, and the Italian banking system's international presence could be further enhanced with top-flight groups. Under the pressure of rapidly rising competition, in the 1990s Italian banks' return on equity was low, below that of other advanced banking systems. This remains true even taking account of the negative externalities of various origins that weigh heavier on Italian banks than on foreign competitors.

At the same time, institutional investors have gained a place and the markets have attained significant size and made remarkable progress in terms of both organizational and informational efficiency. It is noteworthy that these developments have occurred despite the persistence of traditional financial habits among Italian households and firms. There has been a radical reorientation of the Italian financial system, historically centred on banks and intermediaries, towards markets and institutions that are integrally bound up with markets.

The limitations of this process are threefold. European monetary integration, moving towards continent-wide markets through the complex interplay of coordination, alliance and competition, has caught the Italian institutions at varying stages of readiness amidst a delicate transition from public to private, from one legal order to another one, from a smaller to a larger scale. Institutional investors and market structures are still all but totally controlled by the banks. In this sense the system remains bank-centred; indeed, it has become even more so. This has potentially negative implications for the system's diversification and effective openness to departures from the old ways. Above all, the ranks of institutional investors still essentially lack pension funds, which could contribute not only a vast pool of resources for long-term investment but also positive stimulus for corporate governance, an expression of financial capital, which is different from industrial capital but also from bank capital. The Italian economy, the banking system itself and the market's structures reflect this shortcoming in several respects.

8
A Stagnant Economy

Inflation in Italy was gradually brought down during the 1980s and then almost completely eliminated in the second half of the 1990s. Since 1993 the current account of the balance of payments has been in surplus. The external debt was gradually reduced and Italy became a creditor country. Since 1995 the public debt, although still enormous, has shown a clear downward trend in relation to GDP. After it re-entered the EMS in 1996, the lira did not fluctuate significantly with respect to the other European currencies. Italy adopted the euro when it was introduced at the beginning of 1999. A 'culture of stability', which seemed lost, has revived.

These valuable results in the government of the monetary and financial aspects of the economy have been accompanied, however, by a decline in the GDP growth rate, which was particularly unsatisfactory in the 1990s.

This chapter briefly sets out a belief: that the mediocre growth of the economy has been due to the slowness of the transition from a mixed economy to a market economy and to the crushing burden of public debt accumulated in the 1980s; that the banking and financial system has not caused the stagnation but rather has suffered its adverse effects.

The stagnation of the Italian economy in the 1990s

After accomplishing the 'economic miracle', Italian growth decelerated in each decade that passed. From 1950 to 1969 GDP expanded at a record average annual rate of 6 per cent. Since then the slowdown has been continuous and significant: growth averaged 3.6 per cent in the 1970s, 2.4 per cent in the 1980s and just 1.4 per cent in the 1990s. Similar slowdowns have occurred in other countries that reached maturity in the postwar period, but Italy's has been the most pronounced. The European Union significantly underperformed the United States in the 1990s, but even so the average slowdown in Italy's growth rate compared with the 1980s was one percentage point, as against one-third of a point for the Union. Thus one of Europe's most dynamic economies has become one of the most sluggish; Italy's low rate of economic expansion in the 1990s puts it last, together with Sweden, in the ranking of EU countries (Table 8.1). Turning to per capita income and putting the European average (including the relatively poor East Germany) equal to 100, Italy's score was 105 in 1991; according to Community estimates, it had fallen to 99 in 2000. As regards the output gap, the 1990s was the worst decade since the unification of Italy. The growth rate of 1.4 per cent was not far from the minimum of 0.7 per cent recorded in the second and third decades of Italy's history (the 1870s and 1880s). At that time, however, the growth of potential output was much slower than today and, given the predominantly agricultural nature of the economy, much closer to that of actual output. Various estimates have been made of the growth irreparably lost in the 1990s, and it is certainly substantial, on the order of several percentage points of potential GDP.[1] Focusing

Table 8.1   GDP growth, trend growth of per capita GDP and output gap in the EU countries in the 1990s (annual averages)

	GDP growth 1990–9	*Trend growth of per capita GDP 1990–8*	*Output gap[a] 1991–9*
Ireland	6.7	5.6	0.4
Luxembourg	4.9	4.0	n.a.
Netherlands	2.9	2.1	0.1
Portugal	2.9	2.5	−0.2
Spain	2.4	2.2	−0.5
Denmark	2.4	2.1	−0.8
Germany	2.2	0.9	−0.4
Austria	2.2	1.7	0.3
Belgium	2.0	1.7	−0.6
Greece	1.9	1.3	−1.2
United Kingdom	1.9	1.8	−0.6
France	1.7	1.2	−1.5
Finland	1.6	1.3	−4.0
Sweden	1.4	0.9	−2.4
Italy	1.4	1.3	−1.5
European Union	2.0	n.a.	−0.9

[a] Difference between actual output and potential output as a percentage of the latter.
Sources: OECD and national statistics.

on the three five-year periods since 1985 brings out the structural nature of the slowdown in the Italian economy's growth even more clearly. In the 1985–9 sub-period the average annual growth rate was 3.1 per cent in Italy and 3.2 per cent in Europe. In the next sub-period, which includes the 1993 recession, the rate fell to 1.1 per cent in Italy and 1.6 per cent in Europe. After a short-lived recovery in 1995, when Italian GDP grew by 2.9 per cent (the highest rate of the 1990s, fostered by the devaluation of the lira), in the period 1996–9 the average annual expansion of the Italian economy amounted to no more than 1.4 per cent, compared with 2.2 per cent for Europe as a whole.

As is typically the case when growth slows, the disparity between the South and the Centre and North became more pronounced. The growth gap, which had reappeared in the second half of the 1980s, widened in the 1990s. The average annual rate of growth in the South fell to 0.9 per cent (from 2.3 per cent in the 1980s), compared with 1.5 per cent in the rest of the country (2.2 per cent in the 1980s). Investment declined at an average annual rate of 3.3 per cent in the South, while remaining unchanged in the Centre and North. The infrastructure shortfall remains particularly serious. Setting the average national endowment equal to 100, the overall index stood at 77 in the South (compared with 96 in the North-East, 103 in the Centre and 118 in the North-West) and the index for business services provided to enterprises at 60. Employment in the South contracted at an average annual rate of 0.8 per cent, while in the Centre and North it remained unchanged. The unemployment rate soared to 22 per cent, compared with 6.5 per cent in the rest of Italy. Per capita output was equal to 60 per cent of that in the Centre and North in 1985; it fell to 58 per cent in 1989 and 53 per cent in 1999. The average income of a family in the South of Italy is 35 million lire, compared with 54 million in the rest of the country; in relation to the national average, it fell from 82 per cent in 1991 to 74 per cent in 1998.

The rate of accumulation of physical capital – the ratio of gross fixed investment to GDP in the economy as a whole – has followed a downward trend: from 28 per cent at the end of the 1960s to just over 19 per cent at the end of the 1990s. This is the sharpest fall registered by any European country and was due entirely to the construction sector (not only residential buildings, but infrastructure, public works and industrial buildings). Investment excluding construction rose from 7.5 to 11 per cent of GDP, which was above the European average. However, the average annual rate of growth of this part of investment slowed in the private sector from 7 per cent in the 1970s to 3 per cent in the 1980s and 2 per cent in the 1990s. Between 1981 and 1990 the contributions of the three fundamental components of GDP growth to the average annual increment of 2.2 per cent were: the net stock of capital, 0.9 percentage points; employment, 0.4 points; and total factor productivity, 0.9 points. In the 1990s the contribution of the latter remained unchanged and the slowdown in GDP growth to an average annual rate of 1.4 per cent was entirely due to employment, whose contribution turned negative (–0.1 points) and capital, whose contribution declined to 0.6 points.

Unsatisfactory levels of output and capital accumulation were bound to be reflected in a poor performance in the job market. On average, employment, the employment rate and the labour force declined and unemployment rose, despite the recovery in 1998–9. In 1999 employment was 1.4 per cent lower than in 1991 in Italy, 1.4 per cent higher in Europe. These developments widened the already large employment rate differential: in Italy the number of persons in work fell to just above half the active population (53.2 per cent in April 2000), 10 percentage points below the European average. The fall occurred despite the simultaneous contraction of the active population, from 39,135,000 in 1991 to 38,809,000 in 1999. The Italian unemployment rate averaged 10.6 per cent in the 1990s, an increase of 2 percentage points compared with the 1980s; in Europe the increase was less than 1 point. At the beginning of the decade the rate was 9 per cent; it peaked at 12 per cent in April 1998 and then fell to 10.7 per cent in April 2000. Nearly 3 million people, above all young people and women in the South, do not have a job. Often when workers lose their jobs they fail to find another. This is the most serious trauma.

The price competitiveness of Italian goods – measured in terms of unit labour costs – was low in 1990–2. The two dramatic slides of the lira, in 1992 and 1995, brought a temporary improvement. In the summer of 1996 there was still a gain of 15 per cent compared with the middle of 1992 *vis-à-vis* both Italy's European trading partners and the rest of the world. The exchange rate parity chosen for the lira's return to the EMS in November 1996, accepted by the other members of the system with some reluctance, left that gain broadly untouched. From then until the middle of 1999 there was a considerable loss of competitiveness: of 4 per cent *vis-à-vis* all of Italy's trading partners (including the United States, which experienced a substantial appreciation of the dollar) and of 11 per cent *vis-à-vis* the euro-area countries. The loss *vis-à-vis* the countries to which the Italian economy was linked by an irrevocably fixed exchange rate was due primarily to the smaller rise in productivity.

The rate of increase in nominal per capita labour costs came into line with that prevailing in the other European countries. On the other hand, by the end of 1999 industrial productivity had risen by only 7 per cent in Italy, compared with 10–12 per cent in France and Germany.

The decline in price competitiveness was particularly serious considering Italy's continued trade specialization in traditional consumer goods and the machinery for their manufacture or the production of components. Industries with a high proportion of unskilled labour still predominate, while those with a high proportion of skilled labour are few.[2] Italian merchandise exports' share of world trade at constant prices declined significantly, from 5 per cent in 1990 to 4 per cent in 1999. Public and private investment in research and development is still inadequate. It declined in relation to GDP during the 1990s and at just over 1 per cent at the end of the decade was half the average for the other industrial countries. Companies' share of R&D investment remains low (58 per cent, compared with 67 per cent on average in the OECD countries and 73 per cent in the United States). Corporate spending on research rose in relation to GDP until 1992 and then fell to a level below that prevailing in the mid-1980s. There has been a perverse correlation: high profits, low innovation. On the basis of patent applications submitted in the United States in relation to population, Italy ranks very low among the OECD and Asian countries. Without research, without innovation and trusting merely in imitation, Italian industry is unlikely to move into sectors with a higher value added or switch to exports with a lower price elasticity of demand that would provide a more solid basis for retaining its market shares.

The level of productivity of the Italian economy as a whole (in terms of output per working hour) is one of the highest in Europe, just as earnings and labour costs are below the EU average, especially in manufacturing, construction and non-financial services. Excluding agriculture and the energy sector, productivity in the private sector – value added per standard labour unit – increased at an average annual rate of 2.8 per cent in the 1970s. After slowing to 1 per cent in the first half of the 1980s, it rose to around 2.5 per cent in the second half and then fell to just over 2 per cent in the first half of the 1990s. Between 1994 and 1999 it again fell to 1 per cent. Estimates and simulations based on the Bank of Italy's econometric model show that had domestic demand grown faster in 1997–9 and had GDP expanded steadily at an average annual rate of 3 per cent (rather than the actual rate of 1.6 per cent), then the average increase in value added per employee would have been 1.5 per cent (instead of 0.6 per cent). In the second half of the 1980s, when the average rate of GDP growth was close to 3 per cent, value added per employee rose at an average annual rate of 2.3 per cent. Thus, all in all, the recent sharp fall in *ex post* labour productivity gains was due largely to the prolonged period of slow economic growth.

An *ex ante* measure of labour productivity, which coincides with the previous one along a path of balanced growth, is given by the trend of the observed values, which approximates labour-augmenting technical progress. The trend rate of increase (1.6 per cent per year, again excluding agriculture and energy) is obtained by simultaneously estimating the labour and capital demand functions using the data for the period from the mid-1970s to the mid-1990s. In non-equilibrium conditions the two measures of productivity may differ as a consequence of changes in capital per employee. In particular, the *ex post* rate of increase in value added per employee will be less than labour-augmenting technical progress if the latter increases faster than capital intensity. It is therefore possible that although the rate of labour-augmenting technical progress remained basically unchanged in the last few decades the slowdown in the accumulation of capital may have caused the recent fall in the rate of increase in value added per employee. Adjusting the latter for the effects of the change in capital intensity[3] gives an average annual rate of growth in the period 1993–9 of 1.4 per cent, which is basically in line with that estimated with the Bank of Italy econometric model for the period 1975–95. The figure for 1998–9 indicates a reduction in labour productivity according to this yardstick; there could be a distortion, however, owing to the changes underway in the labour market. In short, there is no evidence of a significant variation in the rate of labour-augmenting technical progress. The slowdown in value added per employee reflects that in capital accumulation, which, in turn, is correlated with the slower growth of the economy.

The cyclical fluctuations around the slower average rate of growth of the 1990s can be summarized as follows:

- a slowdown between 1990 and 1992 due to the restrictive stance of monetary policy – in parallel with the lira's return to the narrow fluctuation band of the EMS in January 1990 – and the appreciation of the lira in real effective terms (a loss of competitiveness);
- a sharp recession from the third quarter of 1992 to the third quarter of 1993 (when GDP contracted by 2 per cent); domestic demand slumped by 6 per cent owing to the impact of the mid-September slide of the lira and financial instability on the terms of trade and expectations, the monetary tightening to defend the exchange rate,

and the fiscal adjustment that unfortunately did not forestall but followed the critical, and irreparable, currency crisis;

- a relatively strong but short-lived recovery in 1994–5, fuelled by the growth in net exports generated by the depreciation of the lira;
- an end to the expansion in 1996, slow growth in 1997–9 and a moderate recovery in 1999–2000, the combined effect of the severity of the fiscal squeeze and the gradualness of the monetary policy easing made necessary by the convergence criteria for participation in the euro, by the loss of competitiveness owing to the strengthening of the lira in the second half of 1995 and by in 1996, and by the adverse effects of the Asian crisis of 1997 on net exports. The recent recovery has reflected, with a lag, the upturn in world trade and the sharp depreciation of the euro (by 20 per cent since the beginning of 1999). Domestic demand continues to stagnate.

Three factors have probably held back the Italian economy with respect to its European counterparts in recent years, considering that private consumption, thanks in part to the incentives for new car purchases, has expanded since the recession of 1993 in line with the European average (just under 2 per cent per year): (1) the budgetary adjustment achieved; (2) the poor export performance as a consequence of the changes in the composition of world trade (due in part to the Asian crisis), which were particularly unfavourable to Italian products; and (3) the fall in the propensity to invest or in other words a smaller increase in investment than in the past for given values of the determinants of capital accumulation observed in the period.

1. As regards the budgetary adjustment, the general government primary surplus rose from 3.9 per cent of GDP in 1995 to 6.8 per cent in 1997 and then declined to 4.9 per cent in 1999. Over those 5 years overall borrowing fell by 5.7 percentage points of GDP to 1.9 per cent in 1999.

   The short-term effects of the public finances on economic activity can be estimated by means of counterfactual simulations in which each year the GDP ratio of the general government primary surplus and its composition are kept unchanged with respect to the previous year.

   For the period as a whole the impact effects of the public finances estimated in this way reduced overall GDP growth by little more than 1 percentage point (losses of about 0.6 points in 1995, 0.2 points in 1996 and 0.6 points in 1997, a small positive contribution of some 0.2–0.3 points in 1998 and a neutral impact in 1999). Net of these effects, the average annual rate of growth in GDP in the period would have been around 2 per cent, or still below the European average of 2.5 per cent, which was itself depressed by the budgetary adjustments implemented in some other EU countries.

2. World trade expanded at an average annual rate of 7.5 per cent over the period (compared with 5.8 per cent in 1971–94). Italian exports of goods and services grew by 4.5 per cent per year, reflecting the loss of competitiveness, most of which occurred in 1996.

   The Bank of Italy's econometric model overestimates the growth in Italian exports starting with the three years 1995–7, albeit to a limited extent (2.5 percentage points on a cumulative basis). For the two years 1998–9 the overestimate amounted to just under 7 percentage points. The growth in the demand for Italian goods at rates below those to be expected on the basis of the performance observed in the past and incorporated in the econometric model was thus concentrated in the last part of the decade. The performance of imports was the mirror image of that of exports, indicating a higher degree of penetration of the domestic market by goods produced abroad. The changes coincided with the collapse of imports by Asian countries and the increase in the penetration of world markets by exports from that crisis-stricken area. However, they also reflect a more general loss of competitiveness by the Italian economy and not only in terms of price.

3. As for investment, in the three years 1997–9 the forecasting errors of the Bank of Italy's econometric model (excluding construction) did not signal structural variations in the parameters. Capital accumulation in the period was fundamentally consistent with the values of its determinants over the period according to the elasticities incorporated in econometric estimates based on past experience. The hypothesis of parameter stability is largely confirmed by all the usual statistical tests. In no quarter during the period was the forecasting error significantly different from zero; the average error for the period was the sum of positive and negative figures and was close to zero. More specifically, an overestimate of investment in 1997 was followed by a basically correct figure for 1998 and an underestimate for 1999. There is no evidence of decisions by firms to expand their production capacity that would suggest a higher propensity to invest in the light of the prospects deriving from Italy's participation in the euro area.

The growth in potential output – approximated by the production capacity associated with the accumulation of capital – also slowed down. In the 1980s it had averaged just under 3 per cent. In the last 5 years of the 1990s it has not exceeded 2 per cent.

Another econometric exercise measured the amount of additional investment that would have been necessary in the 3 years 1997–9 to raise the rate of growth in the potential output of the private sector by an annual average of one percentage point, from 2 to 3 per cent. The objective adopted in this exercise is equal to the average recorded in 1975–92. It was found that it would have been achieved if the already significant increase in investment in plant and machinery over the period had been supplemented by additional growth amounting to a cumulative total of more than 10 percentage points (1 per cent of GDP).

The causes: 'real', not financial

The facts and statistical analysis described above can be viewed in the context of an interpretative model based on the underlying causes of the unsatisfactory growth of the Italian economy in the 1990s and, above all, in the last 5 years – both the forces that acted to prevent growth and those that would have fostered growth but failed to act.

The determinants of both types operated, moreover, in an adverse longer-term setting that contributed to the slowdown of the economy, both directly and by aggravating the repercussions of the forces that held back growth in the 1990s. I have already mentioned the crisis of the entire allocative paradigm of the Italian economy as a mixed economy and of the resistance, inertia and slowness with which that paradigm was overcome. The crisis developed and came to a head in the 1970s. The 1980s were the crucial years of delays, missed opportunities and wasted chances to move to a market economy with rules. The shift in allocative mechanisms was concentrated in the 1990s, although in several respects – such as company law – it has still to be completed. If the 'market economy with rules' had replaced the 'mixed economy' in the 1980s, the Italian economy would have developed differently in the 1990s, and probably better. The government of the Italian economy in the 1980s thus bears a dual responsibility: for failing to stop the rise in the public debt and for failing to promote, indeed for obstructing, the passage from the old to the new economy.

It has been suggested that the slowdown in the 1990s was the temporary, albeit costly, consequence of curbing still rapid inflation and a surging public debt. According to this view, Italian economic growth paid the price – high, but necessary and one-off – of the correction of historical disequilibria and the return to virtue imposed by the European parameters: a radical cure that had unquestionably left the patient weak for a while but that would ensure its recovery and ability to run with the swiftest in the future. In short, according to this view the adjustment had been achieved at the price of no more than a short-lived decline in growth. The recovery in 2000 was seen as marking the end of the transition.

This edifying account with a happy ending is open to more than one objection.

The counterinflationary monetary policy actually imposed no cost whatever. If the management of the currency, with unusual effectiveness in Italy's monetary history, had not reined in inflationary expectations after the preventive raising of the discount rate in August 1994, if in 1995–8 inflation had remained at 5–6 per cent as in the early part of the decade, if it had accelerated as it risked doing, the economy would have grown even less. This would have been for a series of reasons: higher nominal and real long-term interest rates and thus even weaker investment; an erosion of disposable income and a consequent reduction in consumption and investment; *rentier*-workers hit by the inflation tax on their financial wealth and consequently less willing to accept an incomes policy and a climate of social peace conducive to investment; and a loss of price competitiveness leading to a fall in net exports. In other words a vicious cycle of inflation, depreciation of the lira, loss of confidence and low investment, as in 1992–3. Disinflation and growth were not in conflict in the 1990s, but strictly complementary. The action taken by the Bank of Italy – first to curb (1990–2) and then to root out (1995–8) an inflation that had been endemic for 20 years – fostered growth. It created the essential premise for implementing the government's and Parliament's decision to adopt the euro. Price stability was among the convergence criteria established by the treaty signed at Maastricht in February 1992; decisive in itself, monetary stability also influenced compliance with all the other criteria: interest rates, the exchange rate and the public finances all depend considerably on the price level.

Counterfactual analysis is also possible for budgetary policy. If, especially after the slide of the lira in September 1992, the general government borrowing requirement had not been curbed, the risk premiums for borrowers and the domestic and international loss of confidence would have opened the way to calamitous scenarios for the

Italian economy. Their effects are hard to quantify but they would undoubtedly have involved financial crises and a fall in production and investment. Curing a deadly disease does *not* have an opportunity cost. The alternative of inaction had to be avoided at all costs. Furthermore, while the budgetary policy pursued did make a start on adjusting the public finances, it is important not to overstate its impact effect on demand. We have already seen that the cumulative effect in 1995–9 was barely 1 percentage point of GDP, with peaks of 0.6 points in 1995 and 1997. Even in the absence of these effects, the growth of the Italian economy would have been less than in the previous 10 years and below the European average.

The 'cost' – if we must use the word – of the monetary and budgetary policies is thus not part of the one-off price that had to be paid in terms of growth. Italy's economic problem in the 1990s and after cannot be reduced to just a reduction in the rate of economic growth as a consequence of a variety of causes, some of them certainly contingent. The slower growth has led to an unsatisfactory rate of increase in the economy's potential output, the result not so much of a worsening of the trend of total factor productivity as of inadequate investment, insufficient to keep the increase in potential output in line with the values recorded in 1975–95. The recovery in 2000, driven – with a lag – by the very strong and probably unsustainable expansion of world trade, does not solve the problem. This is confirmed by the poor performance of net exports, qualitatively even more than quantitatively, which was worse than the loss of price competitiveness would have justified. If anything, by obscuring the problem, it threatens to postpone the solution. The ultimate question therefore concerns the accumulation of capital, with special reference to construction and plant and machinery.

Between 1990 and 1999 (Table 8.2) capital spending on construction declined from 10 to 8 per cent of GDP, in line with the trend that had already emerged in the early 1970s. The fall involved residential building and, above all, non-residential construction and public works. High interest rates, the demographic decline, the contraction of major cities, the taxes on residential buildings, and 'institutional' and financial crises affecting public works interacted to varying degrees. Non-construction investment slowed but rose in relation to GDP (from 10.7 to 11.6 per cent). The propensity of firms to invest, for given values of the determinants of capital expenditure, has not fallen in recent years, but it has not risen either. The start made on the adjustment of the public finances, the curbing of inflation, wage moderation, the adoption of the euro and the challenge this entails are events – amounting to

Table 8.2   Gross fixed investment as a ratio to GDP in Italy, 1982–99 [a]

	Total	In machinery equipment and transport equipment	In construction
1982	20.2	9.3	10.9
1983	19.8	8.8	11.0
1984	19.9	9.2	10.6
1985	19.4	9.1	10.3
1986	19.3	9.2	10.1
1987	19.6	9.8	9.8
1988	20.1	10.4	9.7
1989	20.4	10.5	9.8
1990	20.8	10.7	10.1
1991	20.7	10.6	10.1
1992	20.2	10.4	9.9
1993	18.2	8.9	9.3
1994	17.8	9.3	8.5
1995	18.3	10.0	8.3
1996	18.8	10.2	8.6
1997	18.7	10.5	8.2
1998	19.2	11.1	8.1
1999	19.7	11.6	8.1

[a] The values shown are those of the new national accounts drawn up or reconstructed in accordance with ESA95.

a true regime change – that could have led to a surge in investment. Only a higher propensity of firms to invest could have restored the competitiveness of Italian goods in domestic and international markets, made sure exports held up and limited the penetration of imports. Only the accumulation of capital could have prevented the rate of increase in potential output from falling and, on the contrary, fostered its acceleration. This did not happen. Why not?

In various ways Italian entrepreneurs, both individually and through their associations, have pointed to the burden of taxation and the absence of correctives or offsets as the factor that more than any other dims the outlook for profits in the long term, the *structural* disincentive to invest more.

From the time the commitment to the euro was adopted as the top priority, in 1996, the taxation of firms and more generally of investment income has actually decreased, while the taxation of the economy as a whole has increased. At the same time Italian entrepreneurs and capitalists continued to declare their belief in the European idea, their desire that the lira be dissolved into Europe's solid new currency. In the short time that remained to comply with the criteria for membership of the European Monetary Union in 1997, a step increase in tax revenue was the only choice. It was made and the objective was achieved.[4] Even a weak presumption of rationality and consistency between desires, expectations and behaviour is enough to exclude the possibility that the way the intermediate and necessary objective of reducing the budget deficit was achieved, on the revenue side, put a brake on Italian entrepreneurs' otherwise explosive propensity to invest. In 1997 there was no other way.

But a different interpretation is possible. Together with the country's persistent structural problems and the incomplete passage from a mixed to a market economy, the prospect of a longer-run reduction in the taxation of the economy, of capital and firms, may have played and may still be playing a decisive role. The uncertain or highly improbable nature of this prospect, both in absolute terms and in comparison with developments in other euro-area countries, may explain why Italian firms' propensity to invest failed to increase.

The disastrous management of the public finances in the 1980s – which nonetheless saw faster growth than the 1990s and offered opportunities, which were irremediably dissipated, to put the budget back on a sound footing – can be summarized in just a few figures; the adjustment in the following decade can be divided into three stages.

In the last part of the 1980s primary expenditure rose at an annual rate (10 per cent) that was only slightly less than that of taxation. Net borrowing was equal to 9.8 per cent of GDP and the primary balance still showed a deficit (1.1 per cent of GDP). The public debt surged to 95.4 per cent of GDP (taking the increase over the decade to 35 percentage points). This was the culmination of a decade of non-government of the public finances. The belated change of course came in 1990–2, with measures to curb the centrifugal trend that were officially estimated at 11 per cent of GDP over the three years. The measures to correct the budget on a current programmes basis failed to reverse expectations, however, and neither did they prevent the slide of the lira in September 1992. Indeed, owing to hesitancy and procrastination, the budget measures were stiffened just a few days *afterwards*. The delay, disastrous for the currency, occurred despite the Bank of Italy having stressed the emergency and quantified the necessary reduction in the deficit (100 trillion lire or more than 6 per cent of GDP).[5] Between 1989 and 1993 revenue rose from 42 to 48.3 per cent of GDP but, partly owing to the recession of 1992–3, primary expenditure continued to rise, from 43.1 to 45.7 per cent.

Budgetary adjustments amounting to another 8 percentage points of GDP were made between 1994 and 1996, when the primary surplus rose to 4.4 per cent of GDP, net borrowing fell to 7.1 per cent and the public debt declined from the peak of 123.8 per cent in 1994 to 122.1 per cent. The improvement in this period was achieved on the expenditure rather than the revenue side. Primary expenditure fell from 45.7 to 41.4 per cent of GDP (mainly pensions and public salaries). The revenue ratio also declined, from 48.3 to 45.8 per cent.

For the objective of participating in the European Monetary Union from the start, 1997 was the crucial year. The primary surplus rose by another 2.3 percentage points to 6.7 per cent of GDP, an all-time high. Thanks also to the contraction in interest payments, net borrowing decreased by 4.4 points to 2.7 per cent, comfortably below the limit of 3 per cent established by the Maastricht Treaty. Tax revenue and social security contributions rose in just one year by 1.8 percentage points of GDP. The action of the Ministry of Finance was decisive in achieving this result. Between 1996 and 1999, primary expenditure rose from 41.4 to 42 per cent of GDP, almost in line with the rise in revenue, from 45.8 to 46.9 per cent, and with that in tax revenue and social security contributions, from 42.5 to 43.3 per cent. By 1999 the public debt was down to 115 per cent of GDP, despite the budget continuing to show a deficit that can be considered structural in view of the adverse effects of the gap between actual and potential output.

The commitment to bring the debt ratio down to 100 per cent in 2003, according to the plan drawn up by the government in the December 1999 update of the Stability Programme, nonetheless implied tax revenue and social security contributions remaining well above 40 per cent of GDP, despite a fall of about 2 percentage points. Looking beyond the medium-term programmes, the prospects for the public finances are made uncertain by the only partial reform of the public pension systems[6] and the truly worrisome demographic decline and population ageing, the social aversion to immigration and the low level of employment. These factors hinder the emergence of a credible underlying reduction, albeit gradual, in the heavy burden placed on taxpayers since the 1980s.

The European Union will exercise its influence to ensure that Italy uses any improvement in the public finances beyond what is planned to consolidate the budgetary position further and reduce the stock of debt more rapidly, rather than to reduce taxation. The problem is not so much that a public debt larger than GDP poses a threat to financial stability, especially if the primary surplus is smaller than expected, international interest rates are higher and economic growth lower. Rather, the problem is that other countries, especially in the euro area, might seek, because they are in a position to do so, to boost the competitiveness of their economies by reducing taxation. Italy, meanwhile, would be unable to follow their example and dissuaded from trying to by its European partners, which would call upon it to fulfill its debt-reduction commitment.

This summary analysis has been made without any reference to banking or finance. Among the factors that contributed to the stagnation of the 1990s, we can safely exclude the state of the financial industry. No research on the mediocre performance of the Italian economy in this period stresses the financial aspects.[7]

There are several reasons for absolving the financial industry, for not including it among the main determinants of the decade-long stagnation. The explanatory model outlined above – with banking and finance left on the sidelines – is consistent with the facts. Moreover, numerous indicators show that the financial constraints on firms have eased. Above all, as discussed in detail, the financial industry has made significant improvements in terms of costs and prices, quantities produced and product quality. It is hard to accuse a sector that has advanced of being responsible for the stagnation of the economy. Actually, as will be shown in the next chapter, the financial industry has sustained growth and prevented the stagnation from being even worse.

The first point should already be clear. Compared with 'real' questions of major and sometimes political and social significance, such as the *modus operandi* of the economy and the crushing inheritance of public debt, the working of the banking and financial system is less important. The growth of the Italian economy has been and still is hamstrung by the burden of public debt irresponsibly accumulated between the end of the 1970s and 1992. The taxation needed to curb, and not just service, the debt does not appear reducible in the medium term, at least in comparison with other European countries. Nor are Italian entrepreneurs' animal spirits sufficiently stimulated by unequivocal progress in reform on other fronts: pensions, the labour market, company law, infrastructure, education, research. The uncertainty regarding future taxation acts as a brake on investment and hence on the return to acceptable and sustained growth.

As for the second point, several indicators, albeit to some extent correlated or overlapping, show that the 1990s, and especially the second half of the decade, saw an easing of the structural and other credit and financial constraints to which firms were subject.

It is important to note the combination of higher levels of self-financing and lower levels of capital spending. This led to a reduction in the corporate sector's financial deficit in relation to GDP. The debt of Italian firms, especially the large ones, fell in relation to both equity and value added. Their leverage – the ratio of financial debt to the sum of such debt and equity capital – fell from 52 per cent in 1993 to 41 per cent in 1999. Firms' liquid and illiquid financial assets increased. Interest rates fell. Given their initial level and the convergence process, the fall was larger in Italy than in other European countries. Where they are comparable, bank lending rates are now not much higher than abroad. At the end of 1999 those on loans of between 1 and 5 billion lire stood at 6.5 per cent or, for example, about 100 basis points lower than in Germany. Financial costs have accordingly come down in relation to gross operating profit. Net income has risen. In 1990 gross operating profit was equal to 32 per cent of value added and financial costs to 10 per cent; in 1999 gross operating profit had risen to 35 per cent, while financial costs had fallen to 5 per cent.

The removal of all exchange controls in 1990, the insertion of the Italian economy into 'global' finance, and the range of services this offered at competitive conditions and with the additional possibility of remote access meant that real alternatives to the services the Italian financial industry could offer were available to firms, and not only the larger ones. Italian businesses took advantage of this opportunity in the 1990s, especially when real interest rates were much higher in Italy than abroad. Firms could thus raise funds at a lower cost via this channel and better meet their portfolio and risk management needs.

Firms' financial liabilities to non-residents, in both domestic and foreign currency, increased from 145 trillion lire in 1990 to 500 trillion in 1999, that is from 10 to 16 per cent of their total financial liabilities and from 11 to 23 per cent of GDP. In the same period their foreign assets increased to an even greater extent, rising from 90 to 500 trillion lire and from 20 to 44 per cent of their total financial assets. The deficit on 'financial services' of Italy's balance of payments on current account – excluding the services used by Italian banks for their own account – rose steadily from 0.5 trillion lire in 1990 to 1.3 trillion in 1999, thus providing further evidence of firms' greater recourse to international finance.

Small and medium-sized enterprises are highly profitable, partly because of their lower labour costs, but this advantage is counterbalanced by higher financial costs. Despite the fall in interest rates in recent years, financial costs still amount to more than a third of smaller firms' gross operating profit (compared with 17 per cent for firms with more than 1,000 employees). The scale of these costs reflects these firms' substantial bank borrowing, mostly at short term and in the form of overdrafts, which implies less flexibility in making investments and financial fragility in the negative phases of the business cycle. Bank credit accounts for 73 per cent of the financial debt of firms with less than 10 employees, 55 per cent of that of larger firms.

In recent years, however, the financing constraints on small and medium-sized enterprises have become less stringent. Their profits have permitted self-financing and debt repayments. Firms have rarely cited financial constraints, the availability and cost of bank loans, as causes of the decline in investment. These factors have become less important. Notwithstanding small and medium-sized enterprises' low propensity to seek stock exchange listing, the proportion of funds they have raised through share issues has not been small.

The ratio of credit drawn to credit granted has fallen. The share of secured shorter-term loans has contracted. There has been a reduction in firms declaring that they are rationed by the credit system, to less than 5 per cent of the total on average between 1992 and 1998. Smaller firms were not subject to rationing more than the others. The banks that handle the accounts of small and medium-sized enterprises and households know their local economies better than the larger banks. Mutual, cooperative and savings banks have large shares of local credit markets. They can offer local businessmen credit on good terms, together with advice, and build on the relationships of trust and mutual cooperation that they establish with them.

Among the characteristics of firms, neither size nor age is important, while self-financing is. Firms that can generate internal resources obtain bank loans at lower interest rates. An adverse effect on the cost of credit is found, *ceteris paribus*, for firms that have multiple banking relationships. The cost of credit has also declined as a consequence of increased competition. In particular, successful firms have benefited from better conditions in the credit market. They have obtained a larger proportion of long-term credit from the banking system.

A distinctive trait of Italian manufacturing is that 40 per cent of employment is in firms that belong to 'districts', aggregations of small enterprises specializing in a particular branch of industry and benefiting both from their closeness and from external economies connected with the area in which they operate. Other things being equal, these firms are better placed than the average as regards efficiency, ability to export, the correlation between productivity and wages, and profitability. By contrast, there is no evidence of a special relationship – closer and long-term, with consequent information advantages or at any rate more favourable terms for borrowers – between either local or national banks and 'district' firms. The success of the districts does not appear to depend on more favourable access to credit. The banking system has thus not discriminated between small and medium-sized enterprises that belong to a district and those that do not but are otherwise comparable.

Far from having been caused by financial factors, the mediocre performance of the economy in the 1990s had several adverse effects on the banking and financial sector.

Slow economic growth, a decline in investment and a high level of self-financing on the part of non-financial enterprises created one of the least favourable environments possible for banking and finance. Business volumes contracted and risks rose for intermediaries holding corporate liabilities.

There was a high dispersion of firms' performances with respect to the results of the economy as a whole, by sector and size, between exporting firms and those producing for the domestic market, and by geographical area, especially between the South and the rest of the country. For given average values for the corporate sector, high dispersion had two unfavourable repercussions on the banking and financial system, especially in fields where it was weak. On the one hand the more advanced components of Italian capitalism could turn for innovative services to other financial systems operating internationally when these were considered to be more efficient. On the other hand Italian banks tended to end up by having to cope with the difficulties of the less-profitable parts of the productive system.

The sharp fall in households' propensity to save – for a variety of reasons, but above all the slow growth of the economy – eroded one of the strengths of Italian finance. At the beginning of the 1980s households saved more than one-fifth of their disposable income, one of the highest rates of all the OECD countries and the highest rate of the seven leading economies. Since then the decline has been continuous and faster than in other countries; it accelerated in the 1990s. In 2000 the household saving rate was estimated at just 11 per cent in Italy, less than in France (15 per cent) and Japan (12 per cent), and on a par with Germany, where the figure was unchanged.

The factors described above are reflected, against a background of growing competition, in the higher level of banks' bad debts, the variance and variability of their profits, higher default and 'mortality' rates for loan facilities, and the crisis of the banking system based in the South.

9
Finance and Growth

Far from being a factor contributing to the economic stagnation of the 1990s, the Italian banking and financial system with its structural transformation and improved performance worked and is working in the opposite direction, fostering growth. Further gains in the efficiency of the financial industry can make a significant additional contribution to raising the Italian economy's growth potential.

Schumpeter revisited

As a general rule, finance helps to determine not only the *levels* of variables such as the capital/labour ratio, productivity and national income but also their rates of increase. All else being equal, the *growth* of an economy that develops or improves its financial system is likely to be considerably faster.

The financial system contributes to the quantity and quality of resources and the ways they are used by performing the following functions:[1]

- clearing and settling transactions;
- pooling resources and subdividing the participation in economic initiatives;
- allocating resources, especially to firms;
- managing uncertainty and controlling risk;
- providing information through prices;
- dealing with the incentive problems that arise in the relationship between issuers and subscribers of financial instruments.

The fact that a more effective performance of these functions not only influences the economy in the broad sense but also helps to foster growth implies a connection between these functions and variables that are decisive to growth, such as the accumulation of capital – tangible, intangible, 'human' – and technical progress.[2]

The propensity to invest, the propensity to save and the proportion of savings that is channeled into investment are all affected positively by finance as a rule, although in certain very particular conditions a more efficient financial system can lower households' propensity to save. Thus a good financial system tends to increase the scale of capital accumulation, which continues to be seen as important in all models of growth.

No less important is the channel of technical progress. Both the theory of growth and the economics of finance and growth have assigned increasing, indeed prevalent, importance to this factor. This reflects the basic empirical pattern observed by Simon Kuznets half a century ago and confirmed by subsequent studies of economic growth in many countries, namely that the quality of resources and of their utilization is more important than their quantity in determining the wealth of nations:

> [T]he direct contribution of man-hours and capital accumulation would hardly account for more than a tenth of the rate of growth in per capita product...The large remainder must be assigned to an increase in efficiency in the productive resources – a rise in output per unit of input, due either to the improved quality of the resources, or to the effects of changing arrangements, or to the impact of technological change, or to all three.[3]

Finance is closely connected with all three of these factors. In particular, it can have highly productive leverage effects on organizational and technological innovation. It is no surprise, therefore, that the recent literature on growth and on finance and growth is characterized by a 'return to Schumpeter'. For among the giants of economic theory, Schumpeter more than anyone emphasized the link between innovation and finance or, to use his own terms, between the essence of development and the essence of credit.

The mystery that some market economies develop while others with comparable resources and institutions remain mired in backwardness is increasingly explained by reference to *entrepreneurship*, found in the former but lacking in the latter.[4] Differences in growth rates across time and in different places are also increasingly attributed to differences in the degree of advancement of the financial system, particularly in its capacity to select and sustain innovative firms and investment projects. This special quality of the financial system has been defined in a variety of ways. It has also been variously proxied with empirical quantitative and institutional variables. Almost never has the recent literature on finance and growth followed the letter or spirit of Schumpeter's work on the role of banks and bank credit.[5] In this crucial respect, Schumpeter would never recognize himself in the most recent revisitation of his writings. Ignorance of the thought of the economists of yesterday abounds among those of today. For Schumpeter, the banker, through credit, 'makes possible the carrying out of new combinations, authorizes people, in the name of society as it were, to form them.'[6] In order to perform this function, however, the banker 'should know, and be able to *judge*, what his credit is used for' and he should be 'an independent agent'.[7] The banks

> must first be independent of the entrepreneurs whose plans they are to sanction or to refuse. This means, practically speaking, that banks and their officers must not have any stake in the gains of enterprise beyond what is implied by the loan contract... [B]anks must also be independent of politics.[8]

Detachment, the impartial evaluation of the investment project and the firm's ability to carry it out, non-involvement – apart from the redemption of the loan and the payment of interest – in the fate of the initiative, all make the banker the most neutral of resource allocation mechanisms. An arbiter, a credit judge, at the centre of the market economy, if not above it: 'He is the ephor of the exchange economy.'[9] Prudent, conservative, the banker must harbour no 'entrepreneurial' preferences for the investment projects whose objective chances of success he has to calculate. More essentially, he is called upon to make a simultaneous evaluation of the project, the entrepreneur and the enterprise in a dynamic economy. In the Walrasian general equilibrium this is a specific function that cannot be performed by the capital market (which selects projects via the rate of interest) or the product market (which selects firms via competition). Innovation and economic growth stem from the dialectic – friction, collision, not collusion or community of views – between the innovative drive of the entrepreneur and the cool caution of the banker.

The Schumpeterian bank is therefore anything but King and Levine's 'venture capital firm, funding start-up innovative activity, in exchange for (most of) the firm's stock.'[10] Moreover, the essential qualities of banks that Schumpeter so admirably described are very difficult to proxy using quantitative measures of banking business, its composition, or even the efficiency with which it is performed. Yet a great amount of recent econometric work is expressly inspired by a 'neo-Schumpeterian' vision. Despite the historiographic imprecision of much of this literature, its empirical results cannot be ignored. It may not be Schumpeter, but it does have something to tell us. These economists represent an advance upon the pioneering work of Raymond Goldsmith, who concluded, in the midst of enormous statistical difficulties and econometric uncertainty, that historically, in the long run, we find a 'rough parallelism' between finance and growth.

This ample corpus of econometric studies[11] – grounded in enormous databases and new techniques – demonstrates that financial development has a statistically significant and quantitatively important correlation with economic growth. It further holds that the degree of financial development is a good predictor of and makes a substantial contribution to economic growth over a long subsequent period (years, decades). About a third of the disparity between the countries with very fast growth and those with very slow growth can be ascribed to the differing degree of development of the financial system. The measures of financial development used in these empirical studies can certainly be refined, in particular in their ability to capture the qualitative aspects of finance.[12] But whatever measure is used, simple or refined, it always turns out to be correlated with growth. The main objection – reverse causation – actually applies less to the relationship of finance to growth than to other variables held in theory to be determinants of growth.[13] Statistically, this is confirmed by analysis based on instrumental variables. Logically, the relationship appears plausible in view of the amount of time needed to construct or transform a financial system and the special importance of legal and institutional factors, apart from the response of the markets, in the process.

Alongside the banks – in a relationship that is partly complementary and partly alternative – a broad, deep, liquid, efficient capital market also fosters economic growth in several ways. It offers financing possibilities that are supplementary or alternative to self-financing, bank credit and trade credit. It also provides such opportunities to new or innovative firms, to those that want to invest in order to grow, to firms that intend to take over others to realize their latent value or to integrate them. It subjects firms to healthy pressure, a permanent spur to produce value. This is achieved both through the constant monitoring of the return on the capital invested and through the contestability of ownership and control. Above all, the possibility of liquidating one's position attenuates the reluctance to invest in long-term projects with deferred returns.

Study of the nexus between growth and finance is complicated when we ask whether financial markets or banks are better at stimulating growth. Even in financial systems with broad and liquid equity markets, most of firms' outside financing comes from banks. The findings of empirical inquiries into the link between the composition of external finance and the dynamics of sectoral growth are not unequivocal. The importance of the size and depth of the equity market in determining the overall incidence of the financial sector on economic growth is well documented. Specifically, the liquidity of the equity market – proxied by the volume of trading in proportion to the size of the stock exchange or national income – turns out to be correlated with economic growth, just like the level of development of the banking system.[14] Banks and stock exchanges both affect the performance of the economy, all the more beneficially the more efficient they are. They are complementary to one another, not substitutes.

Better finance, more growth

It should be clear enough by now that the Italian financial system made significant progress in the 1980s and perhaps even more in the 1990s. Progress can be seen in the structure of the system, in the legal and institutional framework, in supervisory activity, in the intensity of competition and in the efficiency and performance of intermediaries and markets in various respects. The improvement from the early 1980s involved all six of the functions that a financial system is called upon to perform according to the classification referred to above.

There was improvement in the handling of payments – for 'real' and 'financial', domestic and international transactions – with better procedures and technology, lower costs and better control of risks. The essential qualitative advances consisted in less use of cash and bank deposits, the introduction of derivative instruments, extensive use of gross settlement, and delivery-versus-payment.

There was improvement in the pooling of savings and the sharing of enterprise risk. The broad qualitative and quantitative development of the activity of banks and other credit and non-credit intermediaries and of the capital market was accompanied by the emergence of specific vehicles, such as investment funds, and specific technical forms, such as securitization (only recently introduced in Italy).

There was improvement in the transfer of resources from the present to the future, from place to place, from agent to agent. The key developments here were advances in operating efficiency (lower costs) and allocative efficiency, in the range of markets and in the scale of activity of the financial system as a whole. A better balance between the two main channels of funding enterprise, banks and markets, emerged. Other improvements involved collateral and the procedures for loan disbursement.

There was improvement in the management of risk, markedly through greater and more economical ways of separating, and specializing, real investment and production from activities directed to the assessment and management of risk. Derivative instruments, investment funds and insurance companies contributed to more efficient risk management in its three essential forms: hedging, diversification, insurance.

There was improvement in the financial system's provision of 'price' information (interest rates, spot and forward securities quotes). The informational efficiency of the securities markets increased very considerably, approaching that of the most advanced stock and bond markets. Greater articulation in terms of instruments, contracts and participants made for easier access to such precious information as the implied volatility of the prices of goods, securities and currencies.

There was improvement, finally, in the incentives and disincentives that are directly responsible for curbing such problems as moral hazard, adverse selection and asymmetric information. The main developments in this area were the privatization of banks and the financial markets themselves and the heightening of competition.

It should be underscored that these changes in the six basic *functions* affected all the different *levels* of the financial system:[15] products (for example, options), business lines (for example, corporate loans), institutions (for example, asset management companies), the system of intermediaries and markets taken all together.

Obviously, the decisive level is the last. And it is this level, that is the fundamental design of the entire system, that has been most radically transformed in Italy. In 1980 the financial system was an integral part of a general Italian model, that is the mixed economy. Devised as the response to the emergency of the 1930s, the system had been consolidated in the 1950s and 1960s. Despite severe shortcomings, it had produced extraordinary economic progress in the entire postwar period until 1973. The crisis of the 1970s, no less insidious if less traumatic, required the development of a whole new model for the Italian economy. Starting in the 1980s, adaptation to the prevailing approach in the other leading industrial countries, against a background of financial globalization, directed Italy towards a configuration more closely resembling a market economy. Obviously, it was necessary for the financial system to adapt to this trend, not to impede it but to accompany and favour it. Despite contradictions and the lags we have sought to recount here, in large part this was achieved.

The conclusion is that in the 1990s the Italian banking and financial system, far from acting as a brake on the Italian economy, actually worked to counter its inherent tendency to slow down. The financial system's stepped-up contribution to growth concerned both the scale of capital accumulation and productivity. That growth would have been slower still had the Italian financial system not undergone its radical transformation starting in 1980 is perforce a counterfactual proposition, but one that is abundantly corroborated by our analysis.

Measuring this contribution is fraught with difficulty and requires great faith in the application of econometrics to the relationship between finance and growth. Those who share that faith will wonder what would have happened to Italian economic growth had the variables that the recent literature uses as crude proxies of financial development remained at their 1980 levels rather than rising to the higher values subsequently observed. According to this analytical approach, the best answer is that the rate of growth in per capita GDP would have been significantly lower, by between 0.2 and 0.3 percentage points each year. Rather than growth of 1.8 per cent per year from 1985 to 1998, we would have had about 1.5 per cent.[16] And there is reason to think that this assessment is actually underestimated. If the transformation and development of the financial system had not occurred, the growth performance could have been far worse.[17] The conclusion is that the contribution of finance to Italian economic advance, in one of its most difficult periods, was not negligible.

Quid agendum

The problems for the Italian financial system – aggravated and highlighted by the very progress made over the last two decades – can be reduced to four interrelated areas for action: the cost of labour, the quality of some services, 'environmental' costs and pension funds.

Per capita labour costs are still very high in the Italian financial industry. They are about twice as high as in other industries, on average, and above all they are high by international standards. They are high in terms of both the social contribution component and gross employee compensation. Italian banks' per capita labour costs are 25 per cent higher than those of German banks, for example. For a given size of bank and product composition, technology – above all IT – offers little scope for organizational diversity. The production function coefficients are largely fixed. Even where it is more costly, the labour factor can be replaced only up to a point. Banking remains the most labour-intensive branch of the financial industry. The Italian banking system does not differ substantially from those of other countries in technology or organization, both of which are designed and proposed by a few big management consulting firms that serve all banks on an international scale.[18] It is most unlikely, therefore, in what is now a competitive market, with equal technology and organizational efficiency, that higher per capita labour costs and various external diseconomies can be offset by greater labour productivity.

In recent years the disparity in banking labour costs *vis-à-vis* other European countries with competitive and internationally oriented financial systems has been reduced. The containment of costs in Italy has been accompanied by cost increases elsewhere. However, the latter are reversible. Domestic and international competition obliges Italian banks to seek profit mainly by cutting costs. Competition will persist and intensify. Only the reduction of the price of labour in relative terms can enable Italian banks to recoup competitiveness and profitability in the long run. In the short term, what is needed is a transitional agreement for wage moderation, until the easing of the tax and social contribution burden on banking and finance that the restoration of sound public finances will make possible in the future.

Economies of scale and scope are naturally of great importance. In the span of just a few years conversion into the limited-company legal form, privatizations, mergers and acquisitions have radically transformed the Italian financial system. The average size of Italian banks at the top of the scale has increased substantially. Groups have been expanded, become more articulated. Several groups have emerged that are at least up to European standards in scale and range of business.

In addition to costs, the problem today and in the future is one of quality, involving the services provided, strategies and interactions with the economy. In some branches of activity and some particular services the Italian banking system must improve the quality and distribution of its products.

There is doubt as to the ability of Italian banks to keep the ratio of income to expense on a par with that of their European competitors. The recent improvement in this indicator was due largely to the sudden increase in asset management services to retail customers, driven by strong and rigid demand as bond and share prices rose. In the medium term it remains to be seen whether the proportion of savings entrusted to asset management professionals will continue to converge with the values found in other industrial countries; whether fees, now higher than in other countries, will be lowered; whether the proportion of managed assets invested in shares, which generally bring higher fees, will increase.

The fundamental characteristic of bank–firm relations in continental Europe is greater corporate recourse to bank loans than to the capital market. The volume of corporate loans from banks is three times as great as that of corporate securities issues. In the United States, the three-to-one ratio runs the other way. In some euro-area countries, notably Germany, the banks have very close relations with customer firms that tend to be exclusive, stable in time, and characterized by a high information content.

In Italy, the small size of firms and their reluctance to submit to market scrutiny enhance the role of banks in corporate finance, but the practice of multiple borrowing reduces the banks' incentive to form fiduciary relationships and increases credit risk. In an economy of small firms, with greater risk and higher recovery costs, Italian banks' loan loss provisions are also very large by international standards.

By working closely with small and medium-sized enterprises, following their development and assisting them in times of need, banks can improve the quality of their loan portfolio, develop risk-pooling techniques and market asset-backed securities. For such transactions to work to the benefit of both clients and banks, the market must perceive that the projects financed have been properly screened.

Bank credit to small businesses and households, which has been rising sharply, will be the preferred terrain of regional banks. When banks merge, there is a decline in the share of the new institution's lending that goes to small businesses. Their competitors, often new or smaller banks, take their place in small business lending.

In the past, Italian banks sometimes viewed the development of the private securities market as potentially harmful. Now, with the reduction in net issues of government debt, households' desire for investment diversification and the development of supplementary pensions, the demand for corporate paper will increase. In their dealings with large firms, the banks' role must be to facilitate market access, handling bond issues, syndicated loans and initial public offerings. In the placement of securities of Italian issuers, Italian banks usually head the underwriting syndicate and contribute decisively to the placement of shares, but they are not major players in international markets.

In any event, the problem of quality is more general. It concerns management, the top Italian bankers and financiers. Management has been extensively renewed in recent years, and the winnowing process is still underway. In the past the Italian business system repeatedly showed it was able to produce bankers of international calibre, no matter whether 'public' or 'private'. Today, now that the system has been reprivatized, it is up to shareholders to select, respect and rely on the best men: the fate of an industry that is decisive to the entire economy is in their hands. Of the managing directors and general managers in office in 1994, only a third still held their positions in 2000. The average age of directors has held steady at just over 50. Net of retirements, deaths and transfers to other banks, annual turnover has risen to as much as 20 per cent in private-sector banks. Thus we are not seeing the replacement of one cohort of managers by a successor generation. Nor have developments outside banking, such as electoral politics, had systematic influence. The change in management is related, as it should be, to the performance of the banks (decline in profit, increase in risk) and to changes in ownership (in turn often generated by poor earnings). To a large extent the system has followed the methods of leadership selection and leadership change found abroad. The establishment of new corporate governance mechanisms has been coupled with the reassertion of the central role of shareholders. The process will be completed with further changes in ownership. This is the purpose of the law on banking foundations and one of the reasons why a greater role for institutional investors that monitor the quality of strategic decisions is to be hoped for.

In the third place there is the question of 'environmental' costs. Technically, these have to do mainly with taxation and the legal framework of economic activity. The removal of the fiscal factor certainly depends to a great extent on progress in righting the public finances. But it will also depend on broader agreement, within society and within the political class, that banks and finance, 'unpopular' though they are, are a crucial part of the economy. As we have noted, their product is 'basic' and is increasingly supplied in a competitive international arena, where finance is globalized but in some major countries sustained if not protected by national governments, parliaments, tax systems and the media. The removal of the second type of cost will depend not only on the day-to-day operating efficiency of the administrative and judicial apparatus and the quantity, quality and management of the resources allocated to it. It will also depend on how the entire legal framework of the Italian economy evolves, along the lines of the recent laws on banking and finance and listed companies' corporate governance. If the Italian legal order is also placed at the service of an open economy engaged in fierce international competition, these problems will be resolved.

The fourth grave lacuna in the Italian financial system is pension funds. Here, both legal and behavioural changes are needed to fill the gap. Private retirement schemes are an urgent necessity. In a society more exposed than others to the shocks of demographic stagnation and population ageing, pension funds are needed to produce a retirement system that does not throw the public finances out of kilter and that can honour the commitments made to present and future pensioners. Supplementary retirement schemes are necessary in view of the contribution that pension funds could make to the further growth of the financial system and its orientation to the market, especially the private capital market. And they are necessary to improve corporate governance in the business world, to institute contestable ownership and control, as well as real protection of minority shareholders, and to minimize conflicts of interest.

Stabilizing the ratio of public pension spending to GDP means reducing individual pension benefits. Italy spends more on pensions for citizens older than 60 than the other OECD countries (except Austria), including those where the public finances are in order. The correlation between less public retirement provision and more private pension funds could become unavoidable.

Institutional investors, with long-term horizons, give the share and bond markets depth; they foster equity strengthening and the issue of long-term liabilities by firms; they lengthen the average maturity of the public debt and facilitate its placement. The experience of Britain and the United States confirms the great contribution that pension fund portfolio choices dictated by relative yields can make to the return on savings, to the allocative efficiency of markets, to lower transaction costs, to less volatility in securities prices and to a lower cost of capital.

The essential criterion for pension funds must be diversification. Portfolio choices must not be externally conditioned. No particular class of financial asset must be preferred, no particular firm, branch or area must be favoured, and investment abroad or in foreign currency assets must not be precluded.

The mandate to manage a pension fund must be conditional upon full transparency *vis-à-vis* participants. Transparency reduces the risk inherent in delegating the choice of the asset management service to a third party (the pension fund), as the law requires. Participants must be in a position to verify that the specialist intermediary manages their assets scrupulously in their interest. With respect to the participants, pension fund administrators must act as independent financial advisors, with no salesman's interest in pushing a particular brand of product. With respect to the managers, fund administrators must seek to obtain the best possible contractual terms. This is essential to make sure that the mandate granted to a specialized intermediary is truly in the participants' interest and functional to the financial performance of their retirement assets.

The participation of pension funds at shareholders' meetings gives companies independence. No effective control or director account-ability is possible unless there are substantial independent shareholders not involved directly in management, free of preconceived notions and ready to support the company financially according to its economic performance.

Italian law does not bar multiple directorships. More appropriately, like other countries, Italy regulates conflicts of interest. Voting agreements and shareholder pacts are common in other countries as well, in the name of freedom of contract; in some countries, however, the strength of 'neutral' finance provided by institutional investors whose sole interest is in risk and return means that multiple directorships, pacts among large shareholders and cross-shareholdings, though legal, have less serious consequences. The only solution, therefore, is to make sure that the economy has that strength at its disposal: intense circulation of capital, which can prevent and remove blocks to good governance.

10
The Outlook

The Italian financial system, having completed the metamorphosis described here, now faces two important questions, taking into account the progress made to date and the shortcomings still to be overcome. The first concerns the outlook for Italy's financial industry in the euro area and in the context of globalization. The second relates to the economy's competitiveness and growth, in so far as they depend on the contribution of the financial system.

It is inconceivable that Italy's economy can grow rapidly, supported by European and world finance, while its financial system is progressively 'crowded out' by competition even at home. Such a scenario would imply the emergence of yet another source of dualism, this time between borrowers who resort to international finance and those as yet unable to do so.

The further quantitative and qualitative development of the financial sector that the Italian economy needs and can sustain is considerable. It probably exceeds the potential for financial deepening in most European economies. Whether or not it takes place will depend, possibly to a greater degree than in the past, on the entrepreneurial spirit of Italian bankers and financiers. It will depend on the overall performance of the economy, since the financial sector is unlikely to make progress if the economy continues to stagnate. It will depend on the ability and willingness of Italian firms and households to take advantage of old and new financial products. It will depend on the elimination of the remaining social, legal, administrative and fiscal constraints that hamper Italian banks.

Consequently, further intervention is required on the institutional framework in which the financial industry operates: company, labour law and civil procedure; the consolidation of public finances, on which the expectation of lower taxation depends; the day-to-day activity of all supervisory authorities; and the protection and promotion of competition.

The Bank of Italy will continue to contribute, particularly in this last respect, which is decisive for the efficiency and stability of the whole banking and financial system – competition, the driving force of change. The intermediate objective pursued over two decades has been surpassed: more competition, together with considerable consolidation and a start on reorganizations of financial intermediaries conducive to efficiency. Competition has exerted its influence on the prices of banking and financial services, bringing them down and making them less widely dispersed. The full benefits for the economy – in terms of lower costs, international competitiveness, profitability and capital accumulation – from the wide availability of good quality services are taking time to come through.

In a context of light and shade, there can be no room for disappointment except among those who fail to appreciate that although competition fosters efficiency it can guarantee it only if producers have the ability to respond to its promptings. It is important to understand the depth of the inertia intrinsic in a process that is primarily cultural, as opposed to legal and institutional or market-related. The 'traverse' from oligopoly to competition is never easy in an industry such as banking, which is based on asymmetric information, bilateral customer relations and the reputation of producers. It has been even harder in Italy, given the initial conditions in the early 1980s, of a banking and financial system with high profits and low average efficiency, and consequently a far cry from competitive.

It is doubtful whether faster progress could have been made in such a context. It is sufficient to recall one point mentioned earlier. The recognition of banks as enterprises and the imposition of equal treatment for private and publicly owned banks were only embodied in Italian legislation as a result of a judgement issued in 1989, 10 years after the supervisory authority had firmly reasserted the principle.

The Bank of Italy's policy is to pursue the course embarked upon at the beginning of the 1980s. Two developments taking place at present will produce their effects. By reinforcing each other and competition in the market for bank products they will help to foster the lower costs and better-quality services that are needed. The first of these developments is the privatization of banks. The second relates to exit procedures designed to avoid moral hazard and negligence over costs. The privatization of ownership is a prerequisite for the contestability of control. If banks can rely less on assistance from the state they will be encouraged to conduct their activity according to even stricter principles of independent, sound and prudent management.

However, we cannot declare ourselves satisfied with the way the notion of 'competition' has been incorporated into the body of law. Is its purpose only to protect today's consumers, or is it also to be a crucial force in driving the whole economy? Why should it be regarded only as an economic notion? It is a procedure, a custom, and it affects the whole of civil society. It is part of the democratic process. Montesquieu was also an economist, although Schumpeter did not greatly admire him as such. What is most important is the notion of competition as a value, a value in itself, not as a tool *for* something (replaceable by other tools), nor as an intermediate objective on the way *towards* something (exchangeable for other objectives). Does it exist as such in the law? Should it be included in the law? If the answer is yes, then should not the *pro*-competition approach permeate the whole body of law, all its provisions and levels? Should it not be guarded by the Constitution? We must ask ourselves whether an additional effort is not needed to create effective competition law in Italy.

Imagine that the first paragraph of article 41 of the Constitution, 'Private economic initiative shall be free' – although no-one is freer than a monopolist! – continued 'It must take place in competitive markets.'

Imagine that Einaudi's proposal to the Constituent Assembly were included, half a century later, in the Constitution: 'The law itself must not create monopolies.'

Imagine that articles 2595–96–97 of the Civil Code, which mention competition almost as if to deny it, were replaced or eliminated.

Imagine that article 2082 of the Civil Code, which should be the Magna Charta of the rights of a market economy but instead draws a picture of its central figure, the entrepreneur, in such banal and reductive terms, were rewritten.

Notes

Preface

1 Roberto Violi, of the Economic Research Department, reread the whole text and Mirella Tocci and Cristina Zago took care of the formal aspects.

2 *Interesse e Profitto. Saggi sul sistema creditizio*, Il Mulino, Bologna, 1982; *Banca, Finanza, Mercato. Bilancio di un decennio e nuove prospettive*, Einaudi, Turin, 1991.

1 A Mutation

1 R.W. Goldsmith, *Financial Structure and Development*, Yale University Press, New Haven, CT, 1969.

2 J.G. Gurley and E.S. Shaw, *Money in a Theory of Finance*, Brookings Institution, Washington, DC, 1960.

3 R. Mattioli, 'I problemi attuali del credito', *Mondo economico*, 1962, p. 28.

4 A. Beneduce, *Relazione del consiglio di amministrazione dell'I.R.I. sul bilancio al 31 dicembre 1936*, Rome, 1937.

5 D. Menichella, *Scritti e discorsi scelti, 1933–1966*, Banca d'Italia, Rome, 1986.

6 C. Mayer, 'Financial Systems, Corporate Finance, and Economic Development', in R.G. Hubbard (ed.), *Asymmetric information, Corporate Finance, and Investment*, University of Chicago Press, 1990.

7 G. Carli, *Cinquant'anni di vita italiana*, Laterza, Rome–Bari, 1993, pp. 386 ff.

8 A reconstruction of the events in Italy in the 1930s is in G. Toniolo, *L'economia dell'Italia fascista*, Laterza, Rome–Bari, 1980.

2 The Institutional and Analytical Framework

1 C.A. Ciampi, *Scritti e conferenze*, 7 vols, Banca d'Italia, Rome, 1979–1993.

2 P. Baffi, 'Osservazioni sull'I.R.I.' in Ministero dell'Industria e del Commercio, *L'Istituto per la ricostruzione industriale*, UTET, Turin, 1955, Vol. 2, pp. 575–85.

3 P. Baffi, 'Inflazione e allocazione delle risorse', introductory address, *XXII Riunione scientifica della Società italiana degli economisti*, Rome, 6 November 1981, in *Allocazione delle risorse e politica economica nelle economie contemporanee*, Giuffrè, Milan, 1984.

4 G. Carli (ed.), *Sviluppo economico e strutture finanziarie in Italia* (1977) and *La struttura del sistema creditizio italiano* (1978), Il Mulino, Bologna.

5 The focus of the conference was the paper by M. Sarcinelli, 'Stagflation and Financial Structures in the 1970s: The Case of Italy'. The conference proceedings are in *Credit Systems in the 1970s*, Ente Einaudi, Rome, 1980.

6 Other, general reasons for gradualness are set out in R.G. Rajan and L. Zingales, 'Financial Systems, Industrial Structure, and Growth', mimeo, 1999.

7 M.S. Giannini, 'Osservazioni sulla disciplina della funzione creditizia' in *Scritti giuridici in onore di Santi Romano*, CEDAM, Padua, 1940; and especially 'Istituti di credito e servizi di interesse pubblico', *Moneta e credito*, 1949, pp. 105–19: 'We can certainly say that here we are dealing with legal orders; all three of their typical elements are found: a plurality of actors, organization, rule-making.

These are sector (or section) legal orders, in that they are limited to the agents that perform a given activity' (p. 111).

8   B. Andreatta, 'Sistema finanziario privato e pubblico', address by the minister of the Treasury to the seminar held by Democrazia Cristiana, *Quale finanza per un'economia aperta?*, in *Credito popolare*, 1982, pp. 33–42.

9   J.M. Keynes, *The General Theory of Employment, Interest and Money*, Macmillan, London, 1936, p. viii.

10   R. Orestano, *Introduzione allo studio del diritto romano*, Il Mulino, Bologna, 1987, p. 357, and 'Economia come storia', letter to *Rivista di storia economica*, 1987, pp. 152–4. This letter confirms that Orestano sees economics and economic policy as falling within the notion of 'legal experience'.

11   A. Giuliani, 'Le radici romanistiche della dottrina italiana della concorrenza', *Rivista di storia economica*, 1997, p. 116.

12   There is growing statistical and even econometric evidence of the quantitative importance and the robustness of the connection between the legal order and variables such as the return on shares, the concentration of share ownership, the cost of bank loans, the depth of capital markets and firms' recourse to such markets, and even the size of enterprises. For an extensive survey of this literature, see R. La Porta, F. Lopez-de-Silanes, A. Shleifer and R. W. Vishny, 'Legal Determinants of External Finance', *Journal of Finance*, 1997, pp. 1131–50; and 'Law and Finance', *Journal of Political Economy*, 1998, pp. 1113–55.

13   A. Marshall, *Principles of Economics*, Macmillan, London, 1890; E. Barone, 'Studi di economia finanziaria', *Giornale degli economisti*, 1912, April–May, pp. 309–53, 'Atlantino dei grafici', June, pp. 469–505, July–December pp. 1–75; F.P. Ramsey, 'A Contribution to the Theory of Taxation', *Economic Journal*, 1927, pp. 47–61.

14   C. Cosciani, *Scienza delle finanze*, UTET, Turin, 1977, p. 269.

15   S. Steve, *Lezioni di scienza delle finanze*, CEDAM, Padua, 1976, pp. 273–4.

16   E. Barone, 'Studi di economia finanziaria', p. 25.

17   K.J. Arrow, *Essays in the Theory of Risk-Bearing*, Elsevier, New York, 1970.

18   C. Chamley and P. Honohan, *Taxation of Financial Intermediation*, Working Paper no. 421, World Bank, Washington, DC, 1990.

19   F.P. Ramsey, 'A Contribution . . .' and 'A Mathematical Theory of Saving', *Economic Journal*, 1928, pp. 543–59.

20   W.J. Corlett and D.C. Hague, 'Complementarity and the Excess Burden of Taxation', *Review of Economic Studies*, 1953, pp. 21–30.

21   C. Chamley, 'Optimal Taxation of Capital Income in General Equilibrium with Infinite Lives', *Econometrica*, 1986, pp. 607–22.

22   E.S. Phelps, 'Why It Is Desirable to Tax Wealth and Retire the Public Debt', mimeo, 1999.

23   V. Visco, 'Il riordino della tassazione dei redditi finanziari nella prospettiva dell'UME', *Studi e note di economia. Quaderni*, 3, 1999, p. 20.

24   J. Tobin, *The New Economics One Decade Older*, Princeton University Press, 1974.

25   R.R. West, 'On the Difference between Internal and External Market Efficiency', *Financial Analysts Journal*, 1975, pp. 30–4.

26   E.F. Fama, 'Efficient Capital Markets: A Review of Theory and Empirical Work', *Journal of Finance*, 1970, pp. 387–417.

27   J. Hirshleifer, 'The Private and Social Value of Information and the Reward to Inventive Activity', *American Economic Review*, 1971, pp. 561–74.

28 G.A. Akerlof, *An Economic Theorist's Book of Tales*, Cambridge University Press, 1984.

29 M. Friedman, *A Framework for Monetary Stability*, Fordham University Press, New York, 1959.

30 P. Ciocca, 'Ancora sul credito di ultima istanza', *Moneta e credito*, 1990, pp. 163–80; 'Il principio di autonomia nel "central banking"', *Quaderni di economia e finanza*, 1992, pp. 5–22.

31 J.M. Keynes, *The End of Laissez-Faire*, Hogarth Press, London, 1926, p. 41.

32 J. Stiglitz, 'The Private Uses of Public Interests: Incentives and Institutions', *Journal of Economic Perspectives*, 1998, pp. 3–21.

33 M. Pantaleoni, *Erotemi di economia*, Laterza, Bari, 1925.

34 L. Einaudi, *Lezioni di politica sociale*, Einaudi, Turin, 1949, p. 21.

35 Cited in F. Cotula (ed.), *Stabilità e sviluppo negli anni cinquanta. Politica bancaria e struttura del sistema finanziario*, Laterza, Rome and Bari, 1999, vol. 3, pp. 172–3.

36 G.J. Stigler, 'Perfect Competition, Historically Contemplated', *Journal of Political Economy*, 1957, pp. 1–17.

37 A.C. Harberger, 'Monopoly and Resource Allocation', *American Economic Review*, Papers and Proceedings, 1954, pp. 77–87.

38 K. Cowling and D.C. Mueller, 'The Social Costs of Monopoly Power', *Economic Journal*, 1978, pp. 727–48.

39 H. Leibenstein, 'Allocative Efficiency vs. "X-Efficiency"', *American Economic Review*, 1966, pp. 412–13.

40 J.A. Schumpeter, *The Theory of Economic Development: An Inquiry into Profits, Capital, Credit, Interest, and the Business Cycle* (1911), Oxford University Press, New York, 1961, p. 74.

41 J.R.S. Revell, 'The Complementary Nature of Competition and Regulation in the Financial Sector', *Revue de la Banque*, 1980, pp. 9–33.

42 M.A. Petersen and R.G. Rajan, 'The Effect of Credit Market Competition on Lending Relationships', *Quarterly Journal of Economics*, 1995, pp. 407–43.

3 The Legal Order

1 J.A. Grundfest, 'Securities Regulation', in P. Newman (ed.), *The New Palgrave Dictionary of Economics and the Law*, vol. 3, Macmillan, London, 1998, pp. 410–19.

2 L.R. Cohen, 'Tender Offers', in P. Newman (ed.), *The New Palgrave Dictionary of Economics and the Law*, vol. 3, Macmillan, London, 1998, pp. 580–83 and the literature referred to therein.

3 U. Scarpelli, 'Il linguaggio giuridico: un ideale illuministico', in P. Di Lucia (ed.), *Nomografia. Linguaggio e redazione delle leggi*, Giuffrè, Milan, 1995, p. 28.

4 V. Visco, 'Il fisco giusto. Una riforma per l'Italia europea', *Il Sole 24 Ore*, Milan, 2000.

5 Several empirical analyses confirm that an adequate legal framework, perceived to be such by investors, can have a powerful positive effect on the economy's rate of growth in the long run. See, most recently, R.J. Barro, 'Human Capital and Growth in Cross-Country Regressions', *Swedish Economic Policy Review*, 1999, pp. 237–77.

4 Taxation

1 D.W. Jorgenson and R. Landau (eds), *Tax Reform and the Cost of Capital: An International Comparison*, Brookings Institution, Washington, DC, 1993, p. 28.

2 Visco, *Il fisco giusto*.

5 Supervision

1 Scarpelli, *Il linguaggio giuridico*, pp. 18 ff.

6 Competition

1 Cited in F. Cotula (ed.), *Stabilità e sviluppo*, p. 190.
2 D. Menichella, *Stabilità e sviluppo dell'economia italiana, 1946–1960*, Laterza, Rome and Bari, 1997, vol. 1, p. 705.
3 D. Menichella, *Stabilità e sviluppo*, p. 459.
4 P. Ciocca, C.A. Giussani and G. Lanciotti, *Sportelli, dimensioni e costi: uno studio sulla struttura del sistema bancario italiano*, Quaderni di ricerche dell'Ente Einaudi, Rome, 1974.
5 B.K. Short, 'The Relation between Commercial Bank Profit Rates and Banking Concentration in Canada, Western Europe, and Japan', *Journal of Banking and Finance*, 1979, pp. 209–19.
6 The seminal contribution was that of W.J. Baumol, *The Stock Market and Economic Efficiency*, Fordham University Press, New York, 1965.
7 F. Caffè, 'Di una economia di mercato compatibile con la socializzazione delle sovrastrutture finanziarie', *Giornale degli economisti e annali di economia*, 1971, pp. 664–84.
8 G. Cristini, 'I rendimenti delle azioni e l'efficienza della borsa', *Contributi alla ricerca economica*, no. 8, Banca d'Italia, Rome, 1978. An earlier study of stock exchanges in eight European countries, including Italy, from 1966 to 1971 had reached the following conclusions: 'Deviations from the random walk seem slightly more apparent in the European stock price behavior than in the American price behavior...Explanations for these departures from the random walk can probably be found in some of the technical and institutional characteristics of European capital markets: loose requirements for disclosure of information, discontinuity in trading. With the exception of the British market, where prices seem to behave much like U.S. stock prices, all other markets tend to exhibit quite unexpectedly similar behavior.' (B. Solnik, 'Note on the Validity of the Random Walk for European Stock Prices', *Journal of Finance*, 1973, p. 1158).
9 T.F. Bresnahan, 'Empirical Studies of Industries with Market Power', in R. Schmalensee and R.D. Willig (eds), *Handbook of Industrial Organization*, North-Holland, Amsterdam, 1989, table 17.1, p. 1051; S. Shaffer, 'A Test of Competition in Canadian Banking', *Journal of Money, Credit, and Banking*, 1993, pp. 49–61; S.A. Berg and M. Kim, 'Oligopolistic Interdependence and the Structure of Production in Banking: An Empirical Evaluation', *Journal of Money, Credit, and Banking*, 1994, pp. 309–22; P. Coccorese, 'The Degree of Competition in the Italian Banking Industry', *Economic Notes*, 1998, pp. 355–70; P. Angelini and N. Cetorelli, *Bank Competition and Regulatory Reform: The Case of the Italian Banking Industry*, Working Paper no. 32, Federal Reserve Bank of Chicago, 1999.

7 Performance

1 G. Becattini, *Il concetto d'industria e la teoria del valore*, Boringhieri, Turin, 1962.
2 P. Schure and R. Wagenvoort, 'Economies of Scale and Efficiency in European Banking: New Evidence', *Economic and Financial Reports of the European Investment Bank*, Report 99/01, Luxembourg, 1999, table 7, p. 35.

3 G. Zadra, 'I principali svantaggi competitivi delle banche italiane nel confronto europeo', *Bancaria*, 2000, pp. 2–8.
4 'La valutazione dell'affidabilità della clientela da parte delle banche. Criteri e prassi operative', *Bancaria*, 1983, p. 942.
5 G. Alesii, *Holding Companies Discounts: Some Evidence from the Milan Stock Exchange*, mimeo, 2000.

8 A Stagnant Economy

1 The estimates of the output gap made by international organizations show a basically similar cyclical pattern for the whole period for which data are available but sometimes differ as regards its size. However, for the years from 1990 to 1999, the highest estimates of the output lost, those of the OECD and the IMF, are practically the same: well above 1 per cent of potential output each year and a cumulative total of nearly 13 percentage points. With reference to GDP in 1999, they correspond to nearly 300,000 billion lire.
2 F. Onida, 'Quali prospettive per il modello di specializzazione internazionale dell'Italia?', *Economia italiana*, 1999, pp. 573–629.
3 G. Parigi and S. Siviero, *An Investment-Function-Based Measure of Capacity Utilisation. Potential Output and Utilised Capacity in the Bank of Italy's Quarterly Model*, Temi di discussione no. 367, Banca d'Italia, Rome, 2000.
4 L. Spaventa and V. Chiorazzo, *Astuzia o virtù? Come accadde che l'Italia fu ammessa all'Unione monetaria*, Donzelli, Rome 2000. In this detailed account no reference is made to monetary policy, which played a key disinflationary role between 1994 and 1998.
5 Exceptionally, the econometric scenario was published in the Bank's Annual Report (May 1992). The exercise was subsequently disseminated internationally in English and Japanese. See L. Dini, 'L'economia italiana. I progressi degli anni ottanta, le questioni aperte', mimeo, Tokyo, 4 June 1992.
6 Only a significant increase in the actual retirement age can permanently curb pension expenditure. To achieve such an increase, it may be necessary to supplement social security reforms with measures affecting the labour market. In this respect, see F. Modigliani and M. Ceprini, 'Social Security Reform: A Proposal for Italy', *Review of Economic Conditions in Italy*, 1998, pp. 177–201 and D. Franco, 'Italy. A Never-Ending Pension Reform', NBER-Kiel Institute Conference, Berlin, March 2000. At the same time only the full employment of a growing labour force can sustain pension expenditure, even if it is curbed. See A. Sen, 'L'occupazione: le ragioni di una priorità per la politica economica', in P. Ciocca (ed.), *Disoccupazione di fine secolo. Studi e proposte per l'Europa*, Bollati Boringhieri, Turin, 1997.
7 M. Buti, A. Carparelli, N. Nagarajan, P. Sestito and M. Svardi, *Italy's Slow Growth in the 1990s: Facts, Explanations and Prospects*, European Economy, Reports and Studies, no. 5, 1999. This report uses national accounts data compiled before the revision based on the latest labour force survey.

9 Finance and Growth

1 R.C. Merton and Z. Bodie, 'A Conceptual Framework for Analyzing the Financial Environment', in D.B. Crane *et al.* (eds), *The Global Financial System: A Functional Perspective*, Harvard Business School Press, Cambridge, MA, 1995.

2 R. Levine, 'Financial Development and Economic Growth. Views and Agenda', *Journal of Economic Literature*, 1997, pp. 688–726.

3 S. Kuznets, *Modern Economic Growth: Rate, Structure, and Spread*, Yale University Press, New Haven, CT, 1966, p. 81. In economies in which the service sector is increasingly preponderant, these factors tend to become even more important. An advanced service economy is inconceivable, has no chance of developing, in a society lacking in education. Educational shortcomings block growth both on the supply side and in the demand for services and human capital. For a long-term quantitative treatment, see A. Maddison, *Monitoring the World Economy 1820–1992*, OECD, Paris, 1995, tables 2–6 ('Successive Steps in Growth Accounting, 1820–1992'), pp. 41–2.

4 W.J. Baumol, *Entrepreneurship, Management, and the Structure of Payoffs*, MIT Press, Cambridge, MA, 1993; and above all H. Lydall, *A Critique of Orthodox Economics. An Alternative Model*, Macmillan, London, 1998. On the various theories of the entrepreneur, see also M. Casson, *The Entrepreneur: An Economic Theory*, Martin Robertson, Oxford, 1982.

5 Another illustrious victim of this philological superficiality is Joan Robinson. She has been singled out as the extreme case of a theoretical economist who supposedly considered the financial structure to be entirely endogenous, hence practically irrelevant, to the process of growth. 'Where enterprise leads finance follows' is the phrase of hers most frequently cited, and most tautologically when taken out of context, by this literature. It is remarkable that a student of Keynes's should be accused of underestimating the importance of money and finance. What is most surprising is that in that same book, in those same pages, practically in the same passage, the significance of finance is recognized, and Robinson even refers explicitly to the 'legal and institutional arrangements and the habits of lenders' (J. Robinson, *The Rate of Interest and Other Essays*, Macmillan, London, 1952, p. 86).

6 J.A. Schumpeter, *The Theory of Economic Development*, p. 74.

. 7 J.A. Schumpeter, *Business Cycles: A Theoretical, Historical, and Statistical Analysis of the Capitalist Process*, McGraw–Hill, New York, 1939, vol. 1, p. 116 (italics added).

8 Ibid., p. 118.

9 J.A. Schumpeter, *The Theory of Economic Development*, p. 74. It should be remembered that the 'ephor' was the supreme magistrate elected by the people of Sparta to oversee and judge the government authorities themselves. Schumpeter wrote the definitive account of the qualities, including moral qualities, that the banker should possess.

10 R.G. King and R. Levine, 'Finance, Entrepreneurship, and Growth. Theory and Evidence', *Journal of Monetary Economics*, 1993, p. 521.

11 Summarized in R. Levine, *Financial Development and Economic Growth*.

12 A major refinement for Italy, confirming the quantitatively important relationship between banking efficiency and growth, is R. Lucchetti, L. Papi and A. Zazzaro, 'Efficienza del sistema bancario e crescita economica nelle regioni italiane', *XL Riunione scientifica annuale della Società italiana degli economisti*, mimeo, 1999.

13 'The main outstanding issue here is to disentangle the financial–development effect on growth from the reverse channel' (Barro, *Human Capital and Growth*, p. 275). Barro himself, moreover, 'explains' growth by reference

both to fundamental variables, less exposed to the risk of reciprocal causation (public consumption, the rule of law, democracy, fertility) and to variables (education, inflation, investment, terms of trade) that are if anything more exposed to this risk than is the level of financial development.

14   R. Levine and S. Zervox, 'Stock Markets, Banks, and Economic Growth', *American Economic Review*, 1998, pp. 537–58.

15   This stratification continues to follow the taxonomy given in Merton and Bodie, 'A Conceptual Framework'.

16   The exercise assumes proxy values constant at their 1985 levels, whereas the average historical values of the 1990s ranged between 5 and 10 per cent higher, depending on the proxy considered. The coefficients are taken from R.G. King and R. Levine, 'Finance and Growth: Schumpeter Might Be Right', *Quarterly Journal of Economics*, 1993, table VII, p. 727.

17   King and Levine run regressions on a vast sample of countries. The average annual growth rate of per capita GDP in each decade (the 1960s, 1970s and 1980s) is determined by economic variables and by the initial value of a variable representing the degree of development of the financial system. Using the parameters that they estimate, we can calculate the effect of the financial variables – according to various counterfactual hypotheses – on the rate of growth of Italian per capita GDP. However, the choice of the variables used to proxy financial development was limited, in King and Levine's study, by the availability of data for so many countries. Their four indicators – the ratio of liquid liabilities to nominal GDP (LLY), the ratio of commercial banks' domestic assets to the sum of those assets plus the domestic assets of the central bank, the ratio of the liabilities of the private non-financial sector to total domestic credit, and the ratio of private non-financial sector liabilities to GDP – are only partial approximations of the actual efficiency, or articulation, of the financial system, especially for the more advanced countries.

In Italy, LLY declined steadily starting in 1980. But it would be mistaken to interpret this as a sign of lesser financial development. On the contrary, the declining incidence of liquid liabilities is a sign of progress in portfolio structures, with less use of money as a financial asset. The other three variables are all essentially proxies of the importance of credit to the private sector. In Italy, they all began to rise starting in the mid-1980s. However, the trends in the aggregates as defined by King and Levine do not sufficiently reflect, indeed significantly underestimate, the effective improvement in the Italian financial system in connection with the privatization of both non-financial firms and of banking and the money and capital markets.

18   Adam Smith's remarks on banking remain valid: 'The only trades which it seems possible for a joint stock company to carry on successfully, without an exclusive privilege, are those, of which all the operations are capable of being reduced to what is called a Routine, or to such a uniformity of method as admits of little or no variation. Of this kind is, first, the banking trade.' *An Inquiry into the Nature and Causes of the Wealth of Nations* [1776], Clarendon, Oxford, 1976, p. 756.

References

Akerlof, G.A., *An Economic Theorist's Book of Tales*, Cambridge University Press, Cambridge, 1984.

Alesii, G., *Holding Companies Discounts: Some Evidence from the Milan Stock Exchange*, mimeo, 2000.

Andreatta, B., 'Sistema finanziario privato e pubblico', address by the minister of the Treasury to the seminar held by Democrazia Cristiana, *Quale finanza per un'economia aperta?*, *Credito Popolare*, 1982, pp. 33–42.

Angelini, P. and Cetorelli, N., *Bank Competition and Regulatory Reform: The Case of the Italian Banking Industry*, Working Paper no. 32, Federal Reserve Bank of Chicago, 1999.

Arrow, K.J., *Essays in the Theory of Risk-Bearing*, Elsevier, New York, 1970.

Atkeson, A., Chari, V.V. and Kehoe, P.J., 'Taxing Capital Income: A Bad Idea', *Federal Reserve Bank of Minneapolis Quarterly Review*, 1999, pp. 3–17.

Baffi, P., 'Osservazioni sull'I.R.I.', in Ministero dell'Industria e del Commercio, *L'Istituto per la Ricostruzione Industriale*, vol. 2, UTET, Turin, 1955, pp. 575–85.

Baffi, P., *Inflazione e allocazione delle risorse*, introductory address, XXIIª Riunione Scientifica della Società Italiana degli Economisti, Rome, 6 November 1981, in *Allocazione delle risorse e politica economica nelle economie contemporanee*, Giuffrè, Milan 1984.

Barone E., 'Studi di economia finanziaria', *Giornale degli Economisti*, 1912 (April–May), pp. 309–53 plus 'Atlantino dei grafici'; (June) pp. 469–505; (July–December) pp. 1–75.

Barro, R.J., 'Human Capital and Growth in Cross-country Regressions', *Swedish Economic Policy Review*, 1999, pp. 237–77.

Baumol, W.J., *The Stock Market and Economic Efficiency*, Fordham University Press, New York, 1965.

Baumol, W.J., *Entrepreneurship, Management, and the Structure of Payoffs*, MIT Press, Cambridge, MA, 1993.

Becattini, G., *Il concetto d'industria e la teoria del valore*, Boringhieri, Turin, 1962.

Beneduce, A., *Relazione del Consiglio di Amministrazione dell'IRI sul bilancio al 31 dicembre 1936*, Rome, 1937.

Berg, S.A. and Kim, M., 'Oligopolistic Interdependence and the Structure of Production in Banking: An Empirical Evaluation', *Journal of Money, Credit, and Banking*, 1994, pp. 309–22.

Bresnahan, T.F., 'Empirical Studies of Industries with Market Power', in Schmalensee, R. and Willig, R.D. (eds), *Handbook of Industrial Organization*, North-Holland, Amsterdam, 1989.

Buti, M., Carparelli, A., Nagarajan, N., Sestito, P. and Suardi, M., *Italy's Slow Growth in the 1990s: Facts, Explanations and Prospects*, European Economy. Reports and Studies, no. 5, 1999.

Caffè, F., 'Di una economia di mercato compatibile con la socializzazione delle sovrastrutture finanziarie', *Giornale degli Economisti e Annali di Economia*, 1971, pp. 664–84.

Carli, G. (ed.), *Sviluppo economico e strutture finanziarie in Italia*, Mulino, Bologna, 1977.

Carli, G. (ed.), *La struttura del sistema creditizio italiano*, Mulino, Bologna, 1978.

Carli, G., *Cinquant'anni di vita italiana*, Laterza, Rome-Bari, 1993.

Casson, M., *The Entrepreneur: An Economic Theory*, Robertson, Oxford, 1982.

Cesari, R., *I fondi pensione*, Mulino, Bologna, 2000.

Chamley, C., 'Optimal Taxation of Capital Income in General Equilibrium with Infinite Lives', *Econometrica*, 1986, pp. 607–22.

Chamley, C. and Honohan, P., *Taxation of Financial Intermediation*, Working Paper no. 421, World Bank, Washington, DC, 1990.

Ciampi, C.A., *Scritti e conferenze* (7 volumes: 1979–93), Banca d'Italia, Rome.

Ciocca, P., *L'instabilità dell'economia. Prospettive di analisi storica*, Einaudi, Turin, 1987.

Ciocca, P., 'Ancora sul credito di ultima istanza', *Moneta e Credito*, 1990, pp. 163–80.

Ciocca, P., 'Il principio di autonomia nel "Central Banking"', *Quaderni di economia e finanza*, 1992, pp. 5–22.

Ciocca, P., Giussani, C.A. and Lanciotti, G., *Sportelli, dimensioni e costi: uno studio sulla struttura del sistema bancario italiano*, Quaderni di Ricerche dell'Ente Einaudi, Rome, 1974.

Coccorese, P., 'The Degree of Competition in the Italian Banking Industry', *Economic Notes*, 1998, pp. 355–70.

Cohen, L.R., 'Tender Offers', in Newman, P. (ed.), *The New Palgrave Dictionary of Economics and the Law*, vol. 3, Macmillan, London, 1998, pp. 580–83.

Corlett, W.J. and Hague, D.C., 'Complementarity and the Excess Burden of Taxation', *Review of Economic Studies*, 1953, pp. 21–30.

Cosciani, C., *Scienza delle finanze*, UTET, Turin, 1977.

Cotula, F. (ed.), *Stabilità e sviluppo negli anni Cinquanta. Politica bancaria e struttura del sistema finanziario*, Laterza, Rome–Bari, 1999, vol. 3.

Cowling, K. and Mueller, D.C., 'The Social Costs of Monopoly Power', *Economic Journal*, 1978, pp. 727–48.

Cristini, G., 'I rendimenti delle azioni e l'efficienza della Borsa', *Contributi alla Ricerca Economica*, no. 8, 1978, Banca d'Italia.

Desario, V., *Il controllo pubblico sull'ordinamento finanziario*, Cacucci, Bari, 1995.

Dini, L., *L'economia italiana. I progressi degli anni Ottanta, le questioni aperte*, mimeo, Tokyo, 4 June 1992.

Domar, E.D. and Musgrave, R.A., 'Proportional Income Taxation and Risk-Taking', *Quarterly Journal of Economics*, 1944, pp. 388–422.

Einaudi, L., *Lezioni di politica sociale*, Einaudi, Turin, 1949.

Fama, E.F., 'Efficient Capital Markets: A Review of Theory and Empirical Work', *Journal of Finance*, 1970, pp. 383–417.

Fazio, A., *Il sistema bancario italiano in Europa*, Annual Meeting of A.B.I., Rome, 1998.

Franco, D., *Italy: A Never-Ending Pension Reform*, NBER-Kiel Institute Conference, Berlin, March 2000.

Friedman, M., *A Framework for Monetary Stability*, Fordham University Press, New York, 1959.

Giannini, M.S., 'Osservazioni sulla disciplina della funzione creditizia', in *Scritti giuridici in onore di Santi Romano*, CEDAM, Padua, 1940.

Giannini, M.S., 'Istituti di credito e servizi di interesse pubblico', *Moneta e Credito*, 1949, pp. 105–19.

Giuliani, A., 'Le radici romanistiche della dottrina italiana della concorrenza', *Rivista di Storia Economica*, 1997, pp. 107–16.

Giuliani, A., *Giustizia ed ordine economico*, Giuffrè, Milan, 1997.

Goldberg, L.G. and Rai, A., 'The Structure–Performance Relationship for European Banking', *Journal of Banking and Finance*, 1996, pp. 745–71.

Goldsmith, R.W., *Financial Structure and Development*, Yale University Press, New Haven, CT, 1969.

Gorini, S., 'La teoria del 'second best' e la scelta degli investimenti pubblici', *Rivista di diritto finanziario e scienza delle finanze*, 1969, pp. 454–92.

Grossman, S.J. and Hart, O.D., 'Disclosure Laws and Takeover Bids', *Journal of Finance*, 1980, pp. 323–34.

Grundfest, J.A., 'Securities Regulation', in Newman, P. (ed.), *The New Palgrave Dictionary of Economics and the Law*, vol. 3, Macmillan, London, 1998, pp. 410–19.

Gurley, J.G. and Shaw, E.S., *Money in a Theory of Finance*, Brookings Institution, Washington, DC, 1960.

Harberger, A.C., 'Monopoly and Resource Allocation', *American Economic Review, Papers and Proceedings*, 1954, pp. 77–87.

Hirshleifer, J., 'The Private and Social Value of Information and the Reward to Inventive Activity', *American Economic Review*, 1971, 561–74.

Jorgenson, D.W. and Landau, R. (eds), *Tax Reform and the Cost of Capital: An International Comparison*, Brookings Institution, Washington, DC, 1993.

Keynes, J.M., *The End of Laissez-Faire*, Hogarth, London, 1926.

Keynes, J.M., *The General Theory of Employment Interest and Money*, Macmillan, London, 1936.

King, R.G. and Levine R., 'Finance, Entrepreneurship, and Growth: Theory and Evidence', *Journal of Monetary Economics*, 1993, pp. 513–42.

King, R.G. and Levine R., 'Finance and Growth: Schumpeter Might Be Right', *Quarterly Journal of Economics*, 1993, pp. 717–37.

Kuznets, S., *Modern Economic Growth: Rate, Structure, and Spread*, Yale University Press, New Haven, CT, 1966.

Lamanda, C., *La società per azioni bancaria*, Bancaria, Rome, 1994.

La Porta, R., Lopez-de-Silanes, F., Shleifer, A. and Vishny, R.W., 'Legal Determinants of External Finance', *Journal of Finance*, 1997, pp. 1131–50.

La Porta, R., Lopez-de-Silanes, F., Shleifer, A. and Vishny, R.W., 'Law and Finance', *Journal of Political Economy*, 1998, pp. 1113–55.

Lee R., 'Regulation of Capital Markets in the European Union', in Newman, P. (ed.), *The New Palgrave Dictionary of Economics and the Law*, vol. 2, Macmillan, London, 1998, pp. 228–32.

Leibenstein, H., 'Allocative Efficiency vs. "X-Efficiency"', *American Economic Review*, 1966, pp. 392–415.

LeRoy, S.F., 'Efficient Capital Markets and Martingales', *Journal of Economic Literature*, 1989, pp. 1583–1621.

Levine, R., 'Financial Development and Economic Growth: Views and Agenda', *Journal of Economic Literature*, 1997, pp. 688–726.

Levine, R. and Zervos, S., 'Stock Markets, Banks, and Economic Growth', *American Economic Review*, 1998, pp. 537–58.

Lucchetti, R., Papi, L. and Zazzaro, A., *Efficienza del sistema bancario e crescita economica nelle regioni italiane*, 40th scientific annual meeting of the Società Italiana degli Economisti, mimeo, 1999.

Lunghini, G. and Mori, P.A., 'Per una politica economica della concorrenza', in Lipari, N. and Musu, I. (eds), *La concorrenza tra economia e diritto*, Cariplo-Laterza, Rome–Bari, 2000.

Lydall, H., *A Critique of Orthodox Economics: An Alternative Model*, Macmillan, London, 1998.

Maddison, A., *Monitoring the World Economy 1820–1992*, OECD, Paris, 1995.

Marshall, A., *Principles of Economics*, Macmillan, London, 1890.

Masera, R.S., *Intermediari, mercati e finanza d'impresa*, Laterza, Rome–Bari, 1991.

Mattioli, R., 'I problemi attuali del credito', *Mondo Economico*, 1962, pp. 27–31.

Mayer, C., 'Financial Systems, Corporate Finance, and Economic Development', in Hubbard, R.G. (ed.), *Asymmetric Information, Corporate Finance, and Investment*, University of Chicago Press, 1990.

Menichella, D., *Stabilità e sviluppo dell'economia italiana, 1946–1960*, Laterza, Rome–Bari, 1997.

Merton, R.C. and Bodie, Z., 'A Conceptual Framework for Analyzing the Financial Environment', in Crane, D.B. (ed.), *The Global Financial System: A Functional Perspective*, Harvard Business School Press, Boston, MA, 1995.

Ministero del Tesoro, *Il sistema creditizio e finanziario italiano*, Istituto Poligrafico e Zecca dello Stato, Rome, 1982.

Modigliani, F. and Fabozzi, F., *Mercati finanziari. Strumenti e istituzioni*, Mulino, Bologna, 1995.

Modigliani, F. and Ceprini, M., 'Social Security Reform: A Proposal for Italy', *Review of Economic Conditions in Italy*, 1998, pp. 177–201.

Musu, I., 'Il valore della concorrenza nella teoria economica', in Lipari, N. and Musu, I. (eds), *La concorrenza tra economia e diritto*, Cariplo-Laterza, Rome–Bari, 2000.

Nardozzi, G., 'Money and Credit: Twenty Years of Debate in Italy (1970–1990)', *BNL Quarterly Review*, 1994, pp. 3–51.

Onida, F., 'Quali prospettive per il modello di specializzazione internazionale dell'Italia?', *Economia italiana*, 1999, pp. 573–629.

Orestano, R., *Introduzione allo studio del diritto romano*, Mulino, Bologna, 1987.

Padoa Schioppa, T., *La moneta e il sistema dei pagamenti*, Mulino, Bologna, 1992.

Pantaleoni, M., *Erotemi di economia*, Laterza, Bari, 1925.

Parigi, G. and Siviero, S., *An Investment-Function-Based Measure of Capacity Utilisation: Potential Output and Utilised Capacity in the Bank of Italy's Quarterly Model*, Temi di discussione no. 367, Banca d'Italia, 2000.

Petersen, M.A. and Rajan, R.G., 'The Effect of Credit Market Competition on Lending Relationships', *Quarterly Journal of Economics*, 1995, pp. 407–43.

Phelps, E.S., *Why It Is Desirable to Tax Wealth and Retire the Public Debt*, mimeo, 1999.

Rajan, R.G. and Zingales, L., *Financial Systems, Industrial Structure, and Growth*, mimeo, 1999.

Ramsey, F.P., 'A Contribution to the Theory of Taxation', *Economic Journal*, 1927, pp. 47–61.

Ramsey, F.P., 'A Mathematical Theory of Saving', *Economic Journal*, 1928, pp. 543–59.

Revell, J.R.S., 'The Complementary Nature of Competition and Regulation in the Financial Sector', *Revue de la Banque*, 1980, pp. 9–33.

Robinson, J., *The Rate of Interest and Other Essays*, Macmillan, London, 1952.

Sarcinelli, M., 'Stagflation and Financial Structures in the Seventies: The Case of Italy, in *Credit Systems in the 1970s*, Ente Einaudi, Rome, 1980.

Scarpelli, U., 'Il linguaggio giuridico: un ideale illuministico', in Di Lucia, P. (ed.), *Nomografia. Linguaggio e redazione delle leggi*, Giuffrè, Milan, 1995.

Schumpeter, J.A., *The Theory of Economic Development: An Inquiry into Profits, Capital, Credit, Interest, and the Business Cycle* [1911], Oxford University Press, New York, 1961.

Schumpeter, J.A., *Business Cycles: A Theoretical, Historical, and Statistical Analysis of the Capitalist Process*, McGraw-Hill, New York, 1939.

Schure, P. and Wagenvoort, R., *Economies of Scale and Efficiency in European Banking: New Evidence*, Economic and Financial Reports of the European Investment Bank, Report 99/01, Luxembourg.

Sen, A., 'L'occupazione: le ragioni di una priorità per la politica economica', in Ciocca, P. (ed.), *Disoccupazione di fine secolo. Studi e proposte per l'Europa*, Bollati Boringhieri, Turin, 1997.

Shaffer, S., 'A Test of Competition in Canadian Banking', *Journal of Money, Credit, and Banking*, 1993, pp. 49–61.

Short, B.K., 'The Relation between Commercial Bank Profit Rates and Banking Concentration in Canada, Western Europe, and Japan', *Journal of Banking & Finance*, 1979, pp. 209–19.

Smith, A., *An Inquiry into the Nature and Causes of the Wealth of Nations* [1776], Clarendon, Oxford, 1976.

Solnik, B., 'Note on the Validity of the Random Walk for European Stock Prices', *Journal of Finance*, 1973, pp. 1151–9.

Spaventa, L. and Chiorazzo, V., *Astuzia o virtù? Come accadde che l'Italia fu ammessa all'Unione monetaria*, Donzelli, Rome, 2000.

Steve, S., *Lezioni di scienza delle finanze*, CEDAM, Padua, 1976.

Stigler, G.J., 'Perfect Competition, Historically Contemplated', *Journal of Political Economy*, 1957, pp. 1–17.

Stiglitz, J., 'The Private Uses of Public Interests: Incentives and Institutions', *Journal of Economic Perspectives*, 1998, pp. 3–21.

Tobin, J., *The New Economics One Decade Older*, Princeton University Press, 1974.

Toniolo, G., *L'economia dell'Italia fascista*, Laterza, Rome–Bari, 1980.

Vicarelli, F., 'Credito', in Lunghini, G. (dir.), *Dizionario di economia politica*, Boringhieri, Turin, 1983.

Visco, V., 'Il riordino della tassazione dei redditi finanziari nella prospettiva dell'UME', *Studi e Note di Economia. Quaderni, 3*, 1999, pp. 11–22.

Visco, V., *Il fisco giusto. Una riforma per l'Italia europea*, Il Sole 24 Ore, Milan, 2000.

West, R.R., 'On the Difference Between Internal and External Market Efficiency', *Financial Analysts Journal*, 1975, pp. 30–4.

Zadra, G., *Strutture e regolamentazione del mercato mobiliare*, Giuffrè, Milan, 1988.

Zadra, G., 'I principali svantaggi competitivi delle banche italiane nel confronto europeo', *Bancaria*, 2000, pp. 2–8.